# BANAL NATIONALISM

# BANAL NATIONALISM

Michael Billig

SAGE Publications
London • Thousand Oaks • New Delhi

First published 1995, Reprinted 1997, 1999, 2001, 2002

 SAGE Publications Ltd
6 Bonhill Street
London EC2A 4PU

SAGE Publications Inc
2455 Teller Road
Thousand Oaks, California 91320

SAGE Publications India Pvt Ltd
32, M-block Market
Greater Kailash – I
New Delhi 110 048

**British Library Cataloguing in Publication data**

A catalogue record for this book is available
from the British Library

ISBN 0 8039 7524–4
ISBN 0 8039 7525–2 (pbk)

**Library of Congress catalog record available**

Typeset by Photoprint, Torquay, S. Devon
Printed in Great Britain by The Cromwell Press Ltd,
Trowbridge, Wiltshire

# Contents

# Acknowledgements

I consider myself extremely fortunate, and privileged, to have as my academic home the Department of Social Sciences at Loughborough University. I have certainly benefited from working amongst such intellectually tolerant and diverse colleagues. I would especially like to thank the members of the Discourse and Rhetoric Group who have given friendly criticism on early drafts. In particular, thanks to: Malcolm Ashmore, Derek Edwards, Mike Gane, Celia Kitzinger, Dave Middleton, Mike Pickering and Jonathan Potter. Also, I would like to thank Peter Golding for all he has done to develop (and protect) the Department as an intellectual home.

I am also grateful for the comments and friendly support of Susan Condor, Helen Haste, Greg McLennan, John Shotter and Herb Simons. Transatlantic conversations with the last two are always greatly appreciated.

Parts of Chapter 7 were originally published in *New Left Review*, November/December, 1993, under the title of 'Nationalism and Richard Rorty: the text as a flag for the *Pax Americana*'. I am grateful to the publishers for permitting me to republish the article in the present form.

Lastly, I want to thank my family. It is a pleasurable sign of passing years to be able to thank Becky Billig for reading parts of the manuscript and for correcting my grammatical mistakes. But, as always, the gratitude goes much deeper than grammar. So thanks and love to Sheila, Daniel, Becky, Rachel and Ben.

# 1

# Introduction

All societies that maintain armies maintain the belief that some things are more valuable than life itself. Just what is so valued varies. In previous times, wars were fought for causes which now seem incomprehensibly trivial. In Europe, for example, armies were mobilized in the name of defending religious ritual or chivalric honour. William of Normandy, speaking before the Battle of Hastings, exhorted his troops to avenge the spilling of "noble blood" (Anonymous, 1916). To fight for such matters appears 'barbaric', or, worse still, 'mediaeval' in today's balance of priorities. The great causes for which modern blood is to be spilled are different; and so is the scale of the bloodshed. As Isaiah Berlin has written, "it is by now a melancholy commonplace that no century has seen so much remorseless and continued slaughter of human beings by one another as our own" (1991, p. 175). Much of this slaughter has been performed in the name of the nation, whether to achieve national independence, or to defend the national territory from encroachment, or to protect the very principle of nationhood. None of these matters was mentioned by Duke William on the south coast of England over nine hundred years ago.

Eve of battle rhetoric is always revealing, for the leader will remind the followers why the most supreme of all sacrifices is being called upon. When President George Bush, speaking from the Oval Office in the White House, announced the start of the Gulf War, he expressed the contemporary common sense of sacrifice: "All reasonable efforts to reach a peaceful resolution" had been expended; acceptance of peace at this stage would be less reasonable than the pursuance of war. "While the world waited," claimed Bush, "Saddam Hussein systematically raped, pillaged and plundered a tiny nation no threat to his own." It was not individuals who had been raped or pillaged. It was something much more important: a nation. The President was not just speaking for his own nation, the United States, but the United States was speaking for the whole world: "We have before us the opportunity to forge for ourselves and for future generations a new world order, a world where the rule of law, not the law of the jungle, governs the conduct of nations." In this new order "no nation will be permitted to brutally assault its neighbour" (George Bush, 16 January 1991; reproduced in Sifry and Cerf, 1991, pp. 311–14).

The moral order that Bush was evoking was an order of nations. In the new world order, nations would apparently be protected from their neighbours, who would also be nations. As always, what is left unspecified is revealing. Bush did not justify why the notion of nationhood was so important, nor why its protection demanded the ultimate of sacrifices. He assumed his audience would realize that a war, waged by nations against the nation, which had sought to abolish a nation, was necessary to affirm the sacred principle of nationhood. At the end of his speech he quoted the words of 'ordinary' soldiers. A Marine Lieutenant-General had said "these things are worth fighting for" because a world "in which brutality and lawlessness go unchecked isn't the kind of world we're going to want to live in".

Bush had judged his audience well. As on previous occasions, bold military action against a foreign enemy brought popular support to a US president (Bowen, 1989; Brody, 1991; Sigelman and Conover, 1981). During the campaign, public opinion polls indicated that the President's 'approval rating' had soared from a mediocre 50 per cent to a record level of nearly 90 per cent (Krosnick and Brannon, 1993). Opposition to the war in the United States was minimal and was castigated as unpatriotic by a loyal press (Hackett and Zhao, 1994; Hallin, 1994). A recording of the national anthem went to the top of the popular music charts. T-shirts and hats, with patriotic insignia, were being sold on the streets. Elsewhere in the world, polls showed that Western public opinion could be relied on to support the coalition (Taylor, P.M., 1992). Britain's largest selling news-paper, the *Sun*, carried a full colour front page, depicting a Union Jack with a soldier's face at its heart; readers were invited to hang the display in their front windows.

Within weeks, the enemy army had capitulated. On 27 February 1991, Bush, speaking again from his Oval Office, was able to announce victory. He spoke of flags: "Tonight the Kuwaiti flag once again flies above the capital of a free and sovereign nation and the American flag flies above our embassy." Perhaps a quarter of a million Iraqis – civilian and military – lay dead. The exact figure will not be known. The West was not counting its victims; it was enjoying its victory. The American flag was flying proudly.

The episode illustrated the speed with which Western publics can be mobilized for flag-waving warfare in the name of nationhood. Nine years earlier there had been a smaller scale rehearsal. In 1982 the Argentinian military junta had sent a military force to take over the South Atlantic islands which they called 'the Malvinas', but whose inhabitants and the administering British called 'the Falkland Islands'. As in the Gulf War, the very principle of nationhood was said to be at stake. Both sides claimed that the islands were rightfully theirs, and, in both cases, the claims were made with popular domestic support. On 3 May of that year, the British House of Commons, debating the crisis, was virtually unanimous in urging the Prime Minister, Margaret Thatcher, to take decisive action. Even Michael Foot, the leader of the Labour Party opposition and a life-long anti-militarist, caught the mood. More was at stake, he declared, than the wishes of the few thousand inhabitants of the islands: there was the wider consideration of ensuring that "foul and brutal aggression does not succeed in the world". If it did, then "there will be a danger not merely to the Falkland Islands, but to people all over this dangerous planet" (quoted in Barnett, 1982, p. 32). The Prime Minister agreed, adding her own brand of rhetoric. The Falkland Islanders were, she said, "British in stock and tradition and they wish to remain British in allegiance" (Barnett, 1982, p. 28).

The rhetoric did not fall upon deaf ears. Just a month previously, according to Gallup Polls, 48 per cent of the British population believed Thatcher to be the worst prime minister in history. In the early days of the crisis, nearly 50 per cent of the British population thought that the maintenance of British sovereignty in the Falklands was not worth loss of life. Once the Task Force had been sent, earlier reservations were abandoned; the government's popularity, and especially that of its leader, soared (Dillon, 1989). By the end of May, 84 per cent of the population were declaring themselves satisfied with the way the government was handling the issue, which was dominating the news (but see Sanders et al., 1987, for an analysis which denies that the 'Falklands factor' had a major, long-term effect on the Conservatives' popularity). During the war, the British press largely, and uncritically, supported the government (Harris, 1985; Taylor, J., 1992).

In both the Falklands and the Gulf Wars, the rhetoric of nationhood was much in evidence. Protagonists were not fighting on behalf of God or a political ideology. They claimed, on both sides, to be fighting for rightful nationhood. The American-led coalition in the Gulf, as did the British in the Falklands campaign, spoke of the crime of national invasion. The new world order would, according to Bush, protect nations from aggressive neighbours. He had nothing to say about protecting citizens from the crimes of their own governments. No one had suggested that the British should intervene to stop the Argentinian government murdering left-wing opponents. Nor was the Gulf War prosecuted to rescue Iraqis from their dictatorial president. The gassing of Kurdish women and children did not provoke the sort of global reaction, which followed the abolition of Kuwait, an established nation with UN membership, flag and postage stamps.

During both the Gulf and Falklands Wars, parallels were freely drawn with the Second World War. When Bush first announced that US troops would be sent to Saudi Arabia, five months before the war was started, he referred to Iraq's tanks storming Kuwait "in blitzkrieg fashion" (speech, 8 August 1990, included in Sifry and Cerf, 1991, p. 197). Margaret Thatcher, eight years earlier, had claimed for herself the mantle of Winston Churchill (Aulich, 1992). The parallels are instructive. The Second World War had not been prompted by the German government's mistreatment of its own citizens: no foreign government had committed its soldiery to rescue German Jewry. But once the German government started making national flags, rather than individual citizens, disappear, then war became inevitable.

In this, one can see the force of nationalism within political thinking of the twentieth century. The assumptions of this nationalism are not so much revealed by the actions of ruling cliques that have territorial ambitions over neighbouring nations: after all, such actions harken back to an earlier era before the rise of nation-states. The assumptions are demonstrated in the actions of established and powerful nation-states which will readily fight, with mass popular support, to prevent, or reverse, such annexations. These assumptions are expressed when leaders can cite a world morality of national integrity. It was not ever such. Duke William had no vision of a world order of nations, except that his enemy deserved to be conquered once more because they were "a people accustomed to being conquered" (Anonymous, 1916, p. 3).

In our age, it seems as if an aura attends the very idea of nationhood. The rape of a motherland is far worse than the rape of actual mothers; the death of a nation is the ultimate tragedy, beyond the death of flesh and blood. The aura attached to sovereign nationhood is not, however, absolute, as if all similar incidents produce a similar response. The United States led no coalition of outrage when its ally, the government of Indonesia, annexed East Timor in 1975. A third of the East Timorese population have been subsequently massacred. Unlike the case of Kuwait, the oil fields fell on the wrong side of the abolished border (Chomsky, 1994; Pilger, 1994). The aura of nationhood always operates within contexts of power.

If there is an ideological aura attached to nationhood, then the role of God in this down-to-earth (or rather, down-to-soil) mysticism is interesting. The order of nations is not designed to serve God, but God is to serve the order. Saddam Hussein, using a rhetoric which echoed pre-national times, claimed to be fighting "the army of atheism"; he asserted that the Iraqis were "the faithful and obedient servants of God, struggling for his sake to raise the banner of truth and justice" (Sifry and Cerf, 1991, p. 315). The defender of the new order spoke very differently in his eve of battle address. Only in his closing remarks did President Bush invite God to make a rhetorical appearance. He called on God to bless "our forces" and "the coalition forces at our side". He finished with the imprecation: "May He continue to bless our nation, the United States of America" (1991, p. 314). In this way, God was asked to continue serving the national order.

In all this, an ideological consciousness of nationhood can be seen to be at work. It embraces a complex set of themes about 'us', 'our homeland', 'nations' ('ours' and 'theirs'), the 'world', as well as the morality of national duty and honour. Moreover, these themes are widely diffused as common sense. It is not the common sense of a particular nation, but this common sense is international, to be found across the globe in the nations of the so-called world order. At regular, but intermittent intervals, the crisis occurs, and the moral aura of nationalism is invoked: heads will be nodded, flags waved and tanks will roll.

**Nationalism and Established Nations**

It might seem odd to begin a book on nationalism with the Gulf War. The term 'nationalism' invites us to look elsewhere for exemplars. In both popular and academic writing, nationalism is associated with those who struggle to create new states or with extreme right-wing politics. According to customary usage, George Bush is not a nationalist; but separatists in Quebec or Brittany are; so are the leaders of extreme right-wing parties such as the Front National in France; and so, too, are the Serbian guerrillas, killing in the cause of extending the homeland's borders. A book about nationalism is expected to deal with such figures. It should be discussing dangerous and powerful passions, outlining a psychology of extraordinary emotions.

Yet, there is something misleading about this accepted use of the word 'nationalism'. It always seems to locate nationalism on the periphery. Separatists are often to be found in the outer regions of states; the extremists lurk on the margins of political life in established democracies, usually shunned by the sensible politicians of the centre. The guerrilla figures, seeking to establish their new homelands, operate in conditions where existing structures of state have collapsed, typically at a distance from the established centres of the West. From the perspective of Paris, London or Washington, places such as Moldova, Bosnia and Ukraine are peripherally placed on the edge of Europe. All these factors combine to make nationalism not merely an exotic force, but a peripheral one. In consequence, those in established nations – at the centre of things – are led to see nationalism as the property of others, not of 'us'.

This is where the accepted view becomes misleading: it overlooks the nationalism of the West's nation-states. In a world of nation-states, nationalism cannot be confined to the peripheries. That might be conceded, but still it might be objected that nationalism only strikes the established nation-states on special occasions. Crises, such as the Falklands or Gulf Wars, infect a sore spot, causing bodily fevers: the symptoms are an inflamed rhetoric and an outbreak of ensigns. But the irruption soon dies down; the temperature passes; the flags are rolled up; and, then, it is business as usual.

If that were the extent of nationalism in established nations, then nationalism, when it moves in from the periphery, only comes as a temporary mood. But, there is more. The intermittent crises depend upon existing ideological foundations. Bush, in his eve of battle speech, did not invent his dismal rhetoric: he was drawing upon familiar images and clichés. The flags displayed by the Western publics during the Gulf War were familiar: Americans did not have to remind themselves what this arrangement of stars and stripes was. The national anthem, which topped the US music chart, was recorded at a football final. Each year, whether in peace or war, it is sung before the game.

In short, the crises do not create nation-states as nation-states. In between times, the United States of America, France, the United Kingdom and so on continue to exist. Daily, they are reproduced as nations and their citizenry as nationals. And these nations are reproduced within a wider world of nations. For such daily reproduction to occur, one might hypothesize that a whole complex of beliefs, assumptions, habits, representations and practices must also be reproduced. Moreover, this complex must be reproduced in a banally mundane way, for the world of nations is the everyday world, the familiar terrain of contemporary times.

There is, however, no readily available term to describe the collection of ideological habits (including habits of practice and belief) which reproduce established nations as nations. It is as if the term 'nationalism' only comes in small sizes and bright colours. The word is comfortably wrapped around social movements, which seek to re-draw existing territorial boundaries, and which, thereby, threaten the existing national status quo. With some room for growth, the word can be stretched over moments of eccentricity, such as Thatcher's remarks about the Falklanders being of 'British stock'. But, if one tries to dress the whole 'normal', national status quo in the term, the garment appears to fall apart; the stitching splits; the buttons pop; the customers complain 'this isn't how it normally looks'.

Gaps in political language are rarely innocent. The case of 'nationalism' is no exception. By being semantically restricted to small sizes and exotic colours, 'nationalism' becomes identified as a problem: it occurs 'there' on the periphery, not 'here' at the centre. The separatists, the fascists and the guerrillas are the problem of nationalism. The ideological habits, by which 'our' nations are reproduced as nations, are unnamed and, thereby, unnoticed. The national flag hanging outside a public building in the United States attracts no special attention. It belongs to no special, sociological genus. Having no name, it cannot be identified as a problem. Nor, by implication, is the daily reproduction of the United States a problem.

The present book insists on stretching the term 'nationalism', so that it covers the ideological means by which nation-states are reproduced. To stretch the term 'nationalism' indiscriminately would invite confusion: surely, there is a distinction between the flag waved by Serbian ethnic cleansers and that hanging unobtrusively outside the US post office; or between the policy of the Front National and the support given by the leader of the opposition to the British government's Falkland's policy. For this reason, the term **banal nationalism** is introduced to cover the ideological habits which enable the established nations of the West to be reproduced. It is argued that these habits are not removed from everyday life, as some observers have supposed. Daily, the nation is indicated, or 'flagged', in the lives of its citizenry. Nationalism, far from being an intermittent mood in established nations, is the endemic condition.

One point needs stressing: banal does not imply benign. A number of observers have claimed that 'nationalism' as a phenomenon is 'Janus-faced', or that it possesses a Jekyll and Hyde duality (Bhabha, 1990; Forbes, 1986; Freeman, 1992; Giddens, 1985; Smith, M., 1982; Tehranian, 1993). According to this reckoning, some forms of nationalism, most notably movements for national liberation from colonialism, tend to be classed as positive, whilst others, such as fascist movements, belong to the shadowed half. It would be wrong to assume that 'banal nationalism' is 'benign' because it seems to possess a reassuring normality, or because it appears to lack the violent passions of the extreme right. As Hannah Arendt (1963) stressed, banality is not synonymous with harmlessness. In the case of Western nation-states, banal nationalism can hardly be innocent: it is reproducing institutions which possess vast armaments. As the Gulf and Falklands Wars indicated, forces can be mobilized without lengthy campaigns of political preparation. The armaments are primed, ready for use in battle. And the national populations appear also to be primed, ready to support the use of those armaments.

## Identity and Ideology

The popular reaction of support for the Gulf War in the United States cannot be understood by what happened during the moments of crisis. A banal, but far from benign, preparation must have been routinely accomplished to make such readiness possible. It is easy to think of these things in terms of 'identity'. One might say that the popular reaction occurred because of the strength of 'national identity'. Identity, in common talk, is something which people have or search for. One might think that people today go about their daily lives, carrying with them a piece of psychological machinery called 'a national identity'. Like a mobile telephone, this piece of psychological equipment lies quiet for most of the time. Then, the crisis occurs; the president calls; bells ring; the citizens answer; and the patriotic identity is connected.

Actually, the notion of an 'identity' does not take the argument very far. It is seldom clear what an identity is. What is this thing – this identity – which people are supposed to carry around with them? It cannot be an object like a mobile phone. Some analysts have said that a national identity is based upon 'primordial ties'. The concept of 'primordial ties' is just as mysterious. As Eller and Coughlan (1993) have argued, social scientists, who make reference to such primordial ties, have not specified how these ties might operate and how they might be reproduced. Just to call nationalism an identity or a tie explains little in itself.

The problems start when one expects to find the 'identity' within the body or the mind of the individual. This is to look in the wrong place for the operation of identity. As far as nationality is concerned, one needs to look for the reasons why people in the contemporary world do not forget their nationality. When George Bush made his eve-of-battle-speech, he could assume that his audience would know whether or not they were

American. He also could assume that they would recognize what a nation was; and, of course, they would believe that a nation was something precious. These assumptions were not created during the moment of crisis. Nor do they disappear in between crises. But on ordinary days, they can be seen bobbing about, brought home daily on the familiar tides of banal nationalism.

The central thesis of the present book is that, in the established nations, there is a continual 'flagging', or reminding, of nationhood. The established nations are those states that have confidence in their own continuity, and that, particularly, are part of what is conventionally described as 'the West'. The political leaders of such nations – whether France, the USA, the United Kingdom or New Zealand – are not typically termed 'nationalists'. However, as will be suggested, nationhood provides a continual background for their political discourses, for cultural products, and even for the structuring of newspapers. In so many little ways, the citizenry are daily reminded of their national place in a world of nations. However, this reminding is so familiar, so continual, that it is not consciously registered as reminding. The metonymic image of banal nationalism is not a flag which is being consciously waved with fervent passion; it is the flag hanging unnoticed on the public building.

National identity embraces all these forgotten reminders. Consequently, an identity is to be found in the embodied habits of social life. Such habits include those of thinking and using language. To have a national identity is to possess ways of talking about nationhood. As a number of critical social psychologists have been emphasizing, the social psychological study of identity should involve the detailed study of discourse (Shotter 1993a, 1993b; Shotter and Gergen, 1989; Wetherell and Potter, 1992). Having a national identity also involves being situated physically, legally, socially, as well as emotionally: typically, it means being situated within a homeland, which itself is situated within the world of nations. And, only if people believe that they have national identities, will such homelands, and the world of national homelands, be reproduced.

In many ways, this book itself aims to be a reminder. Because the concept of nationalism has been restricted to exotic and passionate exemplars, the routine and familiar forms of nationalism have been overlooked. In this case, 'our' daily nationalism slips from attention. There is a growing body of opinion that nation-states are declining. Nationalism, or so it is said, is no longer a major force: globalization is the order of the day. But a reminder is necessary. Nationhood is still being reproduced: it can still call for ultimate sacrifices; and, daily, its symbols and assumptions are flagged.

The investigation of banal nationalism should be a critical study. The gaps in language, which enable banal nationalism to be forgotten, are also gaps in theoretical discourse. The social sciences have used habits of thinking which enable 'our' nationalism to pass by unnoticed. Thus, the mundane ways of thinking, which routinely lead 'us' to think that 'others', but not 'ourselves', are nationalist, are paralleled by habits of intellectual thinking. For this reason, banal nationalism cannot be studied simply by applying ready-made methodologies or theories. If orthodox social psychological theories of identity define 'our' nationalism away, or if they consider it 'natural' to have national identities, then they are not suitable for analysing how banal nationalism is so forgettable. Such theories will not so much provide tools for analysis, as offer further examples of the way that the specificities of nationalism have been overlooked.

Nor is national identity to be explored by taking a scale from the psychological library of tests and administering it to suitable populations. Most scales deal with issues of individual differences, and, thus, as Serge Moscovici (1983, 1987) has emphasized, are unsuited for studying common-sense thinking. The question behind the present investigation is not why some people have 'stronger national identities' than others. It concerns widespread and common habits of thinking, which transcend individual differences.

These habits of thinking also transcend national differences. Nationalism, as an ideology, is not confined to national borders, but its assumptions have been diffused internationally. George Bush, in announcing the start of the Gulf War, was addressing 'the world'. He was speaking as if all nations would (or should) recognize the morality of nationhood – as if this morality were a universal morality. Nationalism in the contemporary world makes universal claims. The talk of a new world order suggests how intertwined the national and the international are. Yet, one nation, in particular, is seeking to represent this order. At the present juncture, special attention should be paid to the United States and its nationalism. This nationalism, above all, has appeared so forgettable, so 'natural' to social scientists, and is today so globally important.

## Outline of the Book

The present book attempts to provide an investigation of 'banal nationalism', setting out some of the basic issues and providing examples. As such, it provides an investigation of contemporary 'national identity', which, broadly speaking, is a social psychological topic. But, as has been said, the sort of social psychology appropriate for the task has to be created. Therefore, as the interlocking themes, outlined above, are explored, so inevitably the exemplars of banal nationalism have to be accompanied by theoretical and critical analyses. In many respects, this must be a preliminary study, which feels its way around the topic. More detailed empirical investigation will still be required, in order to show the operations of banal nationalism in their detail.

Chapter 2 argues that nationalism, far from being an age-old 'primordial' condition, has been produced by the age of the modern nation-state. The rise of the state has brought about an ideological transformation of common sense. Building upon the ideas of Ernest Gellner, Benedict Anderson and Anthony Giddens, it is suggested that nation-states are not founded upon 'objective' criteria, such as the possession of a discrete language. Instead, nations have to be 'imagined' as communities. Because of this imaginary element, nationalism contains a strong social psychological dimension. This chapter argues that the imagining of the nation is part of a wider ideological, discursive consciousness. For example, national languages also have to be imagined, and this lies at the root of today's common-sense belief that discrete languages 'naturally' exist. It might seem obvious that there are different spoken languages; but, this assumption itself is an ideological notion, which has been vital for the achievement of order and hegemony in modern nation-states. The assumption that different languages 'naturally' exist illustrates just how deeply nationalist conceptions have seeped into contemporary common sense.

The following chapter discusses the notions of banal nationalism and the banal flagging of nationhood. A distinction between the waved and unwaved flag is made. The reproduction of nation-states depends upon a dialectic of collective remembering and forgetting, and of imagination and unimaginative repetition. The unwaved flag, which is so forgettable, is at least as important as the memorable moments of flag waving. In line with the strategy of examining the theoretical and the mundane, this chapter also criticizes the narrow view of nationalism to be found in orthodox social science, especially in conventional sociology. Orthodox theories have preferred to talk of 'societies', rather than nations; and they have treated nationalism as something 'surplus', rather than being endemic in the world of nation-states. Here, as throughout the book, particular attention is paid to the case of the United States of America, the source of much sociological thinking about 'society'. American theories of 'society' have frequently ignored the ways that American nationhood is flagged, as school pupils daily pledge their allegiance to the national flag. Such theoretical amnesia is not ideologically neutral.

Chapter 4 examines some of the major themes in nationalist consciousness. In doing this, it criticizes social psychological theories that see nationalism as merely one form of identity amongst countless others. Nationalism is more than this: it is a way of thinking or ideological consciousness. In this consciousness, nations, national identities and national homelands appear as 'natural'. Most crucially, the 'world of nations' is represented as a 'natural', moral order. This imagining of 'us', 'them', homelands and so on must be habitual or unimaginatively accomplished; yet, it also provides a complex way of talking about the world. Nationalism is not an inward-looking ideology, like the pre-modern ethnocentric outlook. It is an international ideology with its own discourses of hegemony. Thus, US presidents, in defending their own national interests, can claim to speak for universal interests, or for the whole world order. The voice of nationalism can employ 'the syntax of hegemony', which claims an 'identity of identities'.

If nationalism has become banal in established democracies of the West, then nationhood should be constantly flagged. Chapter 5 examines the extent to which the flagging occurs and the discursive means by which it is accomplished. Democratic politics is founded on the institutions of nationhood; politicians, in pursuing their public trade, seek to address the nation. Because politicians have become celebrities in the contemporary age, their words, which typically reproduce the clichés of nationhood, are continually reported in the mass media.

Politicians do not provide the only conduit by which nationhood is banally flagged. As an illustrative case study, Chapter 5 also examines British daily newspapers, focusing on one particular day, selected at random. All the papers, whether tabloid or quality, and whether left- or right-wing, address their readers as members of the nation. They present news in ways that take for granted the existence of the world of nations. They employ a routine 'deixis', which is continually pointing to the national homeland as the home of the readers. The little words – mostly overlooked – are crucial components in this routine deixis of the homeland. This chapter also pays special attention to the sports pages, which, day after day, invite 'us', the readers, to support the national cause. The sports pages are predominantly read by men for pleasure. They can be seen as banal rehearsals for the extraordinary times of crisis, when the state calls upon its citizenry, and especially its male citizenry, to make ultimate sacrifices in the cause of nationhood.

A major theme in the present work is that notions of nationhood are deeply embedded in contemporary ways of thinking. Some analysts are currently arguing that the nation-state belongs to the modern age and is being superseded in the postmodern, globalized world. If this is the case, then banal nationalism is a disappearing ideology, with a politics of identity replacing the old politics of nationhood. This thesis is critically discussed in Chapter 6. Not only do some of the theories of postmodernity often take for granted the existence of nationhood, but some of the phenomena, which are being claimed as indicating the end of nations, themselves reveal the continuing hold of nationalist assumptions. There is a central paradox: the theories of national identity and postmodernity, which assert the decline of the nation-state, are being formulated at a time when a powerful nation, the United States of America, is bidding for global hegemony. The global culture itself has a national dimension, as the symbols of the United States appear as universal symbols.

Banal nationalism is not to be corralled into the sports pages or the banal clichés of vote-seeking politicians. It is much more widespread. It even has its philosophical form. Chapter 7 considers in detail the work of Richard Rorty. His philosophy has an engagingly sceptical tone, which seems to dispute the certainties of nationalism and which echoes the spirit of postmodern times. Yet, in so doing, this philosophy illustrates the subtle hold of nationalist assumptions, exactly where they may be least expected. Rorty proposes a philosophy of community, which takes for granted the

nation as the accepted form of community. Moreover, Rorty's own texts
embody the syntax of hegemony, as 'we', that is, the American nation, are
said to speak for all of 'us'. As such, this philosophy can be considered as
an intellectual flag for its place and its times. It is an exemplar of the
nationalist philosophy of a new world order, which is being constructed,
like the coalition in the Gulf, around a US leadership.

The analyst of banal nationalism does not have the theoretical luxury of
exposing the nationalism of others. The analyst cannot place exotic
nationalists under the microscope as specimens, in order to stain the tissues
of repressed sexuality, or turn the magnifying lens on to the unreasonable
stereotypes, which ooze from the mouth of the specimen. In presenting the
psychology of a Le Pen or Zhirinovksy, 'we' might experience a shiver of
fear as 'we' contemplate 'them', the nationalists, with their violent
emotions and 'their' crude stereotyping of the Other. And 'we' will
recognize 'ourselves' among the objects of this stereotyping. Alongside the
'foreigners' and the 'racial inferiors', there 'we' will be – the 'liberal
degenerates', with 'our' international broad-mindedness. 'We' will be
reassured to have confirmed 'ourselves' as the Other of 'our' Other.

By extending the concept of nationalism, the analyst is not safely
removed from the scope of investigation. We might imagine that we
possess a cosmopolitan broadness of spirit. But, if nationalism is a wider
ideology, whose familiar commonplaces catch us unawares, then this is too
reassuring. We will not remain unaffected. If the thesis is correct, then
nationalism has seeped into the corners of our consciousness; it is present
in the very words which we might try to use for analysis. It is naive to think
that a text of exposure can escape from the times and place of its
formulation. It can attempt, instead, to do something more modest: it can
draw attention to the powers of an ideology which is so familiar that it
hardly seems noticeable.

# 2

# Nations and Languages

It was an insignificant item, tucked away on an inside page of a British daily paper, the *Guardian*. It was not even that page's main story. 'Flemish leader calls for split' was the headline. The item, written by the paper's correspondent in Brussels, reported that the leaders of the main Flemish parties had issued a declaration which "has stunned the French-speaking political parties". They had declared that Belgium should be split into a loose confederation of two independent states – Dutch-speaking Flanders and French-speaking Wallonia. Special arrangements should be made for "the small German-speaking community in the east of Belgium". Hitherto, reported the paper, Flemish demands for separation have "been restricted to small nationalist and far-right groups". The Belgian government had hoped that the existing arrangements for devolution would have enabled "Belgium to survive more or less intact" (*Guardian*, 14 July 1994).

The item is revealing both for what it reported, and for what it left unsaid. The possible break-up of Belgium as a nation-state was not sufficiently important to merit the front page of this 'serious' British newspaper. This, in itself, says something about the climate of the times. Although the story was presented as a sudden, stunning declaration, no background explanation was offered to say why Flemish-speakers might wish to establish their own state. By the omission, the paper was indicating that readers could be expected to understand such national aspirations. Other days, the paper might carry stories about French-speaking separatists in Canada, Basque-speakers in Spain or even Welsh-speakers in the United Kingdom. Language groups wanting their own state are not mysterious for newspaper readers today.

Such a story bears two messages. The overt message tells British readers something about 'them', the Belgians, who might soon not be known as 'Belgians'. There is also an implicit message about 'us', the British readers and what 'we' are expected to know. We do not need to be told why communities speaking a particular language might wish to establish their own nation-state. We do not need to be told what a state is; nor what a language is. All this is common sense, or, rather, 'we' are assumed to possess such common-sense ideas about nations.

This sort of common sense is to be found in academic writings, as much as daily newspapers. Social scientists often assume that it is natural that speakers of the same language should seek their own political identity. The author of a book entitled *Varieties of Nationalism* has written, "in the search for security, people who speak the same language are irresistibly drawn together" (Snyder, 1976, p. 21). The word 'irresistibly' suggests that this is an inevitable part of human nature. Thus, if the Flemish-speakers are feeling insecure, then it is little surprise that they are wishing to stick together and to establish a state, in which all citizens speak the same language. John Edwards has observed that "language is still commonly taken to be *the* central pillar of ethnic identity" (1991, p. 269, emphasis in original; see also, Edwards, 1985; Fishman, 1972; Gudykunst and Ting-Toomey, 1990). Indeed, it is sometimes assumed that nations, comprising different linguistic groups, are fragile compromises, which might be torn apart by the next set of crises and insecurities (Connor, 1978, 1993). This way of thinking is not new. In the eighteenth century, Herder and Fichte were declaring that the basis of a nation, and indeed its genius, lay in its language. According to this view, a Belgium, cobbled together out of Flemish speakers and French speakers, not to mention the small community of German speakers, cannot be a 'real' nation. The Flemish separatists, therefore, are seeking to redraw the map of nationhood in a way which accords better with natural human inclinations: little wonder, then, that their demands can seem so comprehensible.

There is a reason for mentioning this. Nationalism is simultaneously obvious and obscure. It appears obvious that the Flemings and the Walloons might wish to have their own separate nation-states. After all, if they can hardly communicate with each other, how can they share a common identity, sense of heritage or feeling of community? The reaction of the Flemish-speakers is understandable; and so is the concern of the French-speaking Prime Minister, who might suddenly find his country cut in half. There is a further question: where does this sense of obviousness come from? Is it 'natural' to think about community, nationhood and language in this way? Or is this sense of naturalness itself the issue?

Eric Hobsbawm (1992), at the beginning of *Nations and Nationalism*, writes that historians of nationalism should distance themselves from nationalist myths, for "no serious historian of nations and nationalism can be a committed political nationalist" (p. 12). Hobsbawm was referring to the sorts of myths which Herder was formulating about the German nation and language. Analogous myths are today being circulated by Flemish nationalists who talk about the inalienable and historic Flemish *volk* (Husbands, 1992). These are the sorts of myth which, according to Hobsbawm, must be discounted. But there is more distancing to be done by the social scientist wishing to study nationalism as an ideology. Certainly, the social scientist should put into brackets the claims of those who, like the Flemish-speaking politicians, wish to create new national units, claiming that these units correspond to natural or age-old facts. In addition, 'our' common sense about nations must be bracketed. This is harder than distancing ourselves from 'them', the Flemings or Walloons and their particular conflict. Something more universal has to be placed in metaphorical brackets.

To achieve this bracketing, we must distance ourselves from ourselves and from that which we routinely accept as obvious or 'natural'. The obviousness must be questioned, if nationalism is to be seen as an ideology, which deeply affects contemporary consciousness – 'our' consciousness, as much as 'theirs'. Ideologies are patterns of belief and practice, which make existing social arrangements appear 'natural' or inevitable (Eagleton, 1991). Thus, patriarchal ideology makes it appear 'natural' (or in accord with the unquestioned, biological way of things) that men rule and that women serve; racist ideology made it seem 'natural' and 'common sense' to Europeans of the eighteenth and nineteenth centuries that the white man was superior in the arts of government to the 'child-like native'. We, who live in nation-states, paying taxes to support the armaments of our nations, do we not, too, have a common sense which makes this world of nation-states seem natural?

If we are to understand this part of ourselves, we have to attempt to stand back from our common-sense assumptions. We cannot rest content that it is actually 'natural' that those who speak the same language will wish to form national groupings. It is not a matter of empirically testing the belief to discover its validity. The analyst of ideology must ask where this belief – our belief – originated from and what it assumes. We must question – or put into ideological brackets – the very concepts which seem so solidly real to us and which enable us to understand the assumptions of the daily news. These include concepts such 'a nation', even 'a language'. Such concepts should not be used uncritically to analyse nationalism, because they do not stand outside the topic which is to be analysed. Instead, the history of nationalism continues to run through the meanings which such concepts routinely bear.

## Studying Nationalism as an Ideology

In general, liberal Western academics today find it easier to recognize nationalism in 'others' than in themselves. Nationalists can be identified as extremists who, impelled by a violently emotional psychology, seek irrational ends; or they can be painted as heroic figures who, in particular, are to be found overseas, battling against repressive colonialists. Nationalism can be seen almost everywhere but 'here'. If nationalism is a widespread ideology, then a different perspective is in order. This would take nationalism to include the patterns of belief and practice which reproduce the world – 'our' world – as a world of nation-states, in which 'we' live as citizens of nation-states. In consequence, nationalism is not merely the ideology which is impelling Flemish speakers to resist the Belgian state. It is also the ideology which permits the states, including the Belgian state, to exist. In the absence of an overt political challenge, like that mounted by the Flemish speakers, this ideology might appear banal, routine, almost invisible.

It is always possible to insist that the term 'nationalism' should be restricted to the beliefs of 'others'. When talking of 'our' beliefs, one might prefer other different words such as 'patriotism', 'loyalty', or 'societal identification'. Such terms banish the word 'nation', and with it the spectre of nationalism, at least in regard to 'our' attachments and identities. The problem is that such terms overlook the object to which the 'loyalty' or 'identification' is being shown: the nation-state. The present approach does not restrict the term 'nationalism' to the ideology of 'others', for, as will be suggested, such a restriction carries ideological implications. Instead, nationalism is broadened as a concept to cover the ways that established nation-states are routinely reproduced. This frequently involves a 'banal' nationalism, in contrast with the overt, articulated and often fiercely expressed nationalism of those who battle to form new nations.

There is another reason for using the term 'nationalism' to describe what is familiar and 'here, at home'. 'Our' common sense about nationhood and 'our' psychology of national attachments should be located within the history of nationalism. By putting 'our' common sense in its historical context, 'our' beliefs about nationhood, and about the naturalness of belonging to a nation, are seen to be the products of a particular historical age. The obviousness of such beliefs is, thereby, questioned. Indeed, they can be made to appear as eccentric as the beliefs of other ages.

Many social scientists, especially sociologists and social psychologists, have not treated the topic of nationalism in this way. They have tended to ignore what is here being called 'banal nationalism'. In using the term 'nationalism' in a limited way, such theorists have often projected nationalism onto others and naturalized 'our' nationalism out of existence. This occurs in two types of theorizing, which often, as will be seen in later chapters, accompany each other.

1  **Projecting theories of nationalism**. These approaches tend to define nationalism in a restricted way, as an extreme/surplus phenomenon. Nationalism is equated with the outlook of nationalist movements and, when there are no such movements, nationalism is not seen to be an issue. By and large, the authors of such theories are not themselves partisans of nationalist movements – although there are exceptions. Such theorists often claim that nationalism is impelled by irrational emotions. Since the theorists are claiming to produce a rational account of something, which they see as being inherently irrational, they are distancing themselves from nationalism. The theorists themselves live in a world of nations: they carry passports and pay their taxes to nation-states. Their theories tend to take this world of nations for granted as the 'natural' environment, in which the dramas of nationalism periodically erupt. Since the nationalism which routinely reproduces the world of nations is theoretically ignored, and nationalism is seen as a condition of 'others', then such theories can be seen as rhetorical

projections. Nationalism as a condition is projected on to 'others'; 'ours' is overlooked, forgotten, even theoretically denied.

2 **Naturalizing theories of nationalism**. Some theorists tend to depict contemporary loyalties to nation-states as instances of something which is psychologically general, or endemic to the human condition. Thus, such loyalties might be theoretically transmuted into 'needs for identity', 'attachments to society' or 'primordial ties', which are theoretically posited to be universal psychological states, and not peculiar to the age of nation-states. As such, 'banal nationalism' not only ceases to be nationalism, but it ceases to be a problem for investigation. Indeed, the lack of such identities (the lack of patriotism in established nations) can be seen as the problem for concern. In this way, such theories make existing conditions of consciousness appear natural, taking for granted the world of nations.

Later chapters will provide examples of the ways in which social scientists have projected and naturalized nationalism. Some do both simultaneously: 'our patriotism' is made to appear 'natural', and thereby invisible, while 'nationalism' is seen as a property of 'others'. Such theories may have the merit of drawing attention to the particular psychological conditions of overtly nationalist movements. However, in so doing, they tend to overlook the nationalist aspects of 'our' common sense. By contrast, the present approach puts the psychological focus back on 'us'. If the world of nations is to be reproduced, then nationhood has to be imagined, communicated, believed in, remembered and so on. An infinite variety of psychological acts is required for the reproduction of nation-states. These psychological acts should not be analysed purely in terms of the motives of the individual actors. An ideological analysis of psychological states stresses that the acts, and, indeed, the motives of the individuals, are constituted through socio-historical processes, rather than vice versa. This necessitates reversing the theoretical frameworks of many conventional theories of social psychology, which presume that psychological variables are universal, rather than historically created (for criticisms of the individualism in most orthodox approaches to social psychology, see, for example: Gergen, 1982, 1985, 1989; Moscovici, 1983; Sampson, 1993; Shotter 1993a and 1993b).

Language plays a vital role in the operation of ideology and in the framing of ideological consciousness. This was stressed over 60 years ago by Mikhail Bakhtin in *Marxism and the Philosophy of Language*, the book he wrote under the name of Voloshinov (Holquist, 1990). Bakhtin argued that "objective psychology must be grounded in the study of ideology", and that forms of consciousness were constituted through language (Voloshinov, 1973, p. 13). Therefore, the social psychological study of ideology should examine the concrete operations of language: "social psychology is first and foremost an atmosphere made up of multifarious *speech performances* that engulf and wash over all persistent kinds of ideological creativity" (p. 19, emphasis in original). Similar points have recently been made by discursive psychologists, who argue that many of the psychological phenomena, that psychologists have assumed to exist internally within the person, are socially and discursively created (Billig, 1987a, 1991; Edwards and Potter, 1992, 1993; Potter and Wetherell, 1987; Potter et al., 1993). Gillett and Harré, (1994) have suggested that emotions, such as anger, fear or happiness, involve judgements as well as outward social acts. This would include so-called emotions of national loyalty or xenophobia (Scheff, 1995; Wetherell and Potter, 1992). These emotions depend upon judgements, shared beliefs, or representations, about nationhood, about 'us' and 'them'. Such emotions are expressed by, and within, complex patterns of discourse, which themselves are part of wider historical processes.

Boswell, in his *Life of Johnson*, recounts how the great doctor used to wander through London at night with Richard Savage, the vagrant poet and convicted murderer. Usually, the two companions were cast down by the misery of those sleeping rough in doorways. But one night, walking around St James's Square, the strange couple were "in high spirits and brimful of patriotism". They traversed the square for several hours, and "inveighed against the minister and 'resolved they would *stand by their country*' " (Boswell, 1906, vol. I, p. 95, emphasis in original).

The words spoken on that evening cannot now be known. The high spirits, which were evident to both, were manifested within the conversation. Each animated the other, until both declared their patriotic resolution, condemning the relevant government minister. Through words, gestures and tones, they created the mood. Similarly, the patriotic spirit, of which they were 'brimful', consisted in declarations, resolutions and judgements. Johnson, in retelling the story to Boswell, could classify the conversation as being 'patriotic' and his biographer could recognize the categorization as appropriate. The patriotism was not something strange lurking beyond the conversation, like the dark figures in the doorways of the Square. But both speakers could recognize this spirit in themselves and in the other.

No doubt, the poet and the future lexicographer uttered commonplace judgements as they displayed their patriotic resolution. To be recognizably brimful of patriotism one must have discourses of patriotism – that is, the phrases and stances which can be conventionally identifiable as 'patriotic'. Johnson and Savage may have repeated stereotypes and uttered declarations of personal feeling. "I am willing to love all mankind, *except an American*", declared Johnson many years later during a conversation at Mr Dilly's house. Johnson's highly charged nature was, to quote Boswell again, bursting "into horrid fire" (vol. II, p. 209, emphasis in original).

Johnson was, of course, expressing his own views and emotions. But he was doing more than that: he was repeating commonplace themes of his times: the virtues of loving all mankind and being brimful with patriotism;

and the naughtiness of enjoying an explosive hatred of Americans. All these matters stretch beyond Johnson, the individual; they reach into the ideological history of nations and nationalism. He was speaking patriotically, at a time when the British nation-state was being established politically, with its government exercising rule over the country in the name of all 'the people', including vagrants and criminals (Colley, 1992). When Johnson was excepting Americans from his love of mankind, the colony was engaged in the violent process of establishing itself as a nation-state, independent from British sovereignty. In other epochs, in other places, people might talk differently about loyalties and hatreds. But Johnson's ways of talking – and his emotions – were part of the ideological consciousness attending the rise of modern nationhood. This ideology accompanied his night-time stroll around London; it strode into Mr Dilly's house, and sat down at his table, as the conversation turned from cookery and religion. Nationalism was filling banal moments of eighteenth-century English life.

## Nationalism and the Nation-State

If nationalism is identified as the ideology that creates and maintains nation-states, then it has a specific socio-historical location. Not all group loyalties are instances of nationalism, but, as Ernest Gellner has argued, nationalism belongs to the era of nation-states. There can be no nationalism without nation-states; and, thus, nationalism, as a way of depicting community, is a historically specific form of consciousness. On the first page of *Nations and Nationalism*, Gellner asserts that "nationalism is primarily a political principle, which holds that the political and the national unit should be congruent" (1983, p. 1). According to Gellner, nationalism emerges only when the existence of the state "is already very much taken for granted" (1983, p. 4); nationalism's core tenet is the belief that "the national state, identified with a national culture and committed to its protection, is the natural political unit" (Gellner, 1993, p. 409). Not only does Gellner's definition link nationalism to the nation-state but also, as Gellner suggests, in these circumstances the political principles of nationalism appear as if they were 'natural'.

The milieu of the nation-state is, broadly speaking, the modern world, for, as Hobsbawm asserts, "the basic characteristic of the modern nation and everything associated with it is its modernity" (1992, p. 14). Historians have disputed exactly when the nation-state first made its appearance in European history. Some historians, such as Hugh Seton-Watson (1977) and Douglas Johnson (1993), have claimed that feelings or patriotic loyalty emerged in England and France as early as the seventeenth century. Other scholars, such as Elie Kedourie (1966), put the date later, claiming that nation-states and nationalist attachments cannot be found until the eighteenth century. Elshtain even argues that the notion of 'La France', the female fatherland, "is a rather recent historic development, one of this century" (1987, p. 66). Both camps, however, agree that mediaeval Europe knew no such nation-states.

Anthony Giddens has attempted to specify what new forms of governance were brought into being with the creation of the nation-state. He defines the nation-state as "a set of institutional forms of governance maintaining an administrative monopoly over a territory with demarcated boundaries, its rule being sanctioned by law and direct control of the means of internal and external violence". Boundedness and possession of the means of violence are key components, for the modern nation-state is "a bounded power-container" (Giddens, 1985, p. 120). Most importantly, nation-states do not exist in isolation, but "in a complex of other nation-states" (Giddens, 1987, p. 171). Nationalism embraces ways of thinking – patterns of common-sense discourse – which make this boundedness and monopolization of violence seem natural to 'us', who inhabit the world of nation-states. This world – 'our' world – is a place where nations have their official armies, police forces and executioners; where boundaries are rigorously drawn; and where citizens, and male citizens in particular, might expect to be called upon to kill and die in defence of the national border-post.

A glance at mediaeval and modern maps shows the novelty of the bounded state. Not only are European mediaeval maps less precise; not only do they tend to depict Jerusalem at the centre of things; not only do they typically indicate an incomplete world, with distant lands shading off into nothingness; but there is also a further difference. Mediaeval maps represent a world unobsessed with boundaries (Roberts, 1985). General areas are indicated for kingdoms and empires, without the compulsion to represent the precise place where one kingdom ends and another starts. The modern map of nations is quite different in this respect. It depicts a completed world, divided up by precisely drawn boundaries. This is the sort of map which is familiar to 'us'.

In mediaeval Europe there were few clear territorial boundaries. As Mann (1988) points out, mediaeval Europe comprised small cross-cutting networks; no single power agency controlled a clear-cut territory or the people within it. In any case, territories kept changing shape from generation to generation, as early mediaeval monarchs frequently divided their estates between their heirs. Peasantry might feel an obligation to a local lord, rather than a distant monarch. Even if the local lord actually lived in the locality, almost certainly he would not speak the language of his peasantry. If kings raised armies, they did so through the major lords, who in turn might sub-contract the job to lesser nobility. There was a whole pyramidal structure of rights and obligations. Armies were continually being raised, since politics, on all levels, tended to be conducted through warfare. These wars were seldom announced with official declarations like the outbreaks of modern inter-state hostility; nor were they brought to formal end-points.

In so many respects, the mediaeval world of Europe looks to modern eyes as an unbelievably messy, disorganized place. Throughout the Middle Ages, the mass of inhabitants, living in what is now known as France or England, did not think of themselves as 'French' or 'English' (Braudel, 1988; Seton-Watson, 1977). They had little conception of a territorial nation (a 'country') to which they owed an allegiance stronger than life itself. Community was imagined, and lived, in different ways from now. And this, in part, makes the mediaeval world seem so foreign today.

It is easy for 'us', who accept the naturalness of a 'boundary-consciousness', to think that the nation-state system introduced order and organization into a world of disorder and inefficient chaos. The state, whether represented by monarch or president, now claims the direct and total loyalty of its citizenry. When it comes to war, the rulers of the state do not depend upon the cooperation of feudal barons. Armies are raised directly from the people, who are urged to fight for their 'nation'. Of course, many, who have been so recruited, have been bribed, coerced or compelled through force of law. But also the modern world has seen mass, voluntary recruitment of young men, willingly, even enthusiastically, going to battle in the cause of the nation (Reader, 1988).

As the nation-state established a monopoly on the right to the means of violence within its boundaries, so the era of 'unofficial wars' ended (Hinsley, 1986). Henceforth 'Britain' would fight against 'France' in the Napoleonic wars; 'Russia' would be invaded; the 'United States of America' would watch closely. In this new world of nations-at-war, there was little room for a Duke of Burgundy or an Earl of Warwick to march into the fray at the head of a private retinue. Today, local 'warlords' tend to emerge in places where the state's authority has collapsed, such as Beirut or Somalia. The other states of the world look with horror on the emergence of 'unofficial armies', dreading such forces within their own borders. With the rise of official wars comes, naturally, the rise of official peace. For the past 200 years, the end of wars has been marked by conferences to affirm precisely where state boundaries were to be drawn. The Congress of Vienna, at the end of the Napoleonic Wars, set an example, which has been much repeated. The 'new world order', which President Bush claimed might be established with the military defeat of Iraq, is nothing new. Since the birth of nation-states, powerful states, who have proved their power in war, have sought to impose their own vision of a settled order of well-drawn international boundaries. In this respect, the modern nation-state is the product of an international age.

## The International World of Nations

Giddens has described the nation-state system as having "no precedent in history" (1987, p. 166). Why the system should have emerged in Europe and then spread through the rest of the world is one of the major puzzles of modern history. Analysts have suggested how the new form of state provided a series of solutions to problems in a modernizing world. Gellner (1983, 1987) has claimed that industrialization brought a demand for standardized skills, which could best be dealt with through centrally controlled systems of education. Thus, economic advantage was given to a centrally organized state, which imposed uniform levels of literacy. Kennedy (1988) emphasizes the military advantage of the nation-state. It could recruit professional armies directly from populations who were willing to fight with patriotic fervour and who would not disappear seasonally to gather in their feudal lord's harvest. Other writers have directly linked the rise of nation-states with the rise of capitalism. Anderson (1983) connects the rise of the nation-state with the importance of printing, the replacement of Latin by vernacular languages, and the spread of discursive literacy, all of which were necessary for capitalist development. Mann (1992) agrees but stresses the role of commercial, rather than industrial, capitalism in the formation of the state: in the eighteenth century, the imperialist conquests, which were to finance the industrial revolutions of western Europe, required state support for their continuing success. Nairn (1977) pointed to the uneven spread of capitalism, suggesting that the state became a means by which peripheral regions could haul themselves into capitalist modernity. Hroch (1985), developing this point, claims that capitalist economies needed the sort of central direction, especially in relation to educational and commercial policy, which could only be provided by the modern sort of nation-state.

Whatever may have been the reasons for the emergence of the nation-state, there is no doubting its success. Nationhood, spreading from Europe to the Americas and elsewhere, was established as the universal form of sovereignty. The world's entire land surface, with the exception of Antarctica, is "now divided between nations and states" (Birch, 1989, p. 3). If nationalism is the ideology which maintains these nation-states as nation-states, then nationalism is "the most successful ideology in human history" (p. 3). Liberalism and Marxism have been territorially limited, as was Christendom or Islam in the Middle Ages, but nationalism is an international ideology. The nation-state system abhors a territorial vacuum; every space must be corralled behind official national boundaries. Thus, the boundary-consciousness of nationalism has itself known no boundaries in its historical triumph.

Nationalism, in its triumphant march, has swept aside rival ideologies. At the beginning of the twentieth century, Marxists were predicting the end of national division: the imminent collapse of capitalism would herald a world of universal class consciousness, joining together the working classes from different states. In the event, Marxist revolutions accommodated themselves to national boundaries. One of the first tasks for the leaders of the 1917 Revolution in Russia was to secure the borders of the socialist state. The treaty with Germany and its allies at Brest-Litovsk signed away territory to Turkey. In the ensuing struggles to defend the revolution from outside attack, the Bolsheviks actually extended the borders of the old Russian empire by annexing Bokhara and Khiva and tightening Russian control over Outer Mongolia (Seton-Watson, 1977). Thus, the Bolshevik regime from the outset represented a nation-state among nation-states. First, Lenin, and then Stalin, played the parts of national leader, planning for 'socialism within one country' and willing to defend the nation against foreign invaders. So it has continued. As Benedict Anderson (1983) points out, in the late 1970s the Marxist regimes of Vietnam, Cambodia and China fought nationalist wars with each other, underlining the fact that "since World War II every successful revolution has defined itself in *national* terms" (p. 12, emphasis in original).

There is something decidedly odd about the nation-state system. Nation-states come in all shapes and sizes. They include entities such as the Republic of China, with its population numbering more than 100 million, as well as Tuvalo with its 10,000 citizens. The idea of the nation-state has not come with a model of ideal size, like the Renaissance city-state. Some land masses, like North America, have few national boundaries, most of which tend to follow straight lines, lakes or rivers. By contrast, Europe is dense with boundaries which whirl and loop across mountains, plains and rivers. Some groups of islands form a single nation, such as Japan, whilst in the Caribbean each island seems to boast its own state (with Haiti and the Dominican Republic sharing the same island). Why Liechtenstein? Why Nauru? Why the United States of America? But no United States of South America? And no national state of Corsica nor of Hawaii? In short, one could not find a set of 'objective' geographical principles, which, if expressed in a computer program, would produce the present crop of jealously guarded, national boundaries. Instead, the world of nations has been divided into a hotchpotch of bizarrely shaped and sized entities, lodging tightly, sometimes uncomfortably, up against one another.

Nor does the hotchpotch reflect some underlying logic of language or religion. There are monoglot states, and there are polyglot states. There is a state like Iceland with comparative cultural and linguistic homogeneity, and a state like India with its mass of religions and languages. Sometimes, different religious groups have nationalist struggles, such as in Northern Ireland, and sometimes the same groups do not, as in Scotland. Sometimes language is a symbol of nationalist aspirations, as in Quebec. Sometimes it is not: there appear to be few nationalist rumblings by linguistic minorities in Scandinavian countries (Elklit and Tonsgaard, 1992). The balance between religion and language can change. When the Belgian state was founded in 1830, religious affinities seemed stronger than linguistic differences, but, apparently, the position is now reversed (Vos, 1993). In Switzerland, a sense of Swiss nationality holds together a state which does not threaten to fragment along linguistic lines. The so-called 'Jura question' concerns the issue of seceding from the Berne canton, in order to form a new canton within Switzerland (Voutat, 1992). And what computer program – let alone what theory of objective historical development –

would have predicted that the vast Spanish-speaking, Catholic areas of
Central and Southern America would be criss-crossed by national boundaries? Why should Venezuela, Costa Rica and Bolivia boast their
independence, raise their own armies and patrol their own borders?

The system of nation-states does not seem to follow a neat pattern for
global division. Historical forces may have combined to produce the
nation-state as modernity's logical form of governance. Yet, a wilful
anarchy seems to have accompanied the way that the logical principle has
been established in practice.

## Making States and Peoples

If so-called 'objective' variables, such as those of language, religion or
geography, cannot predict where the state boundaries are to be drawn,
then one might presume that 'subjective', or psychological, variables are
the decisive ones. Nations are not 'objective communities', in the sense
that they are constructed around clear, 'objective' criteria, which are
possessed, and seen to be possessed, by all national members: instead, they
are, to use Benedict Anderson's term, 'imagined communities'. Because
there are infinite ways of imagining communities, then one should expect
the world map of nations to be somewhat higgledy-piggledy, as the
boundaries between states follow the boundaries of subjective identity. As
will be suggested, there is a grain of truth in this 'subjective' way of
conceiving nationhood. Nevertheless, it is an oversimplification. Psychological identity, on its own, is not the driving force of history, pushing nation-
states into their present shapes. National identities are forms of social life,
rather than internal psychological states; as such, they are ideological
creations, caught up in the historical processes of nationhood.

The term 'nation' carries two interrelated meanings. There is the 'nation'
as the nation-state, and there is the 'nation' as the people living within the
state. The linkage of the two meanings reflects the general ideology of
nationalism. As Gellner implies, nationalism is based upon a principle
which is "very widely held and even more commonly taken for granted in
the modern world" (1993, p. 409). This is the principle that any nation-as-
people should have their nation-as-state. Obviously, the principle assumes
that there are such entities as national peoples. In this respect, nationalism
involves the construction of the sense of national identity for those who are
said to inhabit, or deserve to inhabit, their own nation-state. However,
nationalism involves more than the construction of a particular identity (a
particular national 'us'), for it includes the general principle: it is right that
'we' possess 'our' own state, because peoples (nations) should have their
states (nations).

In this regard, nationalism combines particular and universal features.
This combination could be seen in the way the victors of the French
Revolution proclaimed their triumph. They declared their victory to be a

triumph of universal principles, such as 'liberty, freedom and equality', which would apply, in theory, to all men – but not necessarily to all women (see Capitan, 1988). They also claimed this to be a general victory of reason over prejudice, enlightenment over darkness, the people over despotism. Yet, at the moment of triumph, 'the people' were not left dangling as an abstract concept, nor as a universal possibility. The great, universal principles were being limited to one particular people, situated in a specific place (Dumont, 1992; Freeman, 1992). The Declaration of the Rights of Man and the Citizen asserted that "the principle of sovereignty resides essentially in the Nation: no body of men, no individual, can express authority that does not emanate from it" (quoted in Kedourie, 1966, p. 12). The Nation was, of course, the French nation. Some sort of indissoluble, ineffable tie was being asserted between state, people and territory.

In claiming that sovereignty rests with the nation, the revolutionaries were speaking as if the idea of the 'nation' was unproblematic. In reading their words today, it is easy to assume that the term 'nation' had a clear, concrete signification. At the time of the Revolution, the conventional symbols of nationhood, which are so taken for granted today, were not yet in place. Under the *ancien régime*, there was no national flag, only regional ones (Johnson, 1993). The language in which the Declaration had been written was only spoken by a minority of the population as their first tongue. North of the Loire, but excluding Britanny and Flanders, it might have been understood by most people, but to the south it was generally incomprehensible (Braudel, 1988). When the Declaration was announced, only a small percentage of those who lived in the territory, now recognized as being France, thought of themselves as being 'French'. As such, 'the nation' was not a concrete entity, whose existence all citizens could take for granted. It was a project to be attained. Because the project was being pursued in its own name (policies were to be justified in the name of 'the nation'), it had to assume its own reality before being effected in practice.

These considerations raise the question 'which comes first: the nation-as-people or the nation-as-state?' There has been much debate between those who claim that nation-states have created national identities and those who trace the genealogy of national identities back to times before the rise of the nation-state. Those who take the former view claim that, as nation-states were being formed, so national identities were often invented. Sometimes, the founders of the state were aware of what they were doing. After the Risorgimento, the nineteenth-century Italian nationalist Massimo d'Azeglio declared: "We have made Italy, now we have to make Italians" (quoted in Hobsbawm, 1992, p. 44). To make 'Italians' it was necessary to present the creation as a revival, as if something ancient were being continued. During the heyday of nation-making in the eighteenth and nineteenth centuries many seemingly ancient traditions were invented. New artefacts, such as Scottish kilts or Coronation rituals, were created, but they were presented as if age-old traditions. 'Ancient' epic poems, extolling the nation, were occasionally forged (Cannadine, 1983; Trevor-Roper, 1983).

Through the invention of traditions, national identities were being created as if they were 'natural', even eternal, features of human existence. As Gellner argues, nationalism presents "itself as the affirmation of each and every 'nationality', and these alleged entities are supposed just to be there, like Mount Everest, since long ago, antedating the age of nationalism" (1983, p. 49). The Victorian journalist Walter Bagehot asserted in *Physics and Politics* that nations "are as old as history". He was suggesting that the particular nations, "which are so familiar to us", have always existed throughout history (1873, p. 83). Bagehot's compatriots might have wished to believe that there had always been Englishmen – a whole trail of bearded Alfreds and Arthurs – stumping off into misty dawns of time, carrying their swords and English sense of play like Dr Grace and his cricket bat. Whether these Alfreds and Arthurs actually nourished a sense of 'Englishness' *qua* Englishness (let alone 'Britishness'), in ways which Bagehot would have recognized in himself, is very much a moot point: and ditto for the 'French' ancient heroes and heroines, who were being rediscovered across the Channel at about the same time.

Even more problematic is the case of some former colonies. No prior sense of peoplehood could explain why a United States of America developed to the north of Mexico, but not to its south. The thirteen colonies, which under George Washington's leadership overthrew colonial rule, developed into a single nation, while the five colonies liberated from Spain by Simon Bolivar went their own national ways. In both cases, the sense of nationhood was to be created after the various declarations of independence, whether it was the sense of 'Americanness' (the 'one nation under God'), or the separate senses of being Bolivian, Peruvian, Venezuelan, Ecuadorian and Colombian.

On the other hand, as Anthony Smith (1981, 1986, 1994) has repeatedly argued, not all nations-as-people have been entirely created *de novo*. Some identities must have existed previously and a general sense of community was not entirely invented in the eighteenth century. 'Ethnies' – or peoples claiming a sense of their own unique history, culture and loyalties – are to be found in most ages. Often, nation-states were created out of older loyalties. The 'ancient' Highland kilt may have been as much a modern invention as the Coronation mug, but both mug and kilt were celebrating the much older traditions of the Highland clan system and the English Coronation oath respectively. Neither of these were entirely invented, at least in the era of the state-making. The peoples whom nation-states were claiming to represent often had nurtured a sense of peoplehood before the age of nationhood, even if this sense was not co-extensive with the peoplehood, claimed by the state. The Declaration of the Rights of Man and the Citizen did not itself invent the identity of being 'French', and certainly not the identity of being Frankish or Gallic. And the new French nation, in developing its sense of Frenchness, adapted, as well as invented, much older traditions, stereotypes and myths. Similarly, Massimo d'Azeglio did not invent the term 'Italia'. If nationhood provided the outward political form for states, then this form often took root within, and adapted, older senses of peoplehood. And, so the argument goes, it is not surprising that the results were at once both uniform and variegated.

The creation of the nation-as-people added something to the pre-existing identities. Seldom has the creation of nation-states been a harmonious process, in which a traditional 'ethnie' grows from small shoot into the full flower of nationality, as if following a process of 'natural' maturation. The process typically is attended by conflict and violence. A particular form of identity has to be imposed. One way of thinking of the self, of community and, indeed, of the world has to replace other conceptions, other forms of life. Italians have to be made: individuals have to stop thinking of themselves merely as Lombardians or Sicilians, or members of this or that village. If only a minority of those living in France at the time of the Revolution thought of themselves as French, then it was this minority's outlook, which was to prevail. Paris was to speak metonymically and literally for the whole of France. The Parisian style of speech was to be imposed, legally and culturally, as 'French'.

The battle for nationhood is a battle for hegemony, by which a part claims to speak for the whole nation and to represent the national essence. Sometimes, metonymically the name of the part comes to stand for the national whole. For example, in Thailand and Burma the identity of the nation has come to be associated with the values and culture of the dominant group, the Thais and Burmese respectively (Brown, 1989). Few nations are so homogeneous that they do not contain sub-sections, which fall under Smith's definition of *ethnie*: namely a group which maintains a sense of its own historic uniqueness and origins. Connor (1993) estimates that only 15 of the current 180 nations are not 'multinational' in this sense. This estimate ignores the long-buried senses of peoplehood cluttering the cemetries of history.

The achievement of national hegemony is well illustrated by the triumph of official national languages and the suppression of rivals – a triumph which has so often accompanied the construction of statehood. The Rights of Man and the Citizen did not spread to the rights of Bretons and Occitans to use their own tongue in the schoolrooms of France: the northern *langue d'oïl* was enforced, with the backing of legal statutes, over *la langue d'oc*. In the nineteenth century, Welsh and Lowland Scottish were officially banned in British schools (Kiernan, 1993). The Argentinian government, in a curious by-way of national history, discouraged the use of Welsh in Patagonia (Williams, 1991). Sometimes when hegemony is assured, or when it is later threatened, this legal suppression of language is relaxed, either in the interests of recapturing a harmless heritage, or to ward off demands from separatist or irredentist groups. The suppression of minority languages is not confined to nationalism's early history. Even in the late twentieth century such policies are pursued, in the name of the people, by governing groups seeking to consolidate their hold on state power. The 1982 Constitution of Turkey specifically forbids any political party from concerning itself "with the defence, development or diffusion of any non-Turkish language or culture" (quoted in Entessar, 1989). After the Indonesian government occupied East Timor, it officially banned the teaching of Timorese in schools, proclaiming that it was bringing 'Indonesian civilization' to the island (Pilger, 1994).

With historical hindsight, it might seem inevitable that the nation-state system emerged, but it is hard to see an inevitability about the particular nations themselves. After each major European war, the political map changes: the map drawn by the Treaty of Berlin differs from that of Versailles and certainly from that of today. Some nation-states, like Poland, change their shape, size and location. Others in the Balkans seem to come and go, sometimes reappearing, sometimes not. Wallerstein (1991) points out that very few states today can boast a continuous administrative entity and geographical location from 1450. Hypothetical possibilities abound. Had forces been deployed otherwise on particular battlegrounds, would there today be other nations and other national identities? Had the Confederate forces not been defeated in the American Civil War, might the territory, currently filled by the USA, now provide the locus for two independent states, each nurturing its own separate culture and historical myths? It is possible to take a longer historical perspective. Seton-Watson (1977) suggests that the defeat of the Albigensians in 1213 was of decisive importance. Had fortunes gone the other way, then, when it came to the making of states several centuries later, a powerful, united Mediterranean sea-power, stretching from Catalonia to Rome, might have emerged. One can predict that the loyalty to this state – perhaps to be known as *Mediterranea* – would have been as fierce and as 'naturally age-old' as that shown to any emerging European state. And *la langue d'oc* might now be established as one of the great languages of the world, instead of languishing in its present state of decay (Touraine, 1985).

If it seems that too much is being made to hinge on the outcome of battles, then it should be remembered that violence is seldom far from the surface of nationalism's history. The struggle to create the nation-state is a struggle for the monopoly of the means of violence. What is being created – a nation-state – is itself a means of violence. The triumph of a particular nationalism is seldom achieved without the defeat of alternative nationalisms and other ways of imagining peoplehood. France might appear to have emerged in its historic place with a sense of French identity nourished over centuries (Smith, 1994). The Declaration of the Rights of Man and the Citizen implies as much. However, the achievement of this nationhood not only entailed the historical failure of hypothetical nationalisms – of potential Mediterraneas – but the actual defeat of rival senses of peoplehood. The Bretons and the Occitans needed to be coerced into being French: any national aspirations which they might have entertained had to be forcefully cropped.

All this is to be done in the name of the people (all the people), the nation (the whole nation) or the father/motherland (the whole country). This has become a commonplace characteristic of the times. Today, rulers, however tyrannical their rule, justify their sovereignty as an expression of their nation's will. Even those who seize power through a minority *coup d'état* feel the need to declare to the world that their power carries national legitimacy. Familiar clichés will be employed. For example, when Ernest Shonekan seized power in Nigeria with the aid of the army and in the face of electoral victory being accorded to rivals, he declared that he was acting "in the greater interests of the fatherland" (*Guardian*, 1 September 1993). Shonekan is another figure, who himself possesses little lasting historical significance, but who follows the modern courtly protocol: political leaders must claim to act in the interests of the nation, variously described as 'the people', 'the motherland' or 'the fatherland'. Mediaeval monarchs would have found these evocations of parent-lands strangely mystical. Their sovereignty was claimed to be derived from God; the monarch's possession of a magic, healing touch was taken as evidence of the divine calling (Bloch, 1973). Modern rulers, by contrast, must claim, as evidence of their calling, a common touch. In the modern state the claim to sovereignty has descended from heaven to earth, from the clouds to the soil of the homeland and to the collectively invoked bodies of its inhabitants.

## Nationhood and the Development of Language

As the ideology of nationalism has spread across the globe, so it has shaped contemporary common sense. Notions, which seem to us so solidly banal, turn out to be ideological constructions of nationalism. They are 'invented permanencies', which have been created historically in the age of modernity, but which feel as if they have always existed. This is one reason why it is so difficult to offer explanations for nationalism. Concepts, which an analyst might use to describe the causal factors, may themselves be historical constructs of nationalism. A prime example is the idea of languages. As was mentioned earlier, many analysts have claimed that language is a prime determinant of nationalist identity: those speaking the same language are liable to claim a sense of national bond. Also, as was mentioned in the previous section, the creation of a national hegemony often involves a hegemony of language. It would not be difficult to construct a model of nationalism around the importance of speaking the same or different languages.

To do so would be to treat language itself as an unproblematic concept. It seems so obvious that there are different languages, and that everyone who speaks must speak an identifiable language. How could the matter be questioned? Bagehot might have thought that there have always been nations. Perhaps he exaggerated; or perhaps he was misled by the apparent solidity of invented national permanencies. But surely languages are different: they have always existed. Yet, a caution should be issued.

Humans might have spoken from the dawn of history, with mutually unintelligible ways of talking being developed in different places, but this does not mean that people have thought of themselves as speaking 'a language'. The concept of 'a language' – at least in the sense which appears so banally obvious to 'us' – may itself be an invented permanency, developed during the age of the nation-state. If this is the case, then language does not create nationalism, so much as nationalism creates language; or rather nationalism creates 'our' common-sense, unquestioned view that there are, 'naturally' and unproblematically, things called different 'languages', which we speak.

Mediaeval Europe, in contrast with today's world, was not a place of official vernacular languages. By and large written communication was in Latin. The grammar, which was taught as a basic subject in the curriculum of the trivium, was Latin grammar (Murphy, 1974). The vernacular tongues, even when used in written form, were not considered grammatical, nor was the spelling of their vocabularies standardized. In this context, there were no right and wrong ways to write the vernacular; and in most cases it simply was not written. The pressures to standardize spelling, to establish correct grammars and to teach an approved form of the native tongue were to come much later. Michel Foucault (1972) has compared the emergence of grammar as an academic discipline in the eighteenth century with the development of medicine and economics at the same time. In each case, the academic study was developing in the context of the emerging modern state, which was imposing uniformity and order on its citizenry and which, according to Foucault, was "a disciplinary society" (1986, p. 206).

In the Middle Ages, according to Douglas Johnson, "it was undoubtedly difficult for the ordinary person in one part of France to be understood in another part of France" (1993, p. 41). Indeed, the situation persisted well into the nineteenth century in France (Braudel, 1988). One can imagine mediaeval peasants' relation to their patterns of speaking. They would share ways of talking with fellow members of their village. They would recognize these patterns – and perhaps distinctive words – especially when encountering fellow villagers away from home. The documents of Montaillou recount one villager, Arnaud Sicre, a shoemaker working in San Mateo, overhearing a woman entering the workshop and speaking "the tongue of Montaillou" (Ladurie, 1978, p. 286). He put down his tools to ask whether she did indeed come from Montaillou. The 'tongue' may have been distinctive, yet it was also comprehensible to those living in neighbouring regions, which would also have their own recognizable ways of speaking. Some words would be unfamiliar to outsiders, whilst others would not be. As one travelled further from one's home village, the ratio of unfamiliar phrases to familiar ones would rise, with problems of communication increasing. If one travelled to a particularly inaccessible village, one might find few common phrases. In the case of fourteenth century Montaillou, Ladurie writes that there was a continuum of communication between Occitania and Catalonia.

In travelling between villages and along the continuum of communication, there would be no point at which the peasant would imagine that they had passed through a linguistic boundary, separating one distinct tongue from another. Moments of intelligibility might get fewer, dribbling away entirely in distant horizons. The travelling peasant, however, would not stop to ask 'do these people speak the same language as myself?', as if there was an actual point at which the ratio between the familiar and the unfamiliar became critical and the speech pattern changed from one grammatical essence to another. This essentialism, by contrast, is insinuated into the core of modern common sense about language. We would want to know whether the speech of Montaillou should be categorized as a dialect of Occitan and whether the inhabitants of San Mateo *really* spoke a variant of Catalan. We assume the reality of underlying different deep grammars. If the modern political map, unlike its mediaeval equivalent, contains precise boundaries, so too does the modernly imagined map of speech. The assumptions of this imagined mapping are easily projected on to other cultures and other times. Clifford (1992) recounts how anthropologists typically assume that each village, or each tribe, which they study, has its own unique language.

The modern imagining of different languages is not a fantasy, but it reflects that the world of nations is also a world of formally constituted languages. The disciplinary society of the nation-state needs the discipline of a common grammar. The mediaeval peasant had no official forms to complete, inquiring whether the respondent speaks Spanish or English. No acts of parliament decreed which language was to be used in compulsory public education or in state broadcasting; nor would the mediaeval subject have dreamt of ever going to war over such matters. The questions about language, which today seem so 'natural' and so vital, did not arise. To put the matter crudely: the mediaeval peasant spoke, but the modern person cannot merely speak; we have to speak *something* – a language.

**Languages and Boundaries**

A world of different languages requires the constitution of categorical distinctions. A problem confronts anyone who attempts to make distinctions between one language and another. Not all the speakers of a language speak in the same way. Thus, some differences of speaking have to be classified as being instances of different languages and some will be classified as differences within the same language. The notion of 'dialect' becomes crucial to maintain the idea of separate languages: it seems to account for the fact that not all speakers of a language speak the same way. The word 'dialect' did not gain its linguistic meaning until the early modern period (Haugen, 1966a). Previously, the linguistic problems, which the word addresses and seems to solve, did not arise. The inhabitants of fourteenth-century Montaillou did not worry whether their tongue was a 'dialect' of a wider language, or whether it was a separate language: the shoemaker was interested in knowing whether he shared a birthplace with the woman, not whether they spoke 'the same language'.

The idea of a dialect had little use before nation-states started establishing official ways of speaking and writing. Differences between languages and dialect, then, became hotly contested political issues, as well as concerns for the discipline of linguistics. If it seems obvious to us that there are different languages, it is by no means obvious how the distinctions between languages are to be made. Suppose one stipulated that speakers of the same language understand each other; and that speakers of different languages do not. This would imply that all the variants (or dialects) of a single language are mutually intelligible, and that different languages are mutually unintelligible. Linguists have emphasized that there is no simple criterion for determining mutual intelligibility. How much comprehension should count as intelligibility? Where on the continuum of comprehensibility is the boundary between understanding and non-understanding to be drawn?

Even if such a criterion could be applied, it would lead to very different distinctions from those which are conventionally accepted and which seem so solid to speakers and non-speakers alike (Comrie, 1990; Ruhlen, 1987). There are instances of 'different' languages, such as Danish, Norwegian and Swedish, which are mutually intelligible. As Eriksen (1993) points out, the spoken language of Norwegian cities like Bergen and Oslo is closer to standard Danish than it is to some of the rural dialects of Norwegian. As well as the problem of different languages which are mutually comprehensible, there is the problem of languages which encompass mutually incomprehensible dialects. Thus, speakers of both Gheg and Tosk dialects imagine themselves to speak the common language Albanian, although the dialects are mutually incomprehensible (Ruhlen, 1987).

More is at stake in drawing the boundary of a language than linguistics. The battle for hegemony, which accompanies the creation of states, is reflected in the power to define language, or in what Thompson has called the power "to make meaning stick" (1984, p. 132). This power resides not merely in the imposition of certain words or phrases, but also in the claim of languages to be languages. The middle class of the metropolitan areas typically will make their meanings stick as the official language, relegating other patterns within the national boundaries to 'dialects', a term which almost invariably carries a pejorative meaning. As Haugen (1966a) suggested, a 'dialect' is frequently a language which did not succeed politically: for example, Piedmontese was relegated to the status of dialect after Tuscan succeeded in becoming the language of Italy.

Nationalists, in attempting to create a separate nation, often will create a language as a distinct language, although they might claim to be creating the nation on the basis of the language, as if the latter were an ancient, 'natural' fact. When Herder was praising the German language as the soul of the German nation, he was arguing to bring both – the language and the nation – into existence, whilst treating both as if age-old. The speech of the territory that was to become Germany comprised several mutually unintelligible ways of talking, none of which had succeeded yet in establishing its status as the 'correct' form of an overall German language. At that time, Prussians spoke Low German and "learnt High German as a second language" (Hawkins, 1990, p. 105). In the following century, with the rise of Prussia, 'standard' German was to emerge as the north German pronunciation of southern High German.

Again and again, the boundaries between languages, and the classification of dialects, have followed the politics of state-making. Where national boundaries are established, then, the differences in speech patterns either side of the boundary are more likely to be seen as belonging to distinctly different languages by the speakers themselves, their national centres and the world in general. When the Dutch went their way politically, their form of lower Franconian was to become a separate language, in contrast to other forms which have become known as dialects of German (Schmidt, 1993). Galician, spoken in Spain, and Portuguese, spoken across the border, are now generally thought to be distinct languages. In linguistic terms, French and Italian merge into each other, but the speech patterns on the French side of the border are likely to be seen as dialects of French, and those on the Italian side as dialects of Italian (Ruhlen, 1987). Similarly, Friul in Northern Italy is similar to Romanesch in Switzerland, but, again, national boundaries reinforce a sense of linguistic separateness (White, 1991). The creation of Norwegian is instructive. The decolonization from Denmark was marked by a struggle for language. First, the state of Norway was to declare its own language, creating a spelling to match so-called Norwegian patterns of talking, rather than Danish ones. Then, there was the internal battle between two rival patterns of speech, the Riksmål and Landsmål, both having claims to be considered as the proper Norwegian (Haugen, 1966b). In all these cases, professional linguists have tended to fall into line with accepted practices, accepting Norwegian and Danish as different languages, High and Low German as variants of the same language etcetera (Comrie, 1990). As Ruhlen (1987) admits, because there are no purely linguistic criteria for classifying languages, linguists follow common beliefs about identifying similar and different languages.

The common practices of naming languages tend to emerge through struggles for hegemony. And what is made into a common practice can, under certain circumstances, be unmade or become a locus of struggle. For example, Italian law makes a distinction between *koine* (dialects) of Italian and full-blown minority languages. Friulan and Sardinian activists campaigned for years to have their speech recognized in law as official languages. Successive central governments, fearful of separatism and the cost of grants for minority languages, resisted their demands. In the debate whether Friulan and Sard were dialects or languages, both sides have their expert linguists, contesting the other side's characterization of what constitutes a language and what is merely a dialect (Petrosino, 1992). More dramatically, the Turkish government officially denies that its Kurdish citizens are Kurds and that there is a Kurdish language: the Kurds really are "mountain Turks", who have forgotten their native, Turkish tongue (Entessar, 1989).

One might suppose that nationalist movements, seeking to form separate states, will seek to convert dialect into language. The power of writing down a way of speaking should not be underestimated: it provides material evidence for the claim that a separate language exists. In order to highlight differences from the 'official' governing language, separate spellings might be adopted and these might highlight the area's distinctive way of talking. These spellings, written on public notices and used in mythic poetry, will proclaim the uniqueness of the speech and its status as a language. Sometimes different orthographies can divide mutually intelligible ways of speaking, as in the case of Serbian and Croat, and also Urdu and Hindu. The status of the writing, however, can be contested or officially branded as dialect. In 1994, for the first time since the 1872 Scottish Education Act banned the use of lowland Scottish (or Lalland) in schools, Glasgow University accepted a dissertation written in Lalland: topic of the 'deisertation' was 'Scots spellin'. Significantly, the university senate only agreed to accept the thesis on the understanding that its writing be classified as a dialect of English, not as a separate language (*Guardian*, 8 July 1994).

Writing down a 'dialect' is not a simple issue, because a particular way of speaking has to be selected. Braudel (1988) writes of the problem faced by those who wished to translate the official French documents of the post-Revolutionary state into local 'patois'. Each village seemed to have its own way of speaking and its own accent. The Director of the *département* of Corrèze spoke about the difficulty of finding acceptable translations: "The translator, who happened to come from the canton of Juillac, did not speak with the same accent as the other cantons which all vary slightly; the difference becomes marked at a distance of seven or eight leagues" (quoted in Braudel, 1988, p. 92). Another official, according to Braudel, proposed translating the Declaration of the Rights of Man into a devised patois, which would be "midway between all the different jargons" of the peoples in the Bordeaux area. One might surmise what might have happened had the authorities accepted the idea of such a compromise language, which did not represent the speaking patterns of any existing person. Had this language been taught in schools, and were it used by later poets to extol the historic romance of the area, then separatist groups today might be demanding its official recognition. The University of Bordeaux might be faced with doctoral 'deisertations' written in this apparently ancient tongue.

The establishment of a distinct language involves its own internal struggles for hegemony, as one way of speaking is to stand as the model for the whole language. Were the Kurdish movement in Turkey to champion an official Kurdish language, then it must select from among its supporters' various ways of talking. In the 1930s and 1940s the Sardinian nationalist movement avoided the language issue. To have promoted Sard as a separate language, and to have held it as the symbol of Sardinian independence, would have invited conflict. Sard contained a variety of different forms: even to refer to 'Sard', as such, implies a contestable uniformity. One form of Sardinian speaking would have to have been selected as the official form, with other variations transformed into mere dialects, or poor relations to 'metropolitan Sard'. In order not to alienate speakers of any variety of Sardinian speech, the leaders of the pre-war Sardinian nationalist movement downplayed the importance of language (White, 1991).

The case of the separatist Lombard League is interesting. In the early 1980s, the League declared Lombardian to be a separate language from Italian (Ruzza, 1993). Activists daubed out the final vowels on street signs in Lombardy. In response, opponents mocked the idea that Lombardian was a proper language. There is little point in turning to the linguistic textbooks to settle the issue: some classify Lombardian as a separate language (Grimes, 1988), whilst others do not (Vincent, 1987). Had the League's programme been successful during the early 1980s, and had Lombardy seceded from Italy, establishing its own state boundaries, a prediction might be made: increasingly Lombardian would have come to be recognized as different from Italian, as Norwegian is from Danish and Swedish. After a while, linguistic textbooks would agree on the matter. However, in the late 1980s the League dropped the language issue, and, indeed, it changed its name from Lombard to Northern League (Ruzza, 1993). The issue of language was alienating potential supporters, who considered themselves Lombardian but did not speak the language. Also, a 'correct' form of Lombardian would have to have been created and few supporters were prepared to volunteer their area of Lombardy as the home of incorrectly spoken Lombardian.

Conflicts over language are commonplace in the contemporary world. They are comprehensible to 'our' common sense: reports about French and Flemish speakers in Belgium, or Urdu and Hindu speakers in India, do not occasion puzzlement. Such conflicts are not just struggles about language, but importantly they are conducted through language (as well as through violence). In this respect, the universal, or international, aspects of nationalism are crucial. Without common notions, which can be translated across particular languages and dialects, the conflicts would not be pursued in their nationalist forms. Foremost amongst such notions are the ideas of 'language' and 'dialect' themselves. These terms must be reproduced in every language which is used by its speakers to claim that they possess a separate language, and that, in consequence, they are a separate nation, whose internal differences of speech are merely differences of 'dialect'.

Notions of language and dialect are not the exclusive property of 'extremists', who pursue narrow national dreams. They are part of 'our' common sense. This has methodological and political implications. Nations may be 'imagined communities', but the pattern of the imaginings cannot be explained in terms of differences of language, for languages themselves have to be imagined as distinct entities. If nationalism is to be studied as a widespread ideology, and if nationalist assumptions are to be found in common-sense notions about what a language is, then nationalism should not be projected on to others, as if 'we' are free from all its effects. In addition, the assumptions, beliefs and shared representations, which depict the world of nations as our natural world, are historical creations: they are not the 'natural' common sense of all humans.

At other times people did not hold the notions of language and dialect, let alone those of territory and sovereignty, which are so commonplace today and which seem so materially real to 'us'. So strongly are such notions embedded in contemporary common sense that it is easy to forget that they are invented permanencies. The mediaeval cobblers in the workshops of Montaillou or San Mateo might, with the distance of 700 years, now appear to us narrow, superstition-bound figures. But they would have found our ideas on language and nation strangely mystical; they would be puzzled why this mysticism could be a matter of life and death.

# 3

# Remembering Banal Nationalism

Because nationalism has deeply affected contemporary ways of thinking, it is not easily studied. One cannot step outside the world of nations, nor rid oneself of the assumptions and common-sense habits which come from living within that world. Analysts must expect to be affected by what should be the object of their study. As was seen in the previous chapter, it is easy to suppose that people 'naturally' speak different languages. The assumption is difficult to shake. What makes the problem even more complex is that there are common-sense assumptions about the nature of nationalism itself. In established nations, it seems 'natural' to suppose that nationalism is an over-heated reaction, which typically is the property of others. The assumption enables 'us' to forget 'our' nationalism. If our nationalism is to be remembered, then we must step beyond what seems to be common sense.

Roland Barthes claimed that ideology speaks with "the Voice of Nature" (1977, p. 47). As others have pointed out, ideology comprises the habits of behaviour and belief which combine to make any social world appear to those, who inhabit it, as the natural world (Billig, 1991; Eagleton, 1991; Fairclough, 1992; McLellan, 1986; Ricoeur, 1986). By this reckoning, ideology operates to make people forget that their world has been historically constructed. Thus, nationalism is the ideology by which the world of nations has come to seem the natural world – as if there could not possibly be a world without nations. Ernest Gellner has written that, in today's world, "a man (sic) must have a nationality as he must have a nose and two ears" (1983, p. 6). It seems 'natural' to have such an identity. In the established nations, people do not generally forget their national identity. If asked 'who are you?', people may not respond by first giving their national identity (Zavalloni, 1993a, 1993b). Rarely, if asked which is their nationality, do they respond 'I've forgotten', although their answers may be not be quite straightforward (Condor, in press). National identity is not only something which is thought to be natural to possess, but also something natural to remember.

This remembering, nevertheless, involves a forgetting, or rather there is a complex dialectic of remembering and forgetting. As will be seen, this dialectic is important in the banal reproduction of nationalism in established nations. Over a hundred years ago, Ernest Renan claimed that forgetting was "a crucial element in the creation of nations" (1990, p. 11).

Every nation must have its history, its own collective memory. This remembering is simultaneously a collective forgetting: the nation, which celebrates its antiquity, forgets its historical recency. Moreover, nations forget the violence which brought them into existence, for, as Renan pointed out, national unity "is always effected by means of brutality" (p. 11).

Renan's insight is an important one: once a nation is established, it depends for its continued existence upon a collective amnesia. The dialectic, however, is more complex than Renan implied. Not only is the past forgotten, as it is ostensibly being recalled, but so there is a parallel forgetting of the present. As will be suggested, national identity in established nations is remembered because it is embedded in routines of life, which constantly remind, or 'flag', nationhood. However, these reminders, or 'flaggings', are so numerous and they are such a familiar part of the social environment, that they operate mindlessly, rather than mindfully (Langer, 1989). The remembering, not being experienced as remembering, is, in effect, forgotten. The national flag, hanging outside a public building or decorating a filling-station forecourt, illustrates this forgotten reminding. Thousands upon thousands of such flags each day hang limply in public places. These reminders of nationhood hardly register in the flow of daily attention, as citizens rush past on their daily business.

There is a double neglect. Renan implied that intellectuals are involved in the creation of amnesia. Historians creatively remember ideologically convenient facts of the past, while overlooking what is discomfiting. Today, social scientists frequently forget the national present. The banal episodes, in which nationhood is mindlessly and countlessly flagged, tend to be ignored by sociologists. They, too, have failed to notice the flag on the forecourt. Thus, Renan's insight can be expanded: historians might forget their nation's past, whilst social scientists can forget its present reproduction.

The present chapter argues that the sociological forgetting is not fortuitous; nor is it to be blamed on the absent-mindedness of particular scholars. Instead, it fits an ideological pattern in which 'our' nationalism (that of established nations, including the United States of America) is forgotten: it ceases to appear as nationalism, disappearing into the 'natural' environment of 'societies'. At the same time, nationalism is defined as something dangerously emotional and irrational: it is conceived as a problem, or a condition, which is surplus to the world of nations. The irrationality of nationalism is projected on to 'others'.

Complex habits of thought naturalize, and thereby overlook, 'our' nationalism, whilst projecting nationalism, as an irrational whole, on to others. At the core of this intellectual amnesia lies a restricted concept of 'nationalism', which confines 'nationalism' to particular social movements rather than to nation-states. Only the passionately waved flags are conventionally considered to be exemplars of nationalism. Routine flags –

the flags of 'our' environment – slip from the category of 'nationalism'. And having slipped through the categorical net, they get lost. There is no other theoretical term to rescue them from oblivion.

The double neglect is critically examined in this chapter. This involves examining the rhetoric of the sociological common sense which routinely reduces nationalism to a surplus phenomenon and which forgets to analyse how established nation-states are daily reproduced as nations. If the narrowing of the concept of 'nationalism' has led to the forgetting of banal nationalism, then it is hoped that a widening of the concept will lead to a remembering. The double neglect is to be reversed by a double remembering: the banal nationalism by which nation-states are reproduced is to be remembered, as are the habits of thought which have encouraged a neglect of this reproduction.


**Waved and Unwaved Flags**


The place of national flags in contemporary life bears a moment's consideration. Particular attention should be paid to the case of the United States, whose filling-station forecourts are arrayed with uncounted Stars and Stripes. The US legislature has decreed strict laws about how the flag should be displayed and what is forbidden to be done, on pain of penalty, to the precious pattern of stars and stripes. Desecration of the flag is met with reactions of outrage (Marvin, 1991). Of all countries, the United States is arguably today the home of what Renan called "the cult of the flag" (1990, p. 17).

The anthropologist, Raymond Firth (1973), in one of the few studies of the role of flags in contemporary life, distinguished between the symbolic and signalling functions of flags. The forerunners of modern national flags were often employed as signals, reducing entropy in situations of uncertainty. The mediaeval gonfanon presented a clear rallying point for soldiers in the confusion of the battleground. The *semeion*, in ancient Greece, indicated the presence of the commander to other ships of the fleet (Perrin, 1922). Since the eighteenth century, a complex system of signalling with flags has been developed for vessels at sea. In all these cases, flags are a pragmatically useful means of communicating messages. By contrast, argues Firth, the national flag today performs a symbolic function, being a 'condensation symbol' and "a focus for sentiment about society" (p. 356). The national flag, according to Firth, symbolizes the sacred character of the nation; it is revered by loyal citizens and ritually defiled by those who wish to make a protest. It carries no informational message, although, as Firth points out, the manner of a flag's display can, on special occasions, provide a signal. A national flag hung at half mast may communicate the death of an important figure. Notwithstanding this, the majority of national flags likely to be seen by the modern citizen in the course of a lifetime will not be signalling a particular message.

Other distinctions, besides that between symbol and signal, can be
made. The signal, if it is to be effective, must pass into the conscious
awareness of its recipients. However, the symbol need not have a direct
emotional impact, as Firth seemed to assume. That being so, one can
distinguish between the ways in which national flags are treated. Some are
consciously waved and saluted symbols, often accompanied by a pageant of
outward emotion. Others – probably the most numerous in the contemporary environment – remain unsaluted and unwaved. They are merely there
as symbols, whether on a forecourt or flashed on to a television screen; as
such they are given hardly a second glance from day to day.

The distinction between the waved and unwaved (or saluted and
unsaluted) flag can be illustrated with reference to Roland Barthes' classic
essay 'Myth Today'. Barthes discussed an issue of the magazine *Paris-
Match*, which he was offered in a barber-shop. On its cover, "a young
Negro in French army uniform is saluting, with his eyes uplifted, probably
fixed on the fold of the tricolor" (Barthes, 1983b, pp. 101f.). Barthes does
not make clear whether the Tricolor which the soldier was saluting was to
be seen in the photograph. For the sake of illustration, let us presume it
was. The three-coloured flag which the soldier actually faced was clearly a
flag to be saluted in the appropriate way. However, the photographed flag
on the *Paris-Match* cover was not for saluting. It could lie around the
corner of the barber-shop. Eyes could flick over it, to be reminded
unconsciously of the myth of imperial power, whose photographic image
Barthes so brilliantly analysed. But no one stops to wave or salute this
image of a symbol. The barber does not straighten up in mid-haircut, his
right hand imitating that of the photographed 'young Negro'. The cus-
tomer in the barber's chair, on catching sight of the cover in the mirror,
does not spring to patriotic attention, risking blade and scissor in the
service of the nation. The magazine is picked up and put down without
ceremony. Ultimately, without risk of penalty, the *Paris-Match* flag is
tossed into the rubbish bin.

The young soldier was saluting a single flag in a unique instant, which
was caught by the photographer. Thousands upon thousands of the *Paris-
Match* flag were distributed, gazed at and discarded. They join other flags,
some of which do have recognizable, signalling functions. The French
Tricolor, when displayed on loaves of bread, can indicate an approved
standard of baking, or *pain de tradition française*. When the government
gives such flags *lettres de noblesse*, as Monsieur Balladur's did in September
1993, the Tricolor not only signals the quality of baking; it also flags the
quality of the national tradition and the quality of the national state,
benevolently supervising the daily bread of its citizenry.

The uncounted millions of flags which mark the homeland of the United
States do not demand immediate, obedient attention. On their flagpoles by
the street and stitched on to the uniforms of public officials, they are
unwaved, unsaluted and unnoticed. These are mindless flags. Perhaps if all
the unwaved flags which decorate the familiar environment were to be

removed, they would suddenly be noticed, rather like the clock that stops ticking. If the reds and blues were changed into greens and oranges, there would be close, scandalized scrutiny, as well as criminal charges to follow.

One can ask what are all these unwaved flags doing, not just in the USA but around the world? In an obvious sense, they are providing banal reminders of nationhood: they are 'flagging' it unflaggingly. The reminding, involved in the routine business of flagging, is not a conscious activity; it differs from the collective rememberings of a commemoration. The remembering is mindless, occurring as other activities are being consciously engaged in.

These routine flags are different from those that seem to call attention to themselves and their symbolic message. Belfast in Northern Ireland is divided into mutually suspicious Catholic and Protestant districts. In the former, the Irish tricolor is widely displayed as a gesture of defiance against British sovereignty. In the backstreets of Protestant neighbourhoods, the kerb-stones are often painted with the pattern of the Union Jack (Beattie, 1993). These are not mindless symbols, for each side is consciously displaying its position and distancing itself from its neighbour. The tricolors, in this respect, differ from those hanging on public buildings south of the border. One might predict that, as a nation-state becomes established in its sovereignty, and if it faces little internal challenge, then the symbols of nationhood, which might once have been consciously displayed, do not disappear from sight, but instead become absorbed into the environment of the established homeland. There is, then, a movement from symbolic mindfulness to mindlessness.

Yassar Arafat, the leader of the Palestine Liberation Organization, declared as a peace deal with Israel was becoming a real possibility:

> The Palestine state is within our grasp. Soon the Palestine flag will fly on the walls, the minarets and the cathedrals of Jerusalem. (*Guardian*, 3 September 1993)

Arafat was using the notion of the flag as a metonym: by citing the flag, he was flagging Palestine nationhood. If he was discursively waving the flag of Palestine, he was hoping that the flags would actually be waved within the recovered homeland. Yet, in a longer view, Arafat's hope was that the waving would stop. The Palestine flags, displayed routinely on walls and roofs in a Palestine state, would be barely noticed by a citizenry freely going about their business. Occasionally, on special days – an Independence Day or an Annual Arafat Thanksgiving Parade – the streets would be filled with waved, commemorating flags.

Flags are not the only symbols of modern statehood. Coins and bank notes typically bear national emblems, which remain unnoticed in daily financial transactions. Naming the unit of currency can be a highly symbolic and controversial business, especially in the early days of a nation. In 1994, President Franjo Tudjman of Croatia decided that the dinar should be replaced by the 'kuna', which was the unit of currency used in the Nazi-backed state of Croatia between 1941 and 1945. 'Kuna' is the term for the furry marten which inhabits the forests of Croatia. The president defended his decision by claiming that "the kuna defends our national tradition and confirms our sovereignty" (*Independent*, 15 May 1994). This tradition and sovereignty would become symbolically banalized when the citizenry exchange their kunas without a second thought for furry creatures, President Tudjman or the victims of Nazism. In this way, the tradition, including the Nazi heritage, would be neither consciously remembered, nor forgotten: it would be preserved in daily life.

Psychologically, conscious remembering and forgetting are not polar opposites which exclude all middle ground. Similarly, traditions are not either consciously remembered (or co-memorated) in flag-waving collective activity, or consigned to a collective amnesia. They can be simultaneously present and absent, in actions which preserve collective memory without the conscious activity of individuals remembering. Serge Moscovici has discussed how most social activity is itself a remembering, although it is not experienced as such: "Social and intellectual activity is, after all, a rehearsal or recital, yet most social psychologists treat it as if it were amnesic" (1983, p. 10). Behaviour and thoughts are never totally created anew, but they follow, and thus repeat, familiar patterns, even when they change such patterns. To act and to speak, one must remember. Nevertheless, actors do not typically experience their actions as repetitions, and, ordinarily, speakers are not conscious of the extent to which their own words repeat, and thereby transmit, past grammars and semantics.

If banal life is to be routinely practised, then this form of remembering must occur without conscious awareness: it occurs when one is doing other things, including forgetting. Pierre Bourdieu's notion of the 'habitus' expresses well this dialectic of remembering and forgetting. The 'habitus' refers to the dispositions, practices and routines of the familiar social world. It describes 'the second nature' which people must acquire in order to pass mindlessly (and also mindfully) through the banal routines of daily life. Bourdieu emphasizes the elements of remembering and the forgetting: "The *habitus* – embodied history, internalized as a second nature and so forgotten as history – is the active presence of the whole past of which it is the product" (1990, p. 56).

Patterns of social life become habitual or routine, and in so doing embody the past. One might describe this process of routine-formation as *enhabitation*: thoughts, reactions and symbols become turned into routine habits and, thus, they become *enhabited*. The result is that the past is enhabited in the present in a dialectic of forgotten remembrance. President Tudjman was hoping that the kuna (and, with it, the history of the previous Croatian republic) would become enhabited as a living, unremembered, collective memory. Once enhabited it would flag the very things which the President could only mention mindfully and controversially.

The forgetting of the national past, of which Renan wrote, is continually reproduced in nation-states. The unwaved national flag – whether literally in the form of the flag itself, or, as will be suggested in Chapter 6, in the routine phrases of the mass media – is enhabited in contemporary daily life. These reminders of nationhood serve to turn background space into homeland space. The flag may be, as Firth suggested, a focus for sentiment, but this does not mean that each flag acts as a psychological magnet for sentiments. Far from it, mostly the flags are ignored. Their flagging and reminding are habitually overlooked in the routines of the inhabited, enhabited national homeland.

## Hot and Banal Nationalism

As has been mentioned, there is a double neglect as far as the social scientific investigation of nationalism is concerned. The neglect of the unwaved flags by citizenry going about their daily business is paralleled by a theoretical neglect. The enhabitation of nationalism within established nations is largely ignored by conventional sociological common sense. Only the waved or saluted flag tends to be noticed. If sociological categories are nets for catching slices of social life, then the net, which sociologists have marked 'nationalism', is a remarkably small one: and it seems to be used primarily for catching exotic, rare and often violent specimens. The collectors of these species tend not to stand in Main Street, USA, with net poised for new varieties.

The standard definitions of nationalism tend to locate nationalism as something beyond, or prior to, the established nation-state. In this respect, the social scientific definitions follow wider patterns of thinking. For example, Ronald Rogowski (1985) defines nationalism as "the striving" by members of nations "for territorial autonomy, unity and independence". He claims that this definition matches "everyday discourse", adding that "we routinely and properly speak of Welsh, Quebecquois and Arab nationalism" (pp. 88–9; for similar treatments of 'nationalism', see, *inter alia*, Coakley, 1992; Schlesinger, 1991). As will be seen, Rogowski is correct in stating that this is the way that 'nationalism' is used routinely – but whether more 'properly' is another matter. The definition, in concentrating on the striving for autonomy, unity and independence, ignores how these things are maintained once they have been achieved. No alternative term is offered for the ideological complex, which maintains the autonomous nation-state.

Nationalism, thus, is typically seen as the force which creates nation-states or which threatens the stability of existing states. In the latter case, nationalism can take the guise of separatist movements or extreme fascistic ones. Nationalism can appear as a developmental stage, which mature societies (or nations) have outgrown once they are fully established. This assumption is to be found in Karl Deutsch's (1966) classic study *Nationalism and Social Communication*. More recently, it underlies Hroch's (1985) valuable study *Social Preconditions of National Revival in Europe*. Hroch postulates three stages of nationalism. The first two stages describe how interest in the national idea is awakened by intellectuals and, then, how it is diffused; and the final stage occurs when a mass movement seeks to translate the national idea into the nation-state. There are no further stages to describe what happens to nationalism once the nation-state is established. It is as if nationalism suddenly disappears.

Nationalism, however, does not entirely disappear, according to this view: it becomes something surplus to everyday life. It threatens the established state and its established routines, or it returns when those orderly routines have broken down. Ordinary life in the normal state (the sort of state which the analysts tend to inhabit) is assumed to be banal, unexciting politically and non-nationalist. Nationalism, by contrast, is extraordinary, politically charged and emotionally driven.

Anthony Giddens describes nationalism as "a phenomenon that is primarily psychological" (1985, p. 116; see also Giddens, 1987, p. 178). Nationalist sentiments rise up when the "sense of ontological security is put in jeopardy by the disruption of routines" (1985, p. 218). In these circumstances, "regressive forms of object-identification tend to occur", with the result that individuals invest great emotional energy in the symbols of nationhood and in the promise of strong leadership (p. 218). Nationalism, according to Giddens, occurs when ordinary life is disrupted: it is the exception, rather than the rule. Nationalist feelings "are not so much a part of regular day-to-day social life" (1985, p. 215), but "tend to be fairly remote from most of the activities of day-to-day social life". Ordinary life is affected by nationalist sentiments only "in fairly unusual and often relatively transitory conditions" (p. 218). Thus, the psychology of nationalism is that of an extraordinary, emotional mood striking at extraordinary times. Banal routines, far from being bearers of nationalism, are barriers against nationalism.

Analysts, such as Giddens, are reserving the term 'nationalism' for outbreaks of 'hot' nationalist passion, which arise in times of social disruption and which are reflected in extreme social movements. In so doing, they are pointing to a recognizable phenomenon – indeed, one which is all too familiar in the contemporary world. The problem is not what such theories describe as nationalist, but what they omit. If the term 'nationalism' is applied only to forceful social movements, something slips from theoretical awareness. It is as if the flags on those filling-station forecourts do not exist.

The issue is wider than that of flags. It concerns national identity and its assumed naturalness in the established nation-state. It might be argued that such identities, far from being maintained by banal routines, are, in fact, supported by extraordinary moments which psychically parallel the extraordinary moments when nationalist movements arise. A dramatic psychology of the emotions, rather than a banal psychology of routines, might be evoked to explain identity in nation-states. All nation-states have occasions when ordinary routines are suspended, as the state celebrates itself. Then, sentiments of patriotic emotion, which the rest of the year have to be kept far from the business of ordinary life, can surge forth. The yearly calendar of the modern nation would replicate in miniature its longer political history: brief moments of nationalist emotion punctuate longer periods of settled calm, during which nationalism seems to disappear from sight.

Certainly, each nation has its national days, which disrupt the normal routines. There are independence day parades, thanksgiving days and coronations, when a nation's citizenry commemorates, or jointly remembers, itself and its history (Bocock, 1974; Chaney, 1993; Eriksen, 1993). It could be argued that these occasions are sufficient to flag nationhood, so that it is remembered during the rest of the year, when the banal routines of private life predominate. Certainly, great national days are often experienced as being 'memorable'. The participants are aware that the day of celebration, on which the nation is collectively remembered, is itself a moment which is to be remembered (Billig, 1990a; Billig and Edwards, 1994). Afterwards, individuals and families will have their stories to tell about what they did on the day the prince and princess married, or the queen was crowned (Billig, 1992; Ziegler, 1977).

These are conventional carnivals of surplus emotion, for the participants expect to have special feelings, whether of joy, sorrow or inebriation. The day has been marked as a time when normal routines are put into abeyance, and when extra emotions should be enacted. Participants may be uncertain how to mark the great national occasion in the banal setting of home, but the uncertainty itself reveals both the specialness and the conventional nature of the occasion. The Mass Observation Study asked Britons to record how they spent their time on the day in 1937 when George VI was crowned as king. A left-wing woman recalled in her diary:

> Woken by conscientious male cook stumping about in kitchen overhead. Troubled by vague necessity for waking husband with suitable greeting. Sleepily wondered whether a 'God Save the King!' would be appropriate (husband likes Happy-New-Years and Many-Happy-Returns). Finally awoke enough to realize that a shaking was sufficient. (Jennings and Madge, 1987, p. 106)

Another routine, or conventional pattern, must be found for the special day which formally breaks the everyday routine. This special routine must enable the actor to perform the expected emotion. Thus, the woman wonders how to accomplish an appropriately patriotic greeting. In this respect, the suitable emotion is not an ineffable impulse, which mysteriously impels the social actor in unforeseeable directions. It is dependent upon, and is sustained by, social forms, which themselves can be modelled upon other familiarly conventional breaks of daily routine, such as birthdays and new year celebrations.

The great days of national celebration are patterned so that the national flag can be consciously waved both metaphorically and literally. However, these are by no means the only social forms which sustain what is loosely called national identity. In between times, citizens of the state still remain citizens and the state does not wither away. The privately waved flags may be wrapped up and put back in the attic, ready for next year's independence day, but that is not the end of flagging. All over the world, nations display their flags, day after day. Unlike the flags on the great days, these flags are largely unwaved, unsaluted, unnoticed. Indeed, it seems strange to suppose that occasional events, bracketed off from ordinary life, are sufficient to sustain a continuingly remembered national identity. It would seem more likely that the identity is part of a more banal way of life in the nation-state.

## The Return of the Repressed

"The repressed has returned, and its name is nationalism", writes Michael Ignatieff at the beginning of his widely publicised *Blood and Belonging*, (1993, p. 2). At once, nationalism is signalled as something which comes and goes. Ignatieff's book illustrates how easily – indeed, how convincingly – such a portrayal of nationalism can appear today. In this portrayal, nationalism appears as dangerous, emotional and the property of others. Ignatieff's argument is worth close attention, because of what it omits. As will be seen, his portrayal of nationalism, together with its omissions, matches themes right at the heart of sociological common sense.

Ignatieff's book expresses a common-sense view of nationalism which straddles the boundaries between academic and more general thinking. *Blood and Belonging* accompanied a television series, made by the British Broadcasting Corporation, with the rights being sold world-wide. It was also serialized in a British Sunday newspaper. Announcing the first extract, the *Independent on Sunday* declared that "modern nationalism is as passionate and violent as ever, a call to come home and a call to arms" (24 October 1993).

Ignatieff's message is one of warning. Concentrating upon six locations – Croatia/Serbia, Germany, Ukraine, Quebec, Kurdistan and Northern Ireland – he describes how the irrational forces of ethnic nationalism are erupting to haunt the contemporary world. The collapse of communism and the growth of global communications, far from heralding a new world of cooperative rationality seem to be unleashing a primordial reaction: "the key narrative of the new world order is the disintegration of nation states into ethnic civil war" (1993, p. 2).

The theme of the repressed returning is easily maintained at present. Throughout Europe, the impulses of fascism are stirring again, in the form of parties which declare a politics of national regeneration. Political parties in Romania and Hungary are attracting large numbers of voters with their anti-gypsy and anti-alien messages. In Russia, the misnamed Liberal Democratic Party, campaigning for a greater, ethnically pure nation, is currently the largest party in parliament. During the 1990s the Front National has regularly attracted between 12 and 15 per cent of the French popular vote, whereas in the previous decade it could barely muster 1 per cent (Hainsworth, 1992). The Vlaams Block has become the most popular party of Antwerp (Husbands, 1992). The most striking example of fascism's return is Italy, where in 1994 the MSI (Italian Social Movement), having changed its name to National Alliance, entered the coalition government of Berlusconi. When this occurs, fascism is returning not on the margins of politics, but in the historical heartlands of Europe. No wonder, then, it seems as if the repressed (and the repressive) is returning.

The theme of nationalism's dangerous and irrational return is becoming commonplace in writings by academic social scientists. Majid Tehranian, like Ignatieff, tells a story of repression and return. He suggests that, during the Cold War, "ethnicity and ethnic discourse . . . remained repressed", because, at that time, "the universalist ideological pretensions of communism and liberalism left little room for the claims of ethnic and national loyalties" (1993, p. 193). According to Tehranian, "the end of the Cold War . . . has unleashed the centrifugal, ethnic and tribal forces within nation states" (p. 193). Now, nationalism threatens to turn the new world order into disorder (or 'dysorder', to adopt Tehranian's spelling).

One feature of these stories of repression and return can be mentioned. The claim that nationalism is returning implies that it has been away. In such comments, the world of settled nations appears as the point-zero of nationalism. The wars waged by democratic states, in contrast to the wars waged by rebel forces, are not labelled nationalist. Ignatieff hardly mentions the Vietnam or Falklands Wars, let alone the various US sorties into Korea, Panama, or Grenada. Nor does he mention the popular support given to US military actions, at least while successfully pursued. He does not label wars, occurring during nationalism's so-called quiescent period, as nationalist, despite their accompanying patriotic rhetoric. Moreover, the Cold War itself was couched in nationalist terms. Yatani and Bramel (1984), examining opinion poll evidence, concluded that the American public viewed the confrontation between two great, universalist ideologies as a conflict between two nations: communism was Russian, and capitalism was American.

To be fair, Ignatieff does not entirely forget the nationalism of established nation-states. He remembers it, only to forget it. He distinguishes between 'ethnic' and 'civic' nationalism. Ethnic nationalism is the hot, surplus variety, being based on sentiments of "blood loyalty" (1993, p. 6). It is the nationalism of the intolerant bigots. Ignatieff dissociates himself from ethnic nationalism, declaring "I am a civic nationalist" (p. 9). Civic nationalism, according to Ignatieff, is a political creed, which defines common citizenship and which emerged from the universalist philosophies of the Enlightenment. It is, he writes, the nationalism of established European democracies at their best. Despite Ignatieff's claim to be a civic nationalist, he personally disavows loyalty to a single nation-state. He does not describe how 'civic nationalists' create a nation-state with its own myths; how the civic nations recruit their citizenry in war-time; how they draw their own boundaries; how they demarcate 'others' beyond those boundaries; how they resist, violently if necessary, those movements which seek to rearrange the boundaries; and so on. In fact, the nationalism of 'civic nationalism' seems to slide away.

Indeed, civic nationalism as a whole slides away textually. When Ignatieff refers to 'nationalism' without qualification, he means the ethnic variety: "Nationalism legitimizes an appeal to blood loyalty" (p. 6). Thus, ethnic nationalism appears as if it were the epitome of all nationalism. The 'nationalism', which was repressed, but which now has returned, is, of course, the dangerous variety. Ignatieff's publishers catch the mood on the book jacket: "Modern nationalism is the language of blood: a call to arms which can end in the horrors of ethnic cleansing." Surplus nationalism has become the genus; its benign form is expelled from the category.

So long as the 'problems of nationalism' are defined in this way, the ideology, by which established Western nations are reproduced as nations, can be taken for granted. The Gulf War disappears from theoretical attention, as does the nationalism of established, democratic nations. This way of presenting nationalism is widespread. In describing political events in Northern Ireland, the British media typically use the term 'nationalist' to describe those who seek to abolish the border between the United Kingdom and Éire, especially if they advocate violence in the pursuit of these aims. The government of the British nation-state, by contrast, is not called 'nationalist', although it, too, can use force to maintain present national boundaries. Often, the term 'nationalist' seems to exert a magnetic pull upon the critical adjective 'extreme' in the force-field of commonplace semantics. The linkage implies that those who desire to change the political map of nations possess an unwarranted surplus of fervour, which is to be identified as nationalist.

Examples can be given from British newspapers. Here, as elsewhere, it is important not to select illustrations from the popular press, whose chauvinistic excesses have been well documented (Taylor, 1991). Nationalism is too general a phenomenon to be projected on to the working-class readers of popular newspapers, as if 'we', the liberal, educated classes, are removed from that sort of thing. 'Our' newspapers, on 'our' daily breakfast tables, present routine flags for 'our' benefit, as do 'our' sociological and psychological theories.

The *Guardian*, Britain's most liberal, left-of-centre quality newspaper, is important in this respect. A detailed analysis would be necessary to sustain the general point about the term 'nationalism', but a couple of illustrative examples can be briefly given. An article on Serbia carried the headline 'Nationalists challenge Milosevic'. The opening sentence asserted: "President Slobodan Milosevic of Serbia's problems (sic) will mount today when extreme nationalists table a no-confidence motion against his Serbian Socialist party government" (7 October 1993). In the article, the writer does not once use the word 'nationalist' to describe the Serbian government or its President. Milosevic, himself the architect of a Greater Serbia, and hence of a lesser Bosnia and Croatia, is described as consolidating his power, having "essentially won the wars in Croatia and Bosnia". The term 'extreme nationalists' refers to the same people as the unqualified 'nationalists' of the headline. Thus, the President and his state are being unmade as 'nationalist'. The territory, gained from the war of expansion, is on its way to international recognition. This flagging of what is nationalism (and by implication what is not nationalism) occurs beyond the level of outward argument. It is ingrained into the very rhetoric of common sense, which provides the linguistic resources for making outward arguments.

A second example also concerns Balkan politics. An article reports the opening of a museum of Serbiana on the Greek island of Corfu. The opening paragraph set the tone:

> As fiery displays of fervent nationalism go, it was a fine one. There was the archbishop with his golden cross giving a blessing that had grown men in tears. Amid flowers and flags, a dinner-jacketed all-male choir sang patriotic melodies. (*Guardian*, 6 September 1993)

The event was not an official state occasion. It was organized by a group which wishes to alter, rather than protect, existing state boundaries. In this context, the adjective 'fiery' takes its textual place as a companion to the word 'nationalism'. The author assumes that readers will be familiar with the notion of 'fiery displays of nationalism', and will appreciate that this was a 'fine' example of a generally understood genus. Official occasions in 'our' established nations, such as dinners for heads of state or the opening of new national monuments, often involve similar elements of display: flags, flowers, divines in funny costumes and suitably patriotic melodies. However, these occasions are rarely described as displays of nationalism, let alone 'fiery nationalism'.

The rhetoric distances 'us' from 'them', 'our' world from 'theirs'. And 'we', writer and readers, are assumed to belong to a reasonable world, a point-zero of nationalism. In these newspaper reports and in Ignatieff's book, nationalism is routinely and implicitly the property of others. Freud claimed that projection depends upon forgetting. He was referring to the individual repressing personal experiences of the past from conscious awareness. There is also, by analogy, a form of collective forgetting and collective projection. Common sense, through gaps in vocabulary and through the pointed rhetoric of cliché, can accomplish what amounts to a collective amnesia. This projection is a social habit of thought. 'Our' nationalism is routinely forgotten, being unnamed as nationalism. Nationalism as a whole is projected on to others. But, again and again, not only 'their' nationalism seems to return; 'ours' does too.

## Forgetting the Saluted Flag

The double neglect of banal nationalism involves academics forgetting what is routinely forgotten. People in established nations overlook the routine flagging of nationhood. The flags melt into the background, as 'our' particular world is experienced as *the* world. The routine absent-mindedness, involved in not noticing unwaved flags or other symbols of nationhood, has its reflection in academic theory. However, it is not merely the unwaved flags which have evaded attention. Even the saluted ones can seem so routinely familiar – so near to home – that they are ignored.

Since the 1880s, school pupils in the United States stand each morning before the national flag. At attention, often with hand on heart, they pledge "allegiance to the flag of the United States of America and to the republic for which it stands, one nation under God, indivisible with liberty and justice for all". The ceremony is a ritual display of national unity. Children, in knowing that this is the way in which the school day starts, will take it for granted that other pupils, the length and breadth of the homeland, are also beginning their day similarly; and that their parents and grandparents, if schooled in the United States, did likewise; they might even suppose that all over the world the school day starts thus. This does not mean that an awareness of national unity bubbles excitedly within the mind of each pupil on each and every school day. But it does mean that the nation celebrates itself routinely.

Here, one might have thought, is a ritual which would have been studied and re-studied endlessly by American sociologists and social psychologists. They should be delighted to have on their doorsteps such a Durkheimian ceremony. Moreover, the ceremony appears with the repeatability of a laboratory experiment, so that micro-processes of gesture, intonation and stance can be repeatedly examined in their controlled conditions. It should be a godsend for functionalists, role-theorists and micro-sociologists, let alone anthropologists, who can do their fieldwork and still return home for lunch. In point of fact, academic interest has been negligible. Anthropologists have headed for the reservations of the native Americans rather than the school-rooms of middle Iowa. When Renan mentioned the 'cult of the flag', ceremonies like the daily saluting were still in their infancy. Their strangeness was apparent. A century later the mysticism of pledging oneself to a coloured piece of cloth has become so familiar as to seem unworthy of attention. The theoretical forgetting of the flag is perhaps as remarkable as the act itself.

One of the few American investigators to draw attention to the ritual has been the psychotherapist, Robert Coles. In his book *The Political Life of Children*, Coles reports conversations with school children in the USA and elsewhere. He notes that the saluting of the flag is not performed in exactly the same way across the States. In predominantly black schools, the ceremony can be somewhat perfunctory; one teacher told Coles that it was "not a good way to start the day" (1986, p. 35). For other children, reports Coles, the saluting "can be an occasion for real emotional expression" (p. 36). A nine-year-old boy told Coles that his uncle was a sergeant in the army; another uncle was in the police department; the boy had visited army bases; he has seen the flag in church; he had prayed for his country. He was the sort of young, white, middle-class child for whom the flag had great meaning. For the majority, and for most of the time, one suspects that the routine is enacted as a routine. Even the young boy, who patriotically told Coles of his uncles, may have fidgeted, whispered, nudged his neighbour at times during the ceremony. Unfortunately, we only have the young boy's words, as he spoke on best behaviour to the visiting adult, and not his conduct day after day.

Coles, however, has noticed what other social scientists overlook. The significance of the ceremony is not diminished if it is treated as routine, rather than as an intense experience. If anything, the significance is enhanced: the sacral has become part of everyday life, instead of being confined to a special place of worship or particular day of celebration. Significantly, Coles does not see nationalism as a passing emotion or a surplus phenomenon: "Nationalism works its way into just about every corner of the mind's life" (1986, p. 60). Nor does he project nationalism on to others: "Nationality is a constant in the lives of most of us and must surely be worked into our thinking in various ways, with increasing diversity and complexity of expression as our lives unfold" (p. 59).

Coles' position is unusual on two counts. First, he treats the saluting of the flag as being psychologically important in the development of young Americans' views on the world. Secondly, unusually for an American investigator, he sees nationalism as pervasive in his own country. An interesting possibility arises: perhaps the two stances are related. Or, rather, perhaps the absence of both in much social science is connected. Maybe, embedded in conventional social scientific thinking is a habit of thinking, which produces an intellectual amnesia. This habit leads analysts, especially in the United States, to forget those flags, which are daily saluted and those which remain unsaluted. Also, it leads analysts to forget 'our' nationalism.

## Nationalism and Sociological Common Sense

If there is such a habit of thought, which produces a theoretical amnesia, then it is not the personal mark of a particular academic. It will reflect something much more widespread and deep-seated: a social scientific, or more particularly a sociological, common sense. Such a common sense will be ingrained into the intellectual habits of those who practise sociology professionally. It will mark out certain topics as interesting and sociologically relevant, while others will be peripheral.

An academic discipline's habits of thinking will be contained in core assumptions and in routine rhetorical practices (Brown, 1977, 1994; McCloskey, 1985; Nelson et al., 1987). These are habits which are widely unquestioned, for to question them might appear to threaten the very basis of the discipline itself. The disciplinary common sense can be found in major, intellectual works, as well as in the glossy textbooks, which are designed for a mass student readership. In fact, textbooks are often good sources for discovering a social science's common sense (Billig, 1990b; Stringer, 1990). Textbooks, in seeking to transmit the disciplinary vision to a new generation of disciples, tend to package the approved view in handy form.

A quick glance at the subject indexes of standard textbooks in sociology would reveal that nationalism is not a major, disciplinary preoccupation. It certainly is not in two textbooks, written during nationalism's so-called quiescent period: *Sociology in a Changing World* by Kornblum (1988) and *Sociology* by Macionis (1989). Both these texts are aimed at the large US undergraduate market. Their subject indexes accord 'nationalism' no more than a couple of pages each. Britain's most widely read textbook, Haralambos and Holborn's *Sociology* (1991), has no index entry for nationalism. Similar absences can also be found in important academic texts. *Social Theory Today*, edited by Turner and Giddens (1987), is an influential compendium, presenting an overview of major trends in contemporary sociological theorizing. The subject index has large entries for class, social structure and so on, but there are only two pages which are indexed for nationalism. These two pages deal with movements of "racial or ethnic minorities" within nations, rather than nationalism *qua* nationalism (Miliband, 1987, p. 342). To cite a further example: Ulrich Beck's important and well-received analysis of the new conditions of modernity, *The Risk Society*, has no entry for nationalism. It does mention briefly the undermining of national borders as part of a condition which "makes the utopia of a world society a little more real or at least more urgent" (1992, p. 47). Nationalism, here, far from returning is not even depicted as repressed. But, if it is to return, the way is opened for it to return as a special subject, rather than as the endemic condition of the times.

Sociology, from the classic works of Durkheim and Weber onwards, has been presented by sociologists as the study of 'society'. Sociologists routinely define their discipline in these terms. Edward Shils, writing on 'Sociology' in *The Social Science Encyclopedia*, describes sociology as "at present an unsystematic body of knowledge gained through the study of the whole and parts of society" (1985, p. 799). According to Kornblum, "Sociology is the scientific study of human societies and human behaviour in the many groups that make up a society" (1988, p. 4). Macionis begins his textbook by defining sociology as "the scientific study of society and the social activity of human beings" (1989, p. 2). Haralambos and Holborn define a sociological theory as "a set of ideas which claim to explain how society or aspects of society work" (1991, p. 8). All these definitions assume that there is such a thing as 'a society' which exists in an unproblematic way.

A number of critics of orthodox sociology have drawn attention to the way that sociologists take the existence of 'society' for granted. According to Giddens, it is a term which is "largely unexamined" in sociological discourse (1987, p. 25). Immanuel Wallerstein claims that "no concept is more pervasive in modern social science than society, and no concept is used more automatically and unreflectively than society" (1987, p. 315). Mann (1986), in making a similar point, announces that, if he were able, he "would abolish the concept of 'society' altogether" (p. 2; see also Bauman, 1992a, 1992b; Mann, 1992; McCrone, 1992; Turner, 1990). The problem is not that sociologists, whether in textbooks or works of theory, leave 'society' undefined. It lies in the assumption that 'we' readers will know more or less what a 'society' is: 'we' have common-sense ways of understanding 'society' (Bowers and Iwi, 1993).

It often turns out that the 'society' which lies at the heart of sociology's own self-definition is created in the image of the nation-state. Indeed, in the case of Max Weber there is evidence that his support for German political nationalism directly influenced his conception of 'society' (Anderson, 1992). The connection is continued in today's textbooks. Macionis (1989), having defined sociology as the scientific study of 'society', unusually goes on to give a definition of 'society': it is "a people who interact with one another within a limited territory and who share a culture" (p. 9). This is, of course, precisely how 'nations' are typically viewed both by themselves and by theorists: as peoples with a culture, a limited territory and distinguished by bonds of interaction. For sociologists it is a banal cliché to define their discipline as the 'science of society'; and it just as banal a habit of thought to imagine 'society' as a bounded, independent entity. A number of years ago Norbert Elias put the issue well: "Many twentieth century sociologists, when speaking of 'society', no longer have in mind (as did their predecessors) a 'bourgeois society' or a 'human society' beyond the state, but increasingly the somewhat diluted ideal image of a nation-state" (1978, p. 241).

There is a further point. The phrase 'science of society' implies that societies can be treated as self-contained units, with 'society' as something to be studied in isolation. The discipline has historically concentrated upon social relations within the 'society', or the groups, to use Kornblum's phrase, that make up a society. In so doing, it neglects the relations between 'societies', even failing to ask why there is a world of 'societies', let alone a world of nations (Wallerstein, 1987). Bauman (1992a) claims that the boundaries of 'society' (as conceived in terms of the nation-state) limit sociologists' conception of the social world. What is outside the 'society' is treated as an unanalysed 'environment'. However, nations (or 'societies') exist in a world of other nations (or 'societies'). Nationalism as an ideology, which spread throughout the world, was always an international ideology. Nations have never been hermetically sealed, but, as Bauman suggests, "nation states, those prototypes of theoretical societies, were porous" (p. 57). If the interrelation between the nation and the world of nations has been largely ignored by orthodox sociology, then sociology has been even less equipped to study cultures and epochs, such as

Mediaeval Europe, where forms of community are not apparently organized into neatly separated entities.

Far from leading to nationhood's being in the forefront of sociological inquiry, the emphasis on 'society' and the implicit modelling of 'society' on nation, has both reified and concealed nationhood. 'Society' is conceived as a universal entity. All human social life is presumed to take place within the orbit of 'society'; 'societies' are to be found wherever humans live socially. The problematic for orthodox sociology, particularly Parsonian sociology, has been to study how members of a 'society' become socialized into adopting the 'values', 'norms' and 'culture' of their 'society'. Haralambos and Holborn (1991), in the opening chapter of their textbook, specifically introduce readers to these concepts. These are all universal terms: it is presumed that all 'societies' have 'norms' and 'values'. Thus, 'our' society is not unique, but is an instance of something which is universal.

The image of 'our' society, however, is a nation-state. Kornblum (1988), in his textbook, asserts that the nation-state is "the social entity that, for most people in the world today, represents 'society' itself" (p. 72). If the nation is merely a variant of something universal (a 'society'), then the processes by which it is reproduced need not be identified by special words. Its particularities can be subsumed under general terms such as 'norm', 'value', 'socialization' etc. 'Nationalism' in this context need not make an appearance. Yet, it can return as a special subject to demarcate those who are striving to have their own 'society', or those who might be threatening the integrity of 'ours', or those who are proposing an extreme, fascistic politics of nationality. If the repressed continues its dramatic return in Eastern Europe and elsewhere, then the textbooks of sociology, in their future editions, are likely to add sub-sections or even whole chapters on nationalism. If they do, nationalism will still be seen as something surplus, even contingent. It will be a special subject. 'Society', modelled on the image of 'our' nation, will continue to be treated as necessarily universal. In this way, 'our' nationalism need not return textually.

This sort of sociological common sense can leave its mark on investigations of individual nations. For example, American sociologists, examining the state of American 'society', often overlook the national dimension of their topic, as they transform the particular into universal categories (Woodiwiss, 1993). For example, Bellah et al.'s *Habits of the Heart* is a superbly executed study, investigating the effects of individualism in contemporary American culture. It is based upon wide-ranging interviews with large numbers of American citizens. The book attracted a wide readership, becoming a non-fiction best-seller in the United States. The authors utter a message of warning, as they argue that individualism is undermining a sense of community. According to Bellah et al., "we live in a society that encourages us to cut free from the past . . . no tradition and no community in the United States is above criticism" (1986, p. 154).

The phrasing of the argument is significant. The sense of community, which is being lost, refers to feelings of township or locality. There is still a presumed locus in which the sense of community and tradition is evaporating. As the authors state, "we live in a society": the 'society', of course, is the United States. And the 'we', whom the authors are invoking, are Americans. Whatever the decline of 'community', the national society continues to exist. The authors' analysis seems to overlook their respondents' sense of being American; this sense is shared by the authors, as their text flags its own national identity. In this way, the authors take the framework of their own nation ('our society') for granted. Despite their other warnings of collapse, they do not suggest that the United States will fail to continue as the United States. Indeed, their text, by treating 'our society' as an assumed context, does its bit to enhabit the nation. And for all the authors' detailed accounts of community, tradition and its absence, they do not specifically point out the tradition in the schools, where the young routinely proclaim the unity of their nation under God.

## Our Patriotism – Their Nationalism

The repressed is not totally forgotten in orthodox social scientific writings, for it can return in a textually changed form. 'Our' loyalties to 'our' nation-state can be defended, even praised. A rhetorical distinction is necessary for accomplishing this defence. 'Our' nationalism is not presented as nationalism, which is dangerously irrational, surplus and alien. A new identity, a different label, is found for it. 'Our' nationalism appears as 'patriotism' – a beneficial, necessary and, often, American force.

In consequence, some social scientists insist that patriotism and nationalism represent two very different states of mind. The distinction would be convincing if there were clear, unambiguous criteria, beyond an ideological requirement to distinguish 'us' from 'them'. Walker Connor, one of today's leading specialists on nationalism, claims that nationalism and patriotism "should not be confused through the careless use of language" (1993, p. 376; see also Connor, 1978). According to Connor, nationalism is an irrational, primordial force, "an emotional attachment to one's people" (1993, p. 374). Nationalists often appeal to 'blood ties', in order to tap into these irrational forces. Nationalism, argues Connor, arises in ethnic groups, which claim common origins of blood. Connor cites the rhetoric of Hitler, Bismark and Mao to illustrate the dangerously irrational force of such appeals. Because nationalism is based upon a sense of the nation's ethnic unity, the national loyalties of 'immigrant' nations should not be described as 'nationalist': "I wish to make it clear that my comments do not refer . . . to immigrant societies such as those within Australia, the United States and non-Quebec Canada" (1993, p. 374).

If the loyalties, engendered in the United States, are not properly called nationalist, then they should be called 'patriotic'. Connor writes of his school days in the United States, when he and fellow pupils were taught to sing 'America' and to think of Washington and Jefferson as the founders of the nation. The United States might have adopted some of the ideas of 'nationalism', but still this was not nationalism proper. It did not possess the emotional depth and irrational force of nationalism. Politically, this puts patriotism at a disadvantage, when competing with the (alien) forces of nationalism:

> Despite the many advantages that the state has for politically socializing its citizens in patriotic values, patriotism – as evident from the multitude of separatist movements pockmarking the globe – cannot muster the level of emotional commitment that nationalism can. (Connor, 1993, p. 387)

The rhetoric tells its story. American loyalties, inculcated in school, are constructed as being 'patriotic'; they do not constitute a problematic irruption of the irrational psyche, unlike nationalism, which provokes "countless fanatical sacrifices" (1993, p. 385). The words 'fanatical', 'irrational', 'instinct' attach themselves to 'nationalism' in Connor's text. 'Patriotic values' (the term has a comforting rhetoric) are threatened by the nationalist movements, which 'pockmark the globe' (and, here, the rhetoric of disfigurement is used). 'Their' emotional bonds, so different from 'ours', are the problem and the threat.

The language is psychological, yet there is no direct psychological evidence to distinguish the rational state of patriotism from the irrational force of nationalism (see also the arguments of Eller and Coughlan, 1993). The evidence lies in the social events themselves: mass movements of nationalism are deemed irrational. The analysis, with its dire warnings, soothingly reassures. So much can be forgotten, as 'we' recall 'their' nationalism with horror. The wars waged by US troops; the bombings in Vietnam and Iraq; the bombast of successive US presidents; and the endless display of the revered flag: all these are removed from the problems of over-heated nationalism. If required, they can be transmuted into the warm glow of patriotism, the healthy necessity rather than the dangerous surplus.

A number of social scientists have attempted to draw a psychological distinction between nationalism and patriotism, in terms of the direction, rather than intensity, of the attitudes. Morris Janowitz (1983), advocating that American schools should instil a patriotic civic consciousness, defined patriotism as "the persistence of love or attachment to a country". He distinguished this love from xenophobia, or hatred of others (p. 194). A similar distinction can be found in Snyder's (1976) *Varieties of Nationalism*. Patriotism is "defensive", being based upon a love of one's country, whereas nationalism "takes on a quality of aggression that makes it one of the prime causes for wars" (p. 43, see also Doob, 1964). The social psychologist Daniel Bar-Tal (1993) has argued that patriotism is a function-ally positive force, providing stability for the 'ingroup' and a sense of identity to its members. He defines patriotism as the "attachment of group members towards their group and the country in which they reside" (p. 48). He distinguishes this positive attachment from chauvinism and nationalism, both of which include negative feelings against outgroups (p. 51).

The problem is how to distinguish in practice these two allegedly very different states of mind. One cannot merely ask potential patriots whether they either love their country or hate foreigners. Even the most extreme of nationalists will claim the patriotic motivation for themselves. Frederick Hertz, writing on nationalism when Hitler was still Chancellor of Germany, put the matter well. If one asked fascists what their creed was, they will invariably say that "it consists in passionate devotion to the nation and in putting its interests higher than anything else" (1944, p. 35). Fascists will protest that they are defenders, not attackers, only taking against foreigners when the latter are a danger to the beloved homeland. Hitler, for example, imagined that he was defending Germany against the Jews, asserting in *Mein Kampf* that "the Jew is not the attacked but the attacker" (1972, p. 293). Today's fascists, likewise, claim that they only desire to protect the homeland from invasion, conspiracy and racial pollution (Billig, 1978, pp. 224f.; Billig, 1991). The hatreds will be justified in the name of love. In the world of nation-states, everyone claims to be acting in defence, going to war through necessity, rather than choice. 'We don't want war, but . . .' is the common phrase of politicians leading their countries to battle (Lauerbach, 1989). Semantically, even the notion of 'jingoism' owes its origin to this stance. "We don't want to fight", went the music hall song of 1878, "but, by Jingo, . . ." (Reader, 1988, p. 46).

The claim that nationalism and patriotism are psychologically distinct needs to be backed by evidence about different states of mind or underlying motivations. Often the force of the claim is stronger than the empirical data cited in support. Kosterman and Feshbach (1989) claim to have found empirical evidence that patriotic attitudes about one's own country are unrelated to negative attitudes about foreign nations. Their claims and their evidence are worth examining: they reveal, not so much an objective difference between nationalism and patriotism, but the readiness to claim such a difference.

Kosterman and Feshbach gave samples of US residents questionnaires, asking them about their views of America. Having factor-analysed the replies, Kosterman and Feshbach argued that patriotism and nationalism formed separate dimensions, which can be assessed by independent scales. The patriotic scale included items such as 'I love my country' or 'When I see the American flag flying, I feel great.' The nationalist items compared America with other countries (i.e. 'generally, the more influence America has on other nations, the better off they are'). The mean scores of the patriotism scale were generally high (significantly higher than the nationalist scale), indicating that the patriotic statements about being emotionally committed to America attracted general assent. Despite Kosterman and

Feshbach's claims about the independence of the patriotism and nationalism scales, the data, in fact, showed the two scales to be significantly
correlated (1989, Table VII, p. 268). Also both scales correlated with other
variables in similar ways: for example, on both scales Republican supporters scored more highly than Democratic supporters (Table X, p. 270).

Kosterman and Feshbach draw wide-ranging conclusions from their
data. They claim that their results supported "a sharp discrimination
between nationalism and patriotism" (p. 273). They warn against nationalism: "one cannot help but be concerned" by nationalism, which encourages "belligerent actions". By contrast, patriotism is valuable because it is
as "important to the well-being of a nation as high self-esteem is to the
well-being of an individual"; patriotism, far from causing wars, may
actually be a means "of *reducing* international belligerence" (p. 273,
emphasis in original). This conclusion comes after evidence that those with
higher nationalist scores tend to have higher patriotic scores. Thus, the
sentiments, which supposedly reduce international belligerence, tend to
accompany those which promote it, despite the protestation that the two
should be sharply distinguished. It would seem that something other than
the empirical results was pushing the authors to their praise of patriotism
and their criticism of nationalism.

Underlying such arguments is the assumption that hatred of the
outgroup (rather than love of the ingroup) provides the motivation for
nationalist warfare. This is almost certainly an oversimplification. In an
important analysis, Jean Bethke Elshtain (1993) argues that, in the past
century, young men have gone to war in their millions motivated not
primarily by hatred of the enemy, but by a 'will-to-sacrifice'. The
willingness to die in the cause of the homeland precedes a motive to kill.
The elements of this will-to-sacrifice in the cause of the nation are
uppermost in the items on the 'patriotism scale': the love of the flag, the
'great pride in that land that is our America', the importance 'for me to
serve my country' and so on. As Kosterman and Feshbach's study shows,
such sentiments are widely held in the United States by men and women.
Arguably, these shared sentiments provide the background for nationally
united responses, should some other nation appear to threaten the pride,
politics or economics of 'our' great America.

This is the context for those doubly forgotten flags. Contrary to what
respondents claimed in response to the questionnaire item, they do not feel
great whenever they see the American flag flying. They see it far too often
to feel that way each time. They see it too frequently even to notice that
they are seeing it. Those flags, together with other routine signs of
nationhood, act as unmindful reminders, preventing the danger of collective amnesia. The citizens, however, do not forget their appropriate
responses, when the social occasions demand: they know to declare that
the flag gives them a great feeling. All the while, the forgetting is doubled.
Social scientists have probed the most intimate parts of modern life. They

have calculated the number of sexual fantasies the average adult American is likely to have per day. But a census of flags has not been undertaken. No one asks how many stars and stripes the average American is likely to encounter in the course of the day. Nor what is the effect of all this flagging.

# 4

# National Identity in the World of Nations

It is easy to think that the problems of nationalism come down to issues of 'identity'. So much about nationalism seems, at first sight, to be explained by 'identity'. To be German or French is, psychologically, to have a German or French 'identity'; nation-states are being threatened by the search for 'identities'; patriotic ceremonies strengthen the sense of national 'identity'; 'identity politics' is a reaction to a crisis of modern 'identity'; and so on. 'Identity' seems to provide familiar diagnoses and explanations. As John Shotter has written, " 'identity' has become the watchword of the times" (1993a, p. 188).

The watchword, however, should be watched, for frequently it explains less than it appears to. The routine flaggings, discussed in the previous chapter, might be said to strengthen 'national identity' in the contemporary, established nation-state. But what does 'national identity' mean in this context? It certainly does not refer to an inward emotion – a glow of patriotic awareness – experienced by all who pass by the unsaluted flag. Nor does it mean that everyone within the nation-state becomes identical. As Stuart Hall affirms, "the notion that identity has to do with people that look the same, feel the same, call themselves the same, is nonsense" (1991a, p. 49).

There seems to be something psychological about an 'identity', but theories of psychology are often unable to explain what this psychological element is. There does not seem to be a particular psychological state, which can be identified as an 'identity'. That being so, an investigation of national identity should aim to disperse the concept of 'identity' into different elements. An 'identity' is not a thing; it is a short-hand description for ways of talking about the self and community (Bhavnani and Phoenix, 1994; Shotter and Gergen, 1989). Ways of talking, or ideological discourses, do not develop in social vacuums, but they are related to forms of life. In this respect, 'identity', if it is to be understood as a form of talking, is also to be understood as a form of life. The saluted and unsaluted flags are not stimuli that evoke 'identity-reactions'; they belong to the forms of life which constitute what could be called national identities.

Serge Moscovici (1983) has argued that the so-called inner psychological states of individuals depend upon culturally shared depictions, or representations of the social world. A person cannot claim to have patriotic feelings for their nation, unless they have assumptions about what a nation is and, indeed, what patriotism is: unless, to use Moscovici's terminology, they have social representations of 'nation', 'patriotism' and much else beside (see also Farr, 1993; McKinlay et al., 1993; Moscovici, 1987). In consequence, the psychological study of national identity should search for the common-sense assumptions and ways of talking about nationhood. The present chapter, therefore, investigates the general themes of nationalist consciousness and its habits of thinking. It involves examining what Roland Barthes (1977) called "banal opinion", or 'the doxa' of common sense (p. 162).

With regard to nationalist thinking, one need not ask 'What is a national identity?' but 'What does it mean to claim to have a national identity?' The general forms of nationalist thinking then need to be outlined. As will be argued, these include ways of conceiving of 'us, the nation', which is said to have its unique destiny (or identity); it also involves conceiving of 'them, the foreigners', from whom 'we' identify 'ourselves' as different. Nationalist thinking involves more than commitment to a group and a sense of difference from other groups. It conceives 'our' group in a particular way. In doing so, it takes for granted ideas about nationhood and the link between peoples and homelands; and about the naturalness of the world of nations, divided into separate homelands. A whole way of thinking about the world is implicated. If this way of thinking seems to be commonplace and familiar, then it, nevertheless, includes mystic assumptions which have become habits of thought.

This nationalist way of thinking, even when it is ingrained as habitual, is not straightforward. Just as a dialectic of remembering and forgetting might be said to sustain 'national identity', so this 'identity' involves a dialectic of inwardness and outwardness. The nation is always a nation in a world of nations. 'Internationalism' is not the polar opposite of 'nationalism', as if it constitutes a rival ideological consciousness. Nationalism, like other ideologies, contains its contrary themes, or dilemmatic aspects (Billig et al., 1988). An outward-looking element of internationalism is part of nationalism and has accompanied the rise of nationalism historically. When US presidents, today, claim to speak simultaneously on behalf of their nation and a new world order, they are not placing, side by side in the same utterance, elements from two, clearly separate ideologies; nor are they creating a novel synthesis from the thesis of nationalism and the antithesis of internationalism. They are using the hegemonic possibilities of nationalism. As will be suggested, these possibilities are endemic in nationalist habits of thinking.

## Theory and Nation

The rise of the nation-state brought about a transformation in the ways that people thought about themselves and about community. It could be said to have brought about a transformation of identity, even bringing into the popular vocabulary the notion of 'identity' itself (Giddens, 1990). Nevertheless, before the vocabulary of identity was set in place – before people could claim that they 'were searching for their identity' – it was still possible to talk of the self and of loyalties to the community. People were able to label themselves, whether in terms of place, religion, tribe or vassalage. But these labels, as it were, bore different packets of meaning than the labels of nationhood.

In *Language and Nationalism*, Joshua Fishman recounts a story of peasants in Western Galicia at the turn of the century. They were asked whether they were Poles. "We are quiet folk", they replied. So, are you Germans? "We are decent folk" (Fishman, 1972, p. 6). The story appears to be about the clash of identities. According to Fishman, the peasants had a concrete consciousness: their identity was with *this* village, or *this* valley, rather than with the more abstract idea of the nation. It is said that rural Slovaks, emigrating to the United States at about the same time, were often unaware of their national identity, only knowing from which specific village they had come (Brass, 1991, p. 39). These are not stories of ignorance: the peasants in the Fishman story seem to know more than they admit. Nor do the stories merely tell of a clash of personal identities, as if the only difference were that the peasants identified themselves with the village, while the officials had a national identity. More was at stake than the way of defining the self.

Fishman's story tells of a conflict between two outlooks, or forms of ideological consciousness. Calling it a clash of 'identities' lessens the full force of what was occurring. Like was not confronting like, as if two 'identities' – two variants of the same genus – were in competition. This was not a conflict between Poles and Germans. The peasants were standing against the very assumptions and forms of life which led to the identities of Pole and German. They were resisting the notion of nationhood, reacting against its theories as well as labels. A world, in which it is natural to have a national identity, was meeting, and overrunning, an older world. And now it appears strange – well worth telling as a good story – that four generations ago there were people who neither knew, nor wished to know, their nationality.

The sort of confrontation described by Fishman has been enacted countless times, in one form or another, throughout nationalism's triumphant march across the globe. In Central Arabia, writes Helms (1981), nationalism was unknown until the twentieth century. Previously, identities had been based on the tribe or on the 'sphere of trade'. The tribal and trading boundaries were constantly changing. A world of fixed boundaries, and clearly delineated identities, was to replace this older world. Sometimes, colonial powers imposed the assumptions of nationalism by means of force. The British often insisted upon treating indigenous leaders as if they headed sovereign states (Hinsley, 1986). In the 1830s the British Resident in New Zealand advised Maori chiefs to form themselves into a

'United Tribes of New Zealand'. Not only would such an arrangement be administratively simpler; also, if sovereign state were appearing to negotiate with sovereign state, then highly unequal treaties could be presented with an outward display of legality and morality. In this, of course, a particular ideological vision of morality was being victoriously imposed.

The new imposed identities (such as belonging to the United Tribes of New Zealand) were part of a more general outlook on the world. In this sense, nationalism involves a theoretical consciousness. Etienne Balibar has written that there is "no racism without theory (or theories)" (1991, p. 18). The racist may hate unthinkingly, yet, as Balibar implies, racism distinguishes between 'our race' and 'other races', 'our racial community' and 'theirs'. At the very minimum, the racist shares some common-sense theory of what a 'race' is; why it appears important; how 'races' differ; and why 'ours' should remain unmixed. By the same token, there is no nationalism without theory. Nationalism involves assumptions about what a nation is: as such, it is a theory of community, as well as a theory about the world being 'naturally' divided into such communities. The theory does not need to be experienced theoretically. Intellectuals have written theoretical tomes about 'nation'. With the triumph of nationalism, and the establishment of nations across the globe, the theories of nationalism have been transformed into familiar common sense.

The assertion of belonging to a 'people', if made in a political context in which 'peoples' are assumed to deserve nation-states, is not an assertion of an inner psychological identity. A movement of national independence will not only claim that 'we are a nation', but, in so doing, it will be demanding the political entitlements which are presumed to follow from being a nation. Demanding such entitlements is not possible without assumptions about the nature of nations (any nation, not just 'ours'). The theory can be expressed theoretically, in terms of abstract principles about what a nation is and should be. However, as the world of nations is set in place as *the* world, so the theory also becomes enhabited in common sense. It ceases to seem theoretical, but is embedded in habits of thought and life. In the Fishman example, the peasants were concretely resisting nationalism's habits of thought, asserting their own practical consciousness.

There is a case for saying that the categories of nationalism come with particular theoretical discourses, which do not accompany other categories. Banton suggests that in the polyethnic society of Malaya, people use ethnic terms concretely. He claims that the residents of Petalingjaya rarely use any general notion of 'ethnicity'. Instead, they use "a practical language embodying proper names such as Malay, Chinese and Indian" (1994, p. 6). In day-to-day life, while shopping at Indian or Malay stores, residents do not theorize about the various groups in Malaya. It is possible that Banton may be exaggerating the lack of theoretical consciousness on the part of the residents of Petalingjaya. Other things may be said on other occasions, especially in the context of political disputes for resources. Banton is, nevertheless, suggesting something important: the residents do not have an overall 'theoretical' category under which to group the categories 'Malays', 'Chinese' and 'Indians', and to stipulate, in theory, what these groups are.

They do have a further category, which sometimes subsumes the ethnic categories: this is the national category of being 'Malaysian'. According to Banton, this category comes to the fore at international sporting occasions. The national category is both concrete and theoretical. It is concrete in the sense that nations confront the inhabitants of today's world as concrete entities: Malaysia concretely exists for its citizenry, just as the United States of America, France and Brazil also concretely exist. Similarly, the Malaysian basketball team concretely exists when it plays the Indonesian team and when all its members, whether Malays or Chinese, are cheered by the partisan crowd as 'Malaysians'. In addition, Malaysia, and other nations, exist theoretically. They can be spoken about as 'nations'; there are general ways of talking about these concrete entities.

In the world of nations, nationhood is both unthinkingly enhabited and is a matter of political controversy. 'Nation' can be an essentially contested concept, to use Gallie's phrase (1962). On occasion, definitions will be produced, to prove what a nation *really* is. As Seton-Watson (1977) suggested, definitions of nationhood generally aim "to prove that, in contrast to the community to which the definer belonged, some other group was not entitled to be called a nation" (p. 4). In this respect, the debates about what a nation is parallel, and sometimes are combined with, those debates, discussed in Chapter 2, about what a language is. Disputants, in arguing their political cases, might disagree about what should count as a *real* nation and or a *real* language, but they will take for granted that nations and languages *really* exist; and that they should exist.

For example, the charter of the Palestine Liberation Organization (pointedly called the Palestinian *National* Charter) declares the Palestinians to be a people and a nation. More than this, it has a rhetorical stake in distinguishing between 'genuine' nations and groups which are not nations. According to the Charter, Jews, whatever status they might claim for themselves, are a religious group, and, unlike the Palestinians, they do not "constitute a single nation with an identity of its own" (Article 20; see Billig, 1987b; Harkabi, 1980). In this, there is a theorizing about what constitutes a nation, a people and a religion: the nation is said to have a distinctive identity of its own. This theorizing, or common-sense sociologizing, is not abstract, but is rhetorically and politically directed.

This type of thinking is not, of course, confined to aspiring nations. Established nations can respond in theoretical kind. For years, leading Israeli politicians denied that the Palestinians were a people: the "so-called Palestinian people" was a phrase used by prime ministers, to be contrasted rhetorically with the so-called genuineness of Jewish peoplehood. Yitzhak Rabin's letter to Yassar Arafat in September 1993, accepting mutual recognition, was discursively historic: "The government of Israel has decided to recognize the PLO as the representative of the Palestinian people" (*Guardian*, 10 September 1993). Not only was the PLO recognized, but so were the Palestinians as a 'people', who were entitled to such a representation. Opponents of the agreement used different terminology. Tehran denounced the agreement as not being "commensurate with ideals for which the Muslim Palestinian nation has fought for decades" (*Guardian*, 1 September 1993). A differently characterized people – the 'Muslim Palestinian nation' – is indicated.

These are not haphazard labels. Not only do they reflect political stances, but these stances are articulated by means of common-sense sociological ideas about 'peoples', 'nations' and 'identity'. Wallerstein (1991) recounts the intense debates in South Africa among those classified by the apartheid regime as being 'coloureds': should they call themselves 'coloureds' or were 'coloureds' merely a 'so-called people', an illegitimately imposed category? The debate was one of identity and self-definition, for the protagonists were speaking deeply of themselves. But it was more than that. The nature of the categories – the meaning of peoplehood – was at issue. In the contemporary world, the issue 'what is a nation?' is not merely an interesting topic for academic seminars. It touches upon issues which contemporary people think worth the sacrifice of life – issues which the Galician peasants in the story could recognize as dangerous missiles, from which evasive cover should be taken.

## Identity and Categories

All this is said as a warning against the temptation to explain nationalist consciousness in terms of 'identity', as if 'identity' were a psychological state, which exists apart from forms of life. Nationalism is more than a feeling of identity; it is more than an interpretation, or theory, of the world; it is also a way of being within the world of nations. The problem is that the historical particularities of nationalism, and its links with the world of nation-states, tend to be overlooked, if national 'identity' is considered as functionally equivalent with any other type of 'identity'. A complex topography of heights and depths then becomes flattened into a single plain.

Unfortunately, this flattening characterizes many social psychological theories of identity. It even characterizes the most creative and important theory of social identity to be produced in recent years. The Social Identity Theory has justly been described as "one of the most ambitious undertakings in research on group processes" (Eiser, 1986, p. 316). The theory was originally formulated by Henri Tajfel (1974, 1981, 1982; see also Brewer, 1979; Brown, 1988), and has been developed, more recently, under the heading of 'self-categorization theory' (e.g., Abrams and Hogg, 1991; Hogg and Abrams, 1988; Taylor and Moghaddam, 1994; Turner, 1984; Turner et al., 1987). Although Tajfel (1969, 1970) was concerned to study national identity, Social Identity Theory is not primarily a theory of nationalism. It is a general theory of group identity, exploring universal psychological principles, which are presumed to lie behind all forms of group identity.

Social Identity Theory assumes that psychological elements are crucial in group behaviour. Tajfel gave the example of nations: a nation will only exist if a body of people feel themselves to be a nation (1981, p. 229). This illustrated, he suggested, a more general point: groups only exist if members identify themselves with the group. Identification, according to Social Identity Theory, is, at root, a form of categorization. For groups to exist, individuals must categorize themselves in group terms. The theory stresses that categorization is divisive, because categories segment the world. The meaning of the category 'table' is derived from the fact that a 'table' is to be distinguished from a 'chair' (Rosch, 1978). Similarly, to be a member of an 'ingroup' entails a categorical distinction from an 'outgroup'. The imagining of 'our' community involves imagining, either implicitly or explicitly, 'them', from whom 'we' are distinct. One of the major strengths of the Social Identity Theory is to emphasize this sense of social division, which group identification and categorization entails.

Tajfel's theory contained a strong motivational theme. Individuals, he claimed, have a need for a positive social identity, or self-conception: "It can be assumed that an individual will tend to remain a member of a group and seek membership of new groups if these groups have some contribution to make to the positive aspects of his (sic) social identity" (Tajfel, 1981, p. 256). To achieve this positive identity, groups will tend to compare themselves positively with contrasting outgroups, and they will seek dimensions of comparison on which they will fare well. For instance, nations will produce flattering stereotypes of themselves, and demeaning stereotypes of those other nations, with which they compare themselves. The dimensions, on which they pride their own qualities, will be accorded extra importance. The flattering stereotypes, held by the ingroup about itself, and the unflattering ones about outgroups, will maintain the positive self-identity, which is necessary for the group's continuing existence.

There are, according to Hogg and Abrams (1988), three stages in the process of group identification. First, individuals categorize themselves as part of an ingroup, assigning themselves a social identity and distinguishing themselves from the relevant outgroup. Then, they learn the stereotypic norms associated with such an identity. Third, they assign these norms to themselves, and "thus their behaviour becomes more normative as their category membership becomes salient" (Hogg and Abrams, 1988, p. 172). In this way, the self-categorization version of the theory links self-identification to stereotyping.

Two critical points can be noted about this important body of social psychological theorizing. The first relates to the universalism of Social Identity Theory and its neglect of the specific meaning of social categories. The second critical point concerns the theory's focus upon individual categorization and its neglect of the ways in which national identity becomes enhabited. This, in turn, leads to a neglect of the central, distinguishing features of banal nationalism.

## Categorizing the Categories

Social Identity Theory describes psychological features which are presumed to be universal and not linked to particular socio-historic contexts. Just as classical sociology assumed the universality of 'societies', in which all humans are presumed to live, so Social Identity Theory, and most other psychological theories of 'group identity', assume 'groups' to be universal. Nations, properly speaking, might belong to the modern period, but 'ingroups' and 'outgroups', 'groups' and 'group identities', are to be found in all eras (Bar-Tal, 1993). Of course, Social Identity Theory recognizes that there are different forms of group, such as caste, nation, religion, tribe and so on; feminist critics, however, have maintained that Social Identity theorists have consistently overlooked gender and its particularities (Condor, 1989; Griffin, 1989; Williams, 1984).

Social Identity Theory assumes that the differences between groups are less important than their psychological similarities. Hogg and Abrams begin their book *Social Identifications* by discussing how ingroups distinguish themselves from outgroups. They mention a variety of different sorts of groupings:

> national groups (Italians, Germans), religious groups (Buddhist, Muslim, Protestant, Catholic), political groups (socialist, conservative), ethnic groups (Tamils and Singalese in Sri Lanka), sex groups (male, female), tribal groups (Karen, Lahu, Akha in Thailand), youth groups (punk, skinhead), university faculty groups (Science, Arts, Law) and so on. (1988, p. 2)

The authors declare that the essential social psychological question is "*how* do people identify with a group, and precisely what are the consequences of such identification?" (p. 2, emphasis in original). The task is to find the psychological similarities behind the different forms of group identity.

As Breuilly (1985) has pointed out, the specific meanings of nationalism are lost if it is seen as just another form of 'group identity' – as if the Galician peasants' 'identity' were of a piece with the national identities of Poles and Germans. Psychologists, working with Social Identity Theory, tend not to ask what it specifically means to declare oneself to be a member of a national group, or to declare one's group to be a national group. Any such declaration – whether of self or of the group – is itself a discursive act, which takes its meaning from what is being said and from the context of its utterance (Edwards, 1991; Edwards and Potter, 1992, 1993; Potter et al., 1993). Also, the categorizations come into the discursive situation carrying their own extra packets of meaning. The PLO, in declaring Palestinians, but not Jews, to be a nation, was doing more than make a personal declaration of identity. A sociological way of thinking was being mobilized to make a political case. This case centres on the notion of nationhood and the claim that the group has a national identity.

Social Identity theorists argue that group members must think the group to be 'real'. Turner points out that members of a nation "do not interact with more than a small minority of their fellows"; nevertheless, "the members tend to define themselves and be defined by others as a nation" (1984, p. 521; see also Turner et al., 1987). Benedict Anderson, in describing the nation as an 'imagined community', makes a similar point: the individual members "will never know most of their fellow members, meet them, or hear of them, yet in the mind of each lives the image of their communion" (1983, p. 15). The same might be said for many other sorts of large grouping, such as religious groups, class groups, or even professional groups such as professors of biochemistry. These, too, have to be imagined.

The point is not that such groupings have to be psychologically imagined, and, therefore, they are all psychologically similar. Quite the contrary, it can be argued that they have to be imagined in different ways, and, thus, are psychologically different. As Anderson suggests, communities are to be distinguished "by the style in which they are imagined" (1983, p. 16). The religious communities of the Middle Ages were imagined in different terms from the modern nation: the imagining of 'Christendom' involved different 'theories', representations of morality and assumptions about the nature of the world than are involved in the imagining of the modern nation. The imagining of the great Islamic *umma*, before the age of nationhood, differed crucially from the imagining, and creation, of particular Islamic nation-states today (Zubaida, 1993). Smaller range identities also imply theories and representations. Academics cannot classify themselves as 'biochemists' or 'professors' without making assumptions about academic disciplines, institutions, professions and, indeed, about the nature of knowledge itself. All these imaginings depend upon wider ideological beliefs. In consequence, grammatically similar statements of identity can have very different meanings. 'I am a sociologist', uttered at professional gathering of anthropologists carries a different meaning from the famous declaration of US President John Kennedy, *'Ich bin ein Berliner'*. To say that both are similar statements of group identity would close down analysis at precisely the point at which it should begin.

Social Identity Theory, especially in its 'self-categorization' variety, flattens out different ways of representing the world. The search for the psychological factors leads the analyst to the psyche of the categorizing individual: identity is understood as an inner response to a motivational need. In conceiving identity in these terms, social psychologists narrow their focus unnecessarily. The significant factor may not be how individuals come to categorize themselves, but how the category is categorized. As far as national identity is concerned, not only do the members have to imagine themselves as nationals; not only do they have to imagine their nation as a community; but they must also imagine that they know what a nation is; and they have to identify the identity of their own nation.

## Enhabiting the Categories

Social Identity Theory assumes that individuals have multiple ways of describing and categorizing themselves. In different contexts, different identities become 'salient' (Turner et al., 1987). Hutnik (1991) claims that self-categorizations "act as 'switches' that turn on (or off) aspects of social identity" (p. 164), as identities are used in 'salient' situations. One might imagine an Italian–American woman: in the delicatessen shop she may engage in ethnic signalling with fellow 'Italians', adjusting gesture and intonation to this saliently 'Italian' situation; in her woman's group, she may signal her solidarity with a wider community of 'women'; there may be times when she is an 'American', a 'New Yorker', or even a 'Neapolitan', courtesy of her grandfather's early life (for detailed examples of such switching of behaviour and accent, see Essed, 1994; Giles et al., 1987; Plotnicov and Silverman, 1978). The cues that elicit the switching of identities can be quite subtle and may not even be consciously registered.

If the use of a particular identity is intermittent, nevertheless the identity itself is a constant latency: "An individual who defines him- or herself as an 'Australian' . . . may never think about nationality for days at a time, yet if that self-definition did not exist as a latent identity, it could hardly become salient in relevant settings" (Turner et al., 1987, p. 54). There is no problem with the idea that there are particular situations in which someone might act in a self-consciously, flag-waving Australian manner: after all, the Australian government does not arrange – with due promotional advertising – bicentenary celebrations each week (Augoustinos, 1993). However, Social Identity Theory has little to say about what happens to the identity in between such national situations: it merely becomes some sort of latency, or internalized cognitive schema, within the individual's 'memory-store'; there it stays, awaiting active service when the next salient situation pops along.

There is much more to be said about national identity and its maintenance. The latency of nationalist consciousness does not depend on the vagaries of individual memory: if it did, then many more people would forget their national identity. Nor does national identity disappear into individuals' heads in between salient situations. The hypothetical Australian, while not consciously acting or thinking in an Australian way, continues to live in a nation-state and in a world of nations. Unlike the Galician peasants of former times, this hypothetical citizen of a nation-state will continually encounter, if not consciously register, flagged signs of nationhood. The apparently latent identity is maintained within the daily life of inhabited nations. The 'salient situation' does not suddenly occur, as if out of nothing, for it is part of a wider rhythm of banal life in the world of nations. What this means is that national identity is more than an inner psychological state or an individual self-definition: it is a form of life, which is daily lived in the world of nation-states.

## Imagining 'Us' as the National Community

The theory of 'self categorization', as its own name suggests, focuses upon the first person singular: it is concerned with the declarations of identity which 'I' make about 'myself'. There is a case for saying that nationalism is, above all, an ideology of the first person plural. The crucial question relating to national identity is how the national 'we' is constructed and what is meant by such construction. The nation has to be conceived as an entity with its own identity. As the PLO charter implies, only if the nation is imagined to have an identity, can 'we' claim 'ourselves' to have a national identity.

Benedict Anderson's idea of the nation as an 'imagined community' is a useful starting-point for examining these themes – at least so long as it is realized that the imagined community does not depend upon continual acts of imagination for its existence. Anderson argues that the nation is to be imagined as a unique entity in terms of time and space. It is imagined as a community stretching through time, with its own past and own future destiny; it is imagined across space, embracing the inhabitants of a particular territory. The temporal dimension ensures that all nations maintain a sense of their own history, which is no one else's. It is no coincidence that the emergence of nation-states has typically been accompanied by the creation of national histories (Colley, 1992; Hobsbawm and Ranger, 1983). Because nations not only have to be imagined, but also have to create their own histories, or interpretations of themselves, Edward Said (1983) insists that they are 'interpretive communities' as well as imagined ones.

As was discussed in Chapter 2, some national histories claim that the nation emerged from the misty dawns of time. The English have often liked to speak in these terms, letting the term 'England' speak for the whole of Britain. The Conservative prime minister of the inter-war years, Stanley Baldwin, in a famous example of populist national sentimentality, spoke of the sight of plough-teams as an "eternal sight of England". These sights, together with the sound of the hammer on the anvil and the corncrake on a dewy morning, "strike down into the very depths of our nature, and touch chords that go back to the beginning of time" (Baldwin, 1937, pp. 16–17; on the importance of Baldwin's type of English nationalism, see, *inter alia*, Schwartz, 1986).

National histories will have their special moments, in which heroes and heroines seem to step out of the banal progress of calendrical time. Sometimes, the stories start with the sudden shock of liberatory gunsmoke, and then a hero – a Washington, Bolivar or Nkrumah – bestrides the scene with bigger steps and larger character than later citizens. The narrative structure of these stories can be well known, with citizens easily able to summarize the story in conventional forms (Wertsch, in press;

Wertsch and O'Connor, in press). If the national hero is obviously a dull character, like George Washington, his ordinariness can always be trans-formed into a mythic ordinariness, in order to symbolize the national genius for ordinary-dealing (Schwartz, 1987).

Nations often do not typically have a single history, but there are competing tales to be told. In Britain, the same people will speak about the national past using conservative and liberal tales: they will talk about 'the good old days' of order and hierarchy; and they will speak of the 'bad old days' of poverty and ignorance (Billig, 1990a). The historical tales emerge from the struggles for hegemony. When Estonia was part of the USSR, an official history, which was taught in schools and which told of Russian liberators, was popularly opposed by an unofficial history of Russian oppressors; this unofficial story has now become official (Tulviste and Wertsch, in press). Different factions, whether classes, religions, regions, genders or ethnicities, always struggle for the power to speak for the nation, and to present their particular voice as the voice of the national whole, defining the history of other sub-sections accordingly. 'The voice of the nation' is a fiction; it tends to overlook the factional struggles and the deaths of unsuccessful nations, which make such a fiction possible. Thus, national histories are continually being re-written, and the re-writing reflects current balances of hegemony. As Walter Benjamin argued, history is always the tale of victors, celebrating their triumphs: "Whoever has emerged victorious participates to this day in the triumphal procession in which the present rulers step over those who are lying prostrate" (1970, p. 258).

National histories tell of a people passing through time – 'our' people, with 'our' ways of life, and 'our' culture. Stereotypes of character and temperament can be mobilized to tell the tale of 'our' uniqueness and 'our' common fate (Wetherell and Potter, 1992). As Balibar (1991) emphasizes, 'we' can speak of culture – 'our' culture – as if it were a precious genetic inheritance, to be transmitted uncontaminated and unweakened (see, also Barker, 1981; Taguieff, 1988; Van Dijk, 1993, for further discussions of the 'racialization' of the idea of national culture). Language, too, can be spoken in these terms. The Académie Française seeks to transmit the unique genius of the French language to future generations, protecting it from interbreeding with contaminating foreign words. Julia Kristeva has claimed that, in France, the foreigners' use of French "discredits them utterly – consciously or not – in the eyes of the natives who identify more than in other countries with their beloved, polished speech" (1991, p. 39).

In all this, a sense of 'our' uniqueness and integrity is conveyed. Integrity is frequently conveyed by the metaphors of kinship and gender: the nation is the 'family' living in the 'motherland' or 'fatherland' (Johnson, 1987; Yuval-Davis, 1993). 'We' do not merely categorize 'ourselves', but claim that the object of 'our' identification possesses an identity, indeed a preciously unique identity. Themes of uniqueness can be readily mobilized should an 'alien' threat to 'our' identity be imagined (Windisch, 1985, 1990).

In late twentieth-century Britain there is much uncertainty about 'national identity', especially as relations within the European Union are negotiated. In a study of English people talking of the monarchy, many speakers claimed that the Royal Family was precious because it was one of the things which distinguished 'us', the English/British, from other nations (see Greenfeld, 1992, for a discussion of the historical basis of this belief). One speaker declared that if 'we' didn't have the Royal Family, then 'we' wouldn't be the "British Isles as we know it, we'll perhaps be another state of America or something like that" (Billig, 1992, p. 34). Then 'we' wouldn't be 'us'. The unique form of life, and, hence, 'our' national identity would be lost. Were these to be lost, then so would be 'our' own sense of 'ourselves' as 'ourselves'.

In 1992 Prime Minister John Major sought to reassure his Conservative Party that the signing of the Maastricht Treaty did not entail a loss of national sovereignty to the European Community. The notion of 'national identity' was itself a rhetorical symbol. At the party conference of that autumn, his speech replayed patriotic themes. "We are all British citizens and we will always remain British citizens", he declared (see report in *Guardian*, 10 October 1992). He continued: "I will never, come hell or high water, let our distinctive British identity be lost in a federal Europe." The national flag and the stereotypes of self-praise were consciously waved: "And if there are those who have in mind to haul down the Union Jack and fly high the star-spangled banner of a United States of Europe, I say to them: you misjudge the temper of the British people!" Never would Britain be browbeaten: "And to those who offer us gratuitous advice, I remind them of what a thousand years of history should have told them: you cannot bully Britain."

Such stereotypes of character, identity and history are summoned with ease. No details had to be specified, nor argument advanced. The speaker did not have to argue with facts and figures that 'Britain' possessed a distinctive national identity; nor did he have to cite the corncrake and the plough-team. He could refer to a thousand years of national history without mentioning any historical detail. These were commonplaces in themselves. It was enough to remind the audience (or 'us') that 'we' have existed for a thousand years in 'our' unique manner. The speaker could presume that his audience would well understand, or recognize, that the nation possessed its own distinctive national identity.

If these themes appear as the epitome of insularity, then the idea of insularity itself is not, strictly speaking, insular, or peculiar to those, like John Major, who claim to be members of an 'island race'. The notion is constructed from the more universal themes of nationalism. The way 'we' assert 'our' particularity is not itself particular. 'We' have a history, identity and flag, just like all those other 'we's. In this, 'we' (whichever national 'we' is to be proclaimed) speak (or imagine ourselves to speak) a universal code of particularity. This mixture of universality and particularity enables nations to proclaim themselves as nations.

If 'we' are to imagine 'ourselves' as unique, 'we' need a name to do so. As Tajfel's Social Identity Theory emphasized, 'we' must categorize 'ourselves' with a distinctive label, so that 'we' are 'French', or 'Belgian' or 'Turkish' (or 'Breton', or 'Flemish' or 'Kurdish'). The category not only categorizes 'us', in our particularity – demarcating 'us' as an 'us' – but the category is to be categorized (or proclaimed) as a national label in its universality. There is, in short, a universal code for the naming of particulars.

National labels would not be able to signify particularity, if two, or even more, nations shared the same name. Two 'Germanies', existing side by side, indicated and preserved an ideology for unification. Two 'United States of America', each recognizing the other, are unthinkable. Codes of national particularity are seriously threatened by a duplication of names. The Greek government claims that the Republic of Macedonia has appropriated the name and ancient insignia of Greek Macedonia, the 'real' Macedonia in its eyes. Separate Macedonias, each claiming the unique emblem of the Sun of Vergina, is "a clear provocation", to quote the words of the Greek Prime Minister (*Guardian*, 6 January 1994). The leader of Macedonia's largest political party claims that his people cannot accept the internationally imposed name of the 'Former Yugoslav Republic of Macedonia': "We are not a former republic and we hope that the two words will be dropped from our country's name very soon" (*Guardian*, 17 December 1993).

Of such matters, major incidents are made in the contemporary world. Conflict can be threatened: 'we' claim the right to call 'ourselves' what 'we' want and to have no one else usurp 'our' name. More than a million Greeks demonstrated on the streets against the allegedly spurious Macedonia, and the mayor of Salonika declared: "We are ready for battle and sacrifices . . . our history goes back 4,000 years . . . We are all united on Macedonia because Macedonia is non-negotiable" (quoted in *Guardian*, 1 April 1994). Such a stance should not be dismissed as something peculiarly 'Balkan' or old-fashioned. One should ask whether the people and government of the United States would stand by idly, should President Castro declare that Cuba would henceforth be known as the 'United States of America' and that its flag would be a pattern of 13 blue and white stripes, with a top left corner of 50 hammer and sickles in a red square.

In proclaiming the uniqueness of 'our' national name, 'we' are not just talking of 'our' own particularity. The imagining of this particularity forms part of a universal code for nationalist consciousness: no one should usurp another's name, nor their right to name themselves. Somehow, in ways difficult to articulate, the magic of 'our' name matters to 'us' deeply, whichever national 'we' are: it indicates who 'we' are, and, more basically, *that* 'we' are. In the secular age, the name of the nation is not to be taken in vain.

**Imagining the National Homeland**

A nation is more than an imagined community of people, for a place – a homeland – also has to be imagined. Many peoples have imagined themselves to be distinct, carrying their own particular sense of destiny into the future, but this does not make them nations in the modern sense. As Smith (1981) points out, peoples from earliest times have nurtured a sense of their own communal distinctiveness "in the specific history of the group, and, above all, in the myths of group origins and group liberation" (p. 65). Nationhood, however, involves a distinctive imagining of a particular sort of community rooted in a particular sort of place. Nationalism, to quote Agnew (1989), is never "beyond geography" (p. 167). But the geography is not mere geography, or physical setting: the national place has to be imagined, just as much as the national community does.

Not all peoples have imagined themselves to be living within a 'country', in the sense that nation-states are countries. The European peasants, described by Fishman (1972), had a deep sense of attachment to their immediate place of living, without possessing a sense of a wider national home stretching beyond the directly apprehended locality. In fourteenth-century Montaillou, the unit of geographical perception was the *terra*, which was any region "with limits at once human and natural", like valleys, uplands or lowlands (Ladurie, 1978, p. 283). The imagining of an overall 'country', in which lived-in localities are united within a wider homeland, does not seem to have been typical in pre-modern Europe. As Nigel Harris writes, "under mediaeval serfdom, each serf was tied to a piece of land and to a particular lord". This differs from present times when "every inhabitant is expected to be tied to one national soil and one government, or to be an outcaste" (1990, p. 258).

The imagining of a 'country' involves the imagining of a bounded totality beyond immediate experience of place. The boundedness of this totality distinguishes the homeland from the shifting spheres of trade which loosely divided pre-national Central Arabia. The imagining of the national place is similar to the imagining of the national community. As Anderson stressed, the community has to be imagined because it is conceived to stretch beyond immediate experience: it embraces far more people than those with which citizens are personally acquainted. Similarly, the mediaeval peasants would know intimately the crags and shallows of their *terra*. By contrast, the citizens of the nation-state might themselves have visited only a small part of the national territory. They can even be tourists, indeed strangers, in parts of 'their' own land; yet, it is still 'their' land. For American patriots, the United States is not merely the America they know: their America is to be conceived as a unique, vast but homely, totality. In this respect, the unity of the national territory has to be imagined rather than directly apprehended.

In the modern nationalist imagination, one national territory does not shade into another. Nations stop and start abruptly at demarcated borders.

Rathzel (1994) suggests that the German word '*Heimat*' expresses "a prime symbol of the nation" (p. 84). *Heimat* and 'homeland' capture a duality of meaning. The country is the place of 'our' personal homes – my home, your home – and, as such, it is the home of all of 'us', the home of homes, the place where all of 'us' are at home. In this sense, the homeland is imagined as a unity. Outlying districts are as integral as the metropolitan areas: the images of the remote countryside are as commonly used as stereotypically national images as are the grand public buildings of the capital city. This image of integral unity is, of course, one of the ideological elements by which the metropolitan areas seek to establish their hegemony over the peripheral districts (Nairn, 1977). The special quality, which marks the homeland as 'ours', continues without dilution right up to the borders: and there it stops, to be separated from the different foreign essence which is marking out the territory on the other side. "In the modern conception", writes Anderson, "state sovereignty is fully, flatly and evenly operative over each square centimetre of a legally demarcated territory" (1983, p. 26).

Each homeland is to be imagined both in its totality and its particularity. The world is too small to bear two homelands with the name 'Macedonia', even if clear borders between the two are agreed. Each homeland must be considered a special place, separated physically and metaphorically from other homelands. In the eighteenth century, it was common for the British, and especially the English, to imagine their island as being God's chosen country (Colley, 1992). Jerusalem was to be built in England's green and pleasant land. Across the Atlantic, Americans were also imagining a new Israel. It is said that German immigrants, on arrival in the United States, sang "America . . . is a beautiful land that God promised to Abraham" (Sollors, 1986, p. 44). As was mentioned in Chapter 1, President Bush, announcing the liberation of Kuwait, asked God to continue blessing "our nation, the United States of America". To this day, American patriotic songs declare 'America the beautiful' and invite God's blessing. In these hymns of praise the beauty is not localized: America is not beautiful because it offers a stunning waterfall near Buffalo or a canyon a couple of thousand miles away in Arizona. The country as a totality is praised as special, as 'the beautiful'.

It has been said that nation-states hate losing territory and that national governments will do all they can to appease separatist movements within their boundaries (Waterman, 1989). However, it is not the loss of territory *tout court* which provokes the special pain, but the loss of territory which is situated within the imagined homeland. Ernest Gellner was quoted in Chapter 3, claiming that the modern person considers having a national identity as natural as having a nose and two ears. Losing a part of the imagined homeland is worse than merely losing an ear: in the case of territory, the lost ear always turns up on someone's else's face. Something beyond utility – some part of 'our' home, 'our' selves – has been illegitimately taken by another. This sense of territory does not depend upon a personal link with the physical place. Iran and Iraq felt it worthwhile to expend hundreds of thousands of lives on a strip of land, which both nations imagined to be an essential part of their respective homelands and whose economic importance was dwarfed by the costs of the struggle. The majority of the population in Argentina believes that the national boundaries should include the Malvinas Islands, although no one personally dreams of returning there, nor any current inhabitant of those islands yearns for the *Anschluss*.

The sense of geographic integrity can be seen in the way that nations do not necessarily hold on to all territory with equal tenacity. Some territory is imagined to be 'ours' and to be fought for; some can be ceded, as not really part of the homeland. Israel, in its peace treaty with Egypt, could hand back the Sinai Peninsular, which was situated beyond the Eretz Yisrael depicted in even the most expansionist of Zionist imaginings. By contrast, East Jerusalem, captured during the same war as Sinai, continues to be imagined as integral to the homeland, even within the less expansionist imaginings. It is a place which occupies a very different side of a psychological boundary. The tragedy is that it occupies a similar position in the imagining of a Palestinian state.

The boundary consciousness of nationalism was at work in the agreement between the British and Irish Prime Ministers over Northern Ireland, issued in December 1993. The so-called 'Downing Street Declaration' asserted that "the people of Britain would wish . . . to enable the people of Ireland to reach agreement on how they may live together in harmony". If the people of Northern Ireland wished to remain within the United Kingdom, then this was to be accepted, as would any decision to support "a sovereign united Ireland". The British government was conveying the message that Ulster was not integral to Britain. Its inhabitants were identified as part of "the people of Ireland", as compared with "the people of Britain". The British government stressed that it "had no selfish strategic or economic interest in Northern Ireland" (full text of the Declaration in *Guardian*, 16 December 1993). In other words, Ulster could be detached from 'Britain'. It was not part of Britain's totality, as imagined by the British and Irish governments; both governments could imagine Ulster becoming part of Éire's totality. The British government's position was in striking contrast with its position on Scottish nationalism. Scotland, declared the Conservative Party at the 1992 General Election, could not be detached without the break-up of the Union, of 'our' nation. Ulster could go without disrupting 'our' national identity, the identity which the party's leader claimed to defend 'come hell or high water'.

The sense of a link between the people and the homeland can be seen clearly in the diaspora consciousness of peoples, who dream of a return to their homeland (Sheffer, 1988). It is not enough for the national community to feel its bonds of communal identification; it claims the need to be situated within, and have control over, a special section of the globe. The leader of the Crimean Tartar assembly declares that "we want to get back to our motherland and to re-establish our national territorial republic" (reported in *Guardian*, 1 September 1993). Only a particular place is imagined to be nationally appropriate. In 1905 the Seventh Zionist Congress overwhelmingly rejected Joseph Chamberlain's idea to establish a Jewish national home in Uganda. It was the right idea in the wrong place.

In such claims, a mystical link between the people and its land is detectable. Sometimes the link can be expressed in outwardly religious terms. Thus, God is to bless America; and to build Jerusalem within England; or to re-build Jerusalem within Jerusalem. The mysticism of place does not depend upon an explicitly religious consciousness. Hazani (1993), describing the early Young Zionist *halutzim*, writes of the "paradox of atheists who tenaciously cling to basically religious beliefs, such as the right of the Jewish people to inherit God's Promised Land" (p. 63). As Anderson and others have commented, nationalist consciousness is essentially secular. God may be cited as a justification for the nation's specialness, but the deity, unlike the claim to a special place, is an optional extra. The national community, as a product of the modern age, has descended from heaven to earth.

In essentials, the theory of nationhood stipulates that a people, place and state should be bound in unity. The nationalist-as-poet is a familiar figure in the early stages of movements to establish new nations (Hroch, 1985; Ignatieff, 1993). The mystic bond between people and place is a much repeated theme in their writings. Once nations are established, and nationalism becomes banal, the poets are typically replaced by prosaic politicians, and the epic ballads by government reports. The imagined community ceases to be reproduced by acts of the imagination. In established nations, the imagination becomes enhabited, and, thereby, inhibited. In this sense, the term 'imagined community' may be misleading. The community and its place are not so much imagined, but their absence becomes unimaginable.

Even though the imagination may become banally habitual, nevertheless, the mysticism which posits the special people in its special place does not disappear. The flags can be waved, and sacrifice offered in the cause of the nation's special identity. A mayor of Salonika, cheered by crowds of compatriots, declares himself ready to protect his ancient nation against the idea of a second Macedonia; a British prime minister, whose image-makers struggle to make insipidity a public virtue, declares that Britain has never and will never be bullied out of its distinctive identity. The rhetoric is familiar: past sacrifices are invoked in the name of the present.

The mystic bond, which can be overtly defended, has in the late twentieth century become banal, seeping into everyday consciousness. It underwrites stodgy government documents, such as the Downing Street agreement on Ulster. In such prose, theory has becomes enhabited in a familiar grammar. Around the world, nation-states use the same basic categories for their 'country' and their 'people'. This is part of the universal code of nationality: the particular nation is affirmed within a general code, which always stipulates that a particular people and particular homeland are to be imagined as special, and, thereby, not so special. The same linguistic root gives rise to the singular name of the state or country (Portugal, Peru, Pakistan); and a collective noun for describing the people, who supposedly possess that state (the Portuguese, the Peruvians, the Pakistanis). One major exception to the code is the United Kingdom, a state not peopled by 'United Kingdonians' (the other major exception, the USSR, has already collapsed into more typically named segments). Significantly, the official title, the 'United Kingdom of Great Britain and Northern Ireland', is hardly used by its inhabitants, especially when describing themselves (Condor, in press; Hall, 1992). The pair 'Britain/British' is more frequently used, although the English will unthinkingly substitute 'England/English' for the wider term. Such semantic habits reveal that the complex nomenclature of the United Kingdom permits the complex continuation of an English hegemony (Nairn, 1988).

Notwithstanding the exception of the United Kingdom, the world of today is represented habitually as a world of countries and peoples, tightly bound in semantic unity and concrete reality. America (or at least the 'United States of') exists as the place of Americans (as if the rest of the geographical Americas did not exist); France as the place of the French and so on. Indeed, these are more than places: they are 'countries', unique totalities, populated by their unique peoples. A form of semantic cleansing operates in these terms: there is no gap between the people and its country. If France exists – and it so obviously does – then so must the French exist; and similarly for Peru and the Peruvians; if there are no more Belgians, only Flemings and Walloons, then Belgium should exist no more. All this appears as if obvious. The bonds linking people and place are held firm by a universal grammar, which promises a cleansed vision of proper peoples in their proper places.

Because countries are materially established in this world, the mysticism of this vision appears as a natural, worldly fact of national life. Much can be daily forgotten, as nations appear as inevitable entities, their histories of bitter hegemonic struggle hidden behind the cleanliness of grammatical symmetry. The language of sacrifice is easily called upon to sustain the vision. And when competing visions of homelands draw different boundaries around the same places, the rivals can dream of cleansing each other's vision, and each other's very being, from the geography of their own imagined homeland. Then, semantic and material 'cleansing' become fatally united.

## Stereotyping 'Them'

If nationalism is an ideology of the first person plural, which tells 'us' who 'we' are, then it is also an ideology of the third person. There can be no 'us' without a 'them'. As Henri Tajfel (1981) stressed, a social category, in describing who 'we' are, indicates who 'we' are not. The national community can only be imagined by also imagining communities of foreigners. The 'foreigner', in the age of the nation-state, is a specific category, not merely any 'other'. The point is well expressed by Julia Kristeva, who points out that, with the establishment of nation-states, "we come to the only modern, acceptable, and clear definition of foreignness: the foreigner is the one who does not belong to the state in which we are, the one who does not have the same nationality" (1991, p. 96).

Kristeva's point is an important one, for it gets to the root of the issue of whether nationalism should be considered as a historically specific outlook, or as an example for a more general outlook, in which outsiders are despised. The Galician peasants, in Fishman's story, could be said to have shared an inward-looking perspective, once characteristic of European peasantry. Those living outside the immediate locality – or the *terra*, to use the old mediaeval term – would be viewed with suspicion, if not downright hostility. This is the state of mind which Marx and Engels described in *The Communist Manifesto* as "national one-sidedness and narrow-mindedness" (1968, p. 39), predicting that such restricted world-views would be swept aside by the international spread of capitalism.

The narrowness of mind of which Marx and Engels were writing, is often now called 'ethnocentrism'. William Graham Sumner, in formulating the concept of 'ethnocentrism', wrote that "each group nourishes its own pride and vanity, boasts itself superior, exalts its own divinities and looks with contempt on outsiders". Sumner went on to claim that "each group thinks its own folkways the only right ones, and if it observes that other groups have other folkways, these excite its scorn" (1906, p. 13; see LeVine and Campbell, 1970). Surely, it might be thought, Sumner's description fits the nationalist *par excellence* (Adorno et al., 1950; Forbes, 1986; Kosterman and Feshbach, 1989). As Gellner has written, "in a nationalist age, societies worship themselves brazenly and openly, spurning camouflage" (1983, p. 57). In worshipping themselves, nationalists disparage foreign nations. Again the question might be asked: why bother to insist upon the specialness of nationalism, when it can be seen as an example of something much older and more general – in this case, as an example of ethnocentrism?

Marx and Engels, however, were both right and wrong in their prediction about national one-sidedness. They were correct in supposing that an inward-looking, one-sided perspective would be supplanted by an international outlook in the modern world of international capital. They were wrong to identify the supplanted ideology with a national consciousness. Traditional ethnocentrism was being swept aside, but nationalism was part of the historical force to do the sweeping. Most crucially, the nationalist outlook, as a product and producer of the modern world of nation-states, differs from the ethnocentric view, as described by Sumner. There is one particularly revealing phrase in Sumner's description: the group is scornful '*if* it observes that other groups have other folkways'. The ingroup is presumed to be so culturally isolated and so wrapped within its own concerns that the outside world might be ignored. This, however, is not the condition of nationalism in the modern world.

Nationalists live in an international world, and their ideology is itself an international ideology. Without constant observation of the world of other nations, nationalists would be unable to claim that their nations meet the universal codes of nationhood. Nor would they have ready access to stereotyped judgements about foreigners. Even the most extreme and unbanal of nationalists do not shut out the outside world from consciousness, but often show an obsessive concern with the lives and outlooks of foreigners. Hitler's *Table-Talk* is filled with speculations about the characters of different nations. One illustrative example, taken from 1942, can be given. Martin Bormann had apparently lent his Führer a book entitled *Juan in America*, itself an indicative action. Hitler opines lengthily, while his admirers listen:

> The British swallow everything they are told . . . [Americans] have the brains of a hen . . . the German Reich has two hundred and seventy opera houses – a standard of cultural existence of which they have no conception . . . Spaniards and Americans simply cannot understand each other . . . the Americans live like sows. (1988, pp. 604–5)

And so on. Hitler speaks a continuing stream of stereotypes, as he surveys the rest of the world from his camp at Rastenburg.

Social psychologists frequently assume that narrow, bigoted thinking is characterized by the use of stereotypes. If the imagining of foreignness is an integral part of the theoretical consciousness of nationalism, then foreignness is not an undifferentiated sense of 'Otherness' (McDonald, 1993). Obsessively fine distinctions can be made between different groups of foreigners. Indeed, debates and controversies can arise about how similar or how different various groups of foreigners are to 'us'. In one of the earliest studies of stereotyping, Katz and Braly (1935) showed the extent to which white, American college students used conventional labels to characterize different ethnic and national groups: Jews were mercenary, Turks were cruel, Germans efficient, etc. Later studies have indicated a decline in respondents' willingness to use such generalizing stereotypes (Gilbert, 1951; Karlins et al., 1969). The stereotypes of other nations tend not to be uniformly scornful. Some foreigners are presumed to be more meritorious than others. Thus, Katz and Braly found that some foreign national types, such as the Germans, were praised in ways which others, especially non-European nations, were not.

Stereotypes are shared, cultural descriptions of social groups. Even respondents, who might themselves claim to be sceptical about the truths of the stereotypes, recognize a culturally shared scale of valuations (Devine, 1989). Some foreigners are identified as being stereotyped as more admirable, and more like 'us', than others (Hagendoorn, 1993a; Hagendoorn and Hraba, 1987; Hagendoorn and Kleinpenning, 1991). Inglehart (1991), examining the national attitudes of members of European nations, found that, with the exception of Italians, members of all nations rated their own nation as the most trustworthy. However, not all foreigners were rated equally untrustworthy. Members of small, non-Mediterranean European nations, such as Danes, Swiss and Dutch, tended to be rated more trustworthy, even by Mediterranean respondents. In short, it is commonplace that stereotyped distinctions are made between different sorts of foreigners.

Public opinion polls suggest that there is nothing static in the stereotyped judgements. Foreign stocks can rise and fall, in accord with the movements of political crises. The favourable stereotypes of Germans, which Katz and Braly (1935) found, declined as the United States prepared to enter the Second World War (Harding et al., 1954). Most dramatic was the change in American judgements of Russians, who, in 1945, switched from being heroic allies to bitterest rivals (Yatani and Bramel, 1989). With the collapse of Soviet communism, the American public has been presented with new enemies – whether Libyans, Iraqis or Arabs in general. With prolonged conflicts, a 'siege mentality' can develop, in which stereotypes become rigid, and the enemy is demonized with regular ferocity (Bar-Tal, 1989, 1990; Silverstein and Flamenbaum, 1989). Sudden crises can produce quickly sharpened stereotypes, as, for example, the emergence of 'the Argie' in the British media during the Falklands War (Harris, 1985). The quickly summoned stereotype will build upon older cultural myths, although there might be some initial uncertainty how these should be combined. One member of the British war cabinet was reported as wondering whether the Argentinians would actually go to war, given their half-Italian and half-Spanish ancestry. "There's no precedent", he said, because "if the Spanish half is uppermost, they'll fight, if the Italian, they won't" (quoted in Young, 1993, p. 278).

Stereotypes are often means of distinguishing 'them' from 'us', thereby contributing to 'our' claims of a unique identity. In the eighteenth century, Britain developed many of its modern symbols of nationhood in conscious contradistinction to French styles of nation-making (Cannadine, 1983; Colley, 1992). English writers debated whether there should be an English Academy, but the idea was rejected as being too French (Haugen, 1966a). The first recorded cartoon, depicting John Bull as an 'Englishman', also shows a Frenchman, as thin and meagre as Bull is fat and generous (Surel, 1989). In this case, the icongraphic stereotype of 'us' was created in contrastive differentiation from the stereotype of 'them'. The point is not merely a historical one, but there is an implicit contrast in the stereotyped judgement of 'them' (McCauley et al., 1980; Stangor and Ford, 1992). Typically, people ascribe more stereotypic traits to outgroups than to ingroups; 'we' often assume 'ourselves' as the standard, or the unmarked normality, against which 'their' deviations appear notable (Quattrone, 1986). If 'they, the French' are stereotyped as 'emotional', it is with implicit reference to 'our' presumed, non-emotional standards. Or conversely another group might be stereotyped as 'cold', whereas 'we' will be neither 'cold' (too cold) nor 'emotional' (too emotional).

There is always the possibility of projection, as Kristeva realized in her descriptions of 'foreignness'. 'We' can claim that 'they' possess the qualities, which 'we' deny in 'ourselves'. In Western democracies, 'our' tolerance is much praised by 'ourselves'. Journalists and politicians, especially when arguing for immigration restrictions, cite 'our' tolerance, and 'their' intolerance, as a reason for excluding 'them', the foreigners (Barker, 1981; Van Dijk, 1991, 1992, 1993). The rhetoric denies 'our' prejudice and it condenses an argumentative structure, which attributes intolerance to 'them': 'our' tolerance is threatened by 'their' presence; 'they' are either intolerant or cause intolerance; thus, 'we' seek to exclude 'them', not because 'we' are intolerant but, quite the reverse, because 'we' are tolerant (Billig, 1991; Wetherell and Potter, 1992). In conditions of the 'siege mentality', it is always the 'other' who breaks faith, acts dishonestly and starts aggressive spirals: 'our' actions are justified by circumstance, but 'theirs' are said to reflect a deficiency of character, indeed, the very deficiencies which 'we' deny in 'ourselves' (Pettigrew, 1979; Rothbart and Hallmark, 1988).

It is important not to stereotype the act of stereotyping, as if ready formed judgements come spilling out of the mouth of the person evoking stereotypes (Billig, 1985). More is at stake than the ascription of character-istics to groups. Respondents have much more to say about 'them', the foreigners, than they are permitted to utter while completing question-naires about stereotypes (Wetherell and Potter, 1992). There are multiple ways of talking about a multiplicity of 'thems', and the same speakers have different 'voices', or different tones, for talking about 'them'. Above all, the voices of the particular and the general can jostle to be heard, even as a single person, in making a single utterance, talks about 'them' (Billig et al., 1988).

Van Dijk (1993) gives the example of the German Minister for the Interior arguing for increased immigration restrictions. The minister declares: "It belongs to this fair balance of interests that further immi-gration of foreigners must be restricted, because for each society there are limits to the ability and the readiness to integrate" (quoted p. 94). The minister, in seeking to exclude 'foreigners' from 'our' homeland, is using, and seeking to be seen to use, the rhetoric of reasonableness. The value of fairness is cited: this is not merely 'our' fairness, but a universal fairness. The minister looks beyond the homeland, to cite a general rule about 'each society'. Thus, 'our' interests are not merely 'our' particular interests; 'we' are claiming to act in a universally reasonable way, so that 'our' society is in accord with a universal sociology, which stipulates what each society can and cannot do. This talk, like most academic sociology, assumes, quite naturally, that 'society' is the nation, or the 'country'.

This is characteristic of nationalist discourse in late twentieth-century democracies. As so often, nationalism combines the particular and the universal. 'We' claim to look beyond 'our' boundaries, even when seeking to close those boundaries. 'We' cite universal principles and general laws, denying 'our' own narrowness. Thus, 'we' speak in 'our' own interests with an authority which appears to stretch beyond 'ourselves'. The authority, in this case, is not a deity nor a cosmic force. It is something much more persuasive for the nationalist consciousness. This is the grandeur of a sociological imperative, to which all nations – 'ours' and others – must apparently conform. In this way, 'we' imagine 'ourselves' and 'foreigners' to be equally ruled by the sociology of nationhood. This governing sociology produces 'countries', in which 'we' and 'them' are reproduced as peoples bound both uniquely and universally to 'our' places. Armed with this vision of nationhood, not only can 'we' claim to speak for 'ourselves', but also 'we' can speak for 'them', or for 'all of us'.

## Imagining a Nation among Nations

Nationalism inevitably involves a mixture of the particular and the universal: if 'our' nation is to be imagined in all its particularity, it must be imagined as a nation amongst other nations. The consciousness of national identity normally assumes an international context, which itself needs to be imagined every bit as much as does the national community: or at least the imagination has to become frozen in a habit of thought. Thus, foreigners are not simply 'others', symbolizing the obverse of 'us': 'they' are also like 'us', part of the imagined universal code of nationhood. Because nationalism involves this universal perspective, or this imagining of the international world of nations, it differs crucially from the secluded ethnocentric mentality.

Historically, the rise of nationalism entailed the creation of internationalism. Robertson has claimed that nationalism involves 'the universalization of particularism and the particularization of universalism' (1991, p. 73; see also Robertson, 1990, 1992). He argues that historically "the idea of nationalism (or particularism) develops *only* in tandem with internationalism" (1991, p. 78). The era of the nation-state is not characterized by growing isolation of national polities. Quite the contrary, the emergence of the nation-state coincides with the emergence of international relations (Der Derian, 1989). The Congress of Vienna in 1815, at which the powerfully victorious nations of Europe decided upon their continent's map, was the first modern international political settlement: it provided rules for the operation of frontiers, the exchange of envoys and navigation on international rivers (Hinsley, 1986). The Congress heralded not merely the era of the sovereign nation-state, but that of the international system, in which each state officially recognizes the internal sovereignty of its neighbours. By virtue of its sovereignty, each state becomes "one among other states which rule their communities in the same sovereign way" (Hinsley, 1986, p. 225). To this day, 'the global political order' continues to be based upon the assumption of sovereign nation-states existing in mutual recognition (Giddens, 1990). As Wallerstein (1987) argues, the racism and chauvinism developed in this new order differs from earlier prejudices of xenophobia, which were based upon rejection and fear, rather than constitutional separation and hierarchy.

Not surprisingly, the new forms of community necessitated the production of new discourses. Traditional ways of talking were inadequate for a world which was creating a system of interrelating sovereign nations. Thus it was that Jeremy Bentham, not for the only time in his life, invented a word – one which today possesses such linguistic solidity, and such apparently concrete signification, that it is hard to imagine it ever absent from the vocabulary. In *An Introduction to the Principles of Morals and Legislation* (1789/1982), Bentham discussed the need for the laws of different nations to coincide in an "international jurisprudence". He added, by way of an explanatory footnote, that "the word *international*, it must be acknowledged, is a new one, though it is hoped sufficiently analogous and intelligible" (1982, p. 296, emphasis in original).

In this new nationalist outlook, not only is the nation imagined as an integral whole, but so is the world, in ways that would have been unthinkable in earlier times. The whole world, no longer lying in the hands of the Deity or Satan, can be imagined as a natural order of independent nations. Moreover, the 'natural' order of nations could be imagined to be subverted by international conspirators. The British cartoonist James Gillray depicted this fear in his famous 'The Plumb Pudding in Danger' (1805). Pitt and Napoleon are seated at a dinner table carving up the globe for themselves. Gillray's cartoon was much copied throughout Europe, inspiring many imitations (Hill, 1966). As Gillray's image was enjoying huge success, so conspiracy theories were being formulated: de Barruel and Robison were claiming that the freemasons were taking over the world, overthrowing the old orders of the aristocracy and seeking to mix the 'naturally' separate nations (Lipset and Raab, 1970; Roberts, 1974). Fantastic though these ideas of world conspiracy might seem, they have had a powerful hold in the past 200 years (Finn, 1990, 1993; Graumann and Moscovici, 1987).

Nazism, the most virulent of all nationalism's forms, involved more than the imagining of stereotypes about 'us', the master race, and 'them', the inferiors. The stereotypes on their own did not lead to a policy of systematic extermination. There was also a global story of conspiracy: the whole world was imagined to be falling into the grip of Jews, who were seeking to destroy races and nations (Billig, 1989a; Cohn, 1967; Katz, 1980; Poliakov, 1974). The covers of anti-semitic tracts portrayed the image of Jewish hands grasping the world, in a manner resembling Gillray's image of Pitt and Napoleon. The mixture of conspiratorial and racial themes ensured that Nazi ideology contained an internal dynamic for extermination: the world could only be saved by destroying the conspirators, who were driven to world conspiracy by their unchanging and unchangeable racial natures. These strange notions cannot be explained away as an anachronistic reversal to an earlier mediaeval way of thinking.

Nazism was intrinsically modern in its nationalist depiction of an international world.

The case of Nazism illustrates the general point that nationalism, even at its most extreme, is never completely inward-looking. To claim to be a nation is to imagine one's group to fit a common, universal pattern. Thus, nationalism has a mimetic quality. This can be seen most clearly in the creation of new nations, especially those that are formed in the wake of an imperial collapse. Colonies, in struggling for independence, fit themselves to a mould which is not of their making, appropriating the model of the Western nation-state (Mercer, 1992). The universal principles of national sovereignty can be turned against colonial masters. John Chilembwe, during the First World War, wrote tracts as a self-proclaimed nationalist, specifically basing his case for Nyasaland's independence on the principles of the Enlightenment (Rotberg, 1966). It was a pattern to be much repeated in Africa and elsewhere. The leaders of independence movements often conceive themselves as creating a new nation on the site of the colony. For example, to Spartacus Monimambo, an early leader of the MPLA in Angola, political education was crucial, and it should be "first of all, nationalist". Talking about the revolutionary struggle shortly before his death, Monimambo explained: "The people must understand that we are all Angolans", so that "tomorrow we will have cultural unity throughout Angola" (1971, pp. 382–3).

After independence, the new states tend to keep their colonial boundaries. The policy of 'cultural unity' often involves, as it did in the creation of established European nations, the attempt by one section of the territory to imposes its hegemony over the rest. Not surprisingly, and again following the European model, civil war frequently is the result. After the old order has been overthrown, the radical rhetoric is sometimes maintained, not to widen the focus of liberation, but to bolster repression in the newly independent state (Akioye, 1994; Ihonvbere, 1994). As Harris (1990) points out, even nationalist movements battling against imperialist exploitation are marked by a deep conformism. They are essentially reformist, because their aspirations are limited to accepting the conventional forms of nationhood and thereby taking for granted "a world order of national states" (1990, p. 276).

Nations do not have to pass a theoretical test of nationhood, showing that they possess some notional criterion of internal unity, whether of ethnicity, language or culture. The tests are concrete, based upon the ability of the state to impose order and monopolize violence within established boundaries (Giddens, 1985, 1990). The major test is international, for the nation will seek recognition from established nations, who, in their turn, will recognize their own nationhood in the successful new claimant. In consequence, the new nation has to resemble other nations to gain their recognition. It must adopt conventional symbols of particularity, which, because of their conventionality, are simultaneously symbols of the universality of nationhood. For example, each nation is expected to have its own flag and national anthem. The new interim constitution of South Africa, which was proposed in November 1993, carefully specified that "a national anthem and flag will be introduced by an act of the new parliament" (*Guardian*, 18 November 1993). When Palestinian and Israeli leaders met officially for the first time in Washington, the Palestinians had to choose which of their anthems would be played (*Independent on Sunday*, 12 September 1993). The universal code forbade the playing of two anthems for one nation: becoming a 'proper' nation would mean selecting a single 'official' anthem.

A national anthem is a universal sign of particularity. The conventions of the oeuvre demand that the uniqueness of the nation be celebrated in a universally stylized manner. The old Soviet anthem fitted praise for communism into a celebration of the nation and its people. Its chorus proclaimed: "Sing to our motherland, home of the free, Bulwark of peoples in brotherhood strong!" Its author, Sergei Mikhalkov, is quoted as saying that "an anthem is a prayer sung by people worshipping their country" and "every nation must have this prayer" (*Independent on Sunday*, 14 February 1993). After the Soviet system fell, the words of the old anthem were deemed inappropriate for the new Russia. Accordingly, the government announced a competition for a new anthem. Recognizing this to be a minor modern art form, whose aesthetics transcend political divisions, the government appointed the elderly Mr Mikhalkov to select the winning entry. Whatever his past political mistakes, he could be trusted to recognize a suitable prayer for the nation.

National anthems not only fit a common pattern, but it is part of their symbolism that they are seen to do so. They flag the nation as a nation among nations, as flags themselves do. Each flag will have its own particular symbols like the *chakra-dhavaja*, or wheel, in the Indian flag, or the Protestant orange and Catholic green in the flag of Éire. Even as a flag indicates particularity, with its own individual patterns (whether the Stars and Stripes, the Union Jack, the Tricolor or whatever), it also flags its own universality. Each flag, by its conventional rectangular pattern, announces itself to be an element of an established, recognizable series, in which all the flags are essentially similar in their conventions of difference. The odd exception, like the pennant-shaped flag of Nepal, only serves to confirm the general rule. New nations, in designing their flags, tend to follow heraldic convention of colour as well as shape: they avoid certain shades like shocking pink and kingfisher blue (Firth, 1973). The hoisting of the newly designed flag indicates that another nation has joined the club of nations: 'we' have become like 'you' (no longer 'them'); 'we' are all nations, with 'our' flags and 'our' anthems, 'our' seats in the United Nations, and 'our' participation, with appropriately designed vests, at Olympic Games and World Cups.

This international consciousness is integral to the modern consciousness of nationalism. The banal symbols of 'our' particularity are also banal symbols of 'our' universality. Nationalism does not provide a single way of talking about the world. In consequence, there are infinite discursive possibilities for talking about 'us' and 'them': and, indeed, 'you'. 'We' are not confined to simple differentiating stereotypes, which downgrade the foreigner as the mysterious Other. Foreign nations are like 'ours', but never completely alike. 'We' can recognize 'ourselves' in 'them'; and, there again, 'we' can fail to recognize 'ourselves'. 'We' can become allies, 'they' becoming 'you'; and 'we' can become enemies. And 'we' can debate amongst 'ourselves' about the value of 'our' allies. 'We' can accuse 'them' of threatening 'our' particularity or of failing to act like proper, responsible nations like 'we' do. And 'we' can claim that 'they', in threatening 'us', threaten the idea of nationhood. In damning 'them', 'we' can claim to speak for 'all of us'.

## Syntax of Hegemony

The infinite possibilities for talking nationally about 'us', 'you' and 'them' illustrate the dilemmatic character of nationalism. It is a mistake to think that an ideology is characterized by a single voice, or a particular attitudinal position. In common with other ideologies, nationalism includes contrary themes, especially the key themes of particularism and universalism. Its contrary themes provide the wherewithal for dilemma and, thus, for controversy and debate (Billig et al., 1988). The debate, however, is conducted within parameters that take nationhood for granted as the natural context of the universe. In this sense, the argument is conducted within, and not against, nationalism.

This is easy to overlook if nationalism is seen in a restricted sense, which expects the ideology to be represented by the 'pure' tones of irrationality, small-mindedness and opposition to internationalism. Nationalism has always had its own, nationalized voice of reason and of hegemony. The national principle of sovereignty has presented itself as a reasonable principle; and within the history of nationalism, one part of the imagined national whole has always sought to present itself as the universal voice of the whole. When a leader claims that 'we are all Angolans' (or all Americans, Peruvians – it matters not) and that a cultural unity needs to be created, the leader is speaking in a voice which is not particularly Angolan (or whatever). Also, in attempting to construct a national, cultural unity, one part – one aspect of the cultural and linguistic mosaic – will become the dominant, metonymic representation of the whole. As was discussed in Chapter 2, other ways of being national will be repressed, forgotten or relegated to the status of dialect.

Mikhail Bakhtin (1981) claimed that utterances generally contain different voices, often simultaneously voicing 'centripetal' and 'centrifugal' tendencies. Nationalist utterances could be said to comprise universal (centripetal) elements and particularist (centrifugal) ones. The French Revolution, with its claim that the French nation stood for the rights of man (sic), has been hailed as the classic example of the way that the universal aspirations of the Enlightenment could be given national expression (for example, Kedourie, 1966; Schwartzmantel, 1992). 'We' the French, linguistically and rhetorically, coincide with 'we', the whole of humanity. Some analysts have claimed that the combination of universalism and particularism was so contradictory that it was bound to collapse. Thus, nationalism moved towards the right, as the universal was rejected in favour of the particular (Dumont, 1992).

Other examples of this apparent movement towards the right could be given. In Greece, the earliest nationalists, like Rhigas Velestinlis, were cosmopolitan in spirit, but their liberal nationalism was brushed aside by forces of absolutism and dogmatism (Kitromilides, 1979). The radicalism of English patriots like John Wilkes in the eighteenth century was overtaken, in the following century, by a John Bull Toryism (Cunningham, 1986). So, one might think that nationalism resolves its early, internal contradictions by discarding its liberalism, and, thereby, becoming an internally consistent ideology.

This sort of account has a problem. It tells of nationalism passing from universal, radical beginnings to parochial endings (with renewed bursts of radicalism from later anti-imperialist nationalisms). The problem is that the tale tends to leave nationalism exclusively in the hands of the right-wing. It also assumes that ideologies operate by some law of cognitive dissonance, which suggests that inner contradictions must inevitably be resolved, so that the contradictory ideology splits into two consistent parts. In the case of nationalism, there is a case for saying that the split between the universal and particular was never fully accomplished. Indeed, it is preserved in the commonplace discourses of nationalism. Right from its earliest times, nationalism used a 'syntax of hegemony', by which the part claimed to represent the whole. One form of speaking might claim to be the language of the whole nation, or one district claim to represent the national culture (see Chapter 2). A further extension can be made. The particular nation can claim to talk for the whole world: 'our' particular interests can appear as the interests of universal reason. The very syntax of the first person plural seems to invite such claims.

The voice of universal reason can accompany the voice of national self-glorification in the most mundane, banal clichés of contemporary political discourse. Immediately after the result of the 1992 US presidential elections had been declared, the candidates gave short addresses. President-elect Clinton, hailing "my fellow Americans", spoke about the "clarion call for our country" and ended by accepting with a full heart the responsibility of being "the leader of this, the greatest country in human history". Outgoing President Bush used a similar rhetoric, addressing "all Americans", who "shared the same purpose, to make this, the world's greatest nation, more safe and more secure" (reported in *Guardian*, 5 November 1992). The self-worship of 'our' nation, 'our' country, as the greatest in history was not a cynical appeal for votes, for, by then, the polling booths had been closed. Both politicians were answering a higher rhetorical duty: they were aware that this is the way American presidents should speak on such occasions. Their phrases of national self-praise contained an unsaid implication: if there is a greatest nation in history, then so there must be all those other nations, overshadowed and imperfect.

Bush, in conceding electoral defeat, talked about respecting "the majesty of the democratic system". This is not merely 'our' majesty, or something which might appear majestic in 'our' eyes; but 'our' democracy is universally 'majestic'. In speaking to 'us', his fellow Americans, Bush was also appealing to what rhetoricians have called 'the universal audience' (Perelman and Olbrechts-Tyteca, 1971; Perelman, 1979; Shotter, 1995). The speaker assumes that any audience of reasonable people, or the hypothetical 'universal audience', would find the arguments persuasive. The outgoing president spoke as if any reasonable person – whether listening or not, whether American or belonging to a less than greatest nation – should recognize this majesty, 'our' democratic majesty. The rhetoric, in reaching towards the audience of 'fellow Americans', also treated that particular audience as a universal audience, and the American greatness as a universal greatness.

If nationalism involves imagining an international context, or international order, as well as imagining 'ourselves' and 'foreigners', then 'we' can claim 'ourselves' to be representing the interests of this international, universal order: 'we', in our great particularity, can be imagined to stand for 'all of us', for a universal audience of humanity. Thus, the modern nation does not go to war merely for particular interests, but claims to be acting in the interests of 'all nations' or the universal order of nations.

Margaret Thatcher, addressing a rally of Conservative Party supporters in Britain after the Falklands War, spoke with the tones of national self-congratulation. The national 'we' was rhetorically and smugly evident. 'We' had shown "that Britain has not changed and that this nation still has those sterling qualities which shine through our history". Again, the details of the history were deemed superfluous to the persuasiveness of the case. Yes, "Britain had rekindled that spirit which has fired her for generations past". At the start of the speech, the Prime Minister had declared that "we are entitled to be proud" because "this nation had the resolution to do what it knew had to be done – to do what it knew was right". She explained: "We fought to show that aggression does not pay and that the robber cannot be allowed to get away with his swag." And 'we' did so with "the support of so many throughout the world" (speech delivered 3 July 1982, text reproduced in Barnett, 1982, pp. 149f.).

Thus, there was a universal principle and a universal audience applauding 'us': 'we' were acting on behalf of a universal morality of right. 'Our' stance and the position of universal morality coincided. From the other side, a similar claim could be heard. The Argentinian news claimed the invasion of the Malvinas to be "a rebirth of Argentine values and simultaneously of Western ideals" (quoted Aulich, 1992, p. 108). 'Western ideals' metonymically stood for universal ideals in this statement of double hegemony. In both cases, 'our' particular rebirth, or rekindling, was claimed to be co-extensive with a wider, universal morality in the world of nations.

The syntax involved in such discourse is not always straightforward. 'We' can become an ambiguous term, indicating both the particularity of 'we', the nation, and the universality of 'we', the universally reasonable world. In this way, 'our' interests – those of party, government, nation and world – can appear to coincide rhetorically, so long as 'we' do not specify what 'we' mean by 'we', but, instead, allow the first person plural to suggest a harmony of interests and identities (Billig, 1991; Maitland and Wilson, 1987; Wilson, 1990).

There has been an extra theme in contemporary, international politics since the fall of the Soviet Union. 'A new world order' is being invoked. The claim to represent the 'world order' appears as a moral claim, which depicts some sort of unity between 'ourselves' and a universal morality. However, the universal aspect of the new order is also highly particular. As Der Derian (1993) points out, the term 'new world order' started appearing in George Bush's speeches in August 1990 and "it was used to describe an American-led, United Nations-backed system of collective security" (p. 117). For example, Bush announced to a joint session of Congress, on 11 September 1990, the new world order to be "an era in which the nations of the world, East and West, North and South, can prosper and live in harmony". As was mentioned in the opening chapter, this is an order of nations in which one particular nation seeks a leading role.

The new world order is producing its own commonplace discourses, which routinely repeat reassuring ambiguities. However, the syntax, by which 'we', the United States, lay claim to a leading role, is of necessity complex. In claiming to represent international principles of justice, order and sovereignty, 'we', as an individual nation, cannot directly lay claim to the world: 'we' cannot appear as a Pitt or a Napoleon tucking into the global plum pudding. 'We' must locate 'ourselves' humbly within that world. 'We' must recognize the rights of others, whilst speaking for these others, and while reminding 'ourselves' that 'we', the greatest nation in history, stand for 'our' own interests.

When President Clinton spoke of US military intervention in Haiti, he declared that "the military authorities in Haiti simply must understand that they cannot indefinitely defy the desires of their own people as well as the will of the world community". He went on: "that path holds only suffering for their nation and international isolation for themselves" (quoted in *Guardian*, 16 October 1993). The American President was speaking in the voice of universal morality: there was a right and a wrong way for nations to behave; and 'the international community', for which he was speaking, upholds the right way, as if it could be imagined as a single actor with a single will. But this was not all. In the same speech, the President commented on "important American interests at stake in Haiti". These included the restoration of democracy and the security of American citizens. 'Our' particular, nationally defined, interests were represented as coinciding with the universal morality of the 'international community'.

General Colin Powell, the chief of US military staff, commented that American withdrawal from Somalia "would be devastating to our hopes for the new world order and our ability to participate in multinational organisations to deal with problems like this" (*Guardian*, 11 September 1993). 'Our ability to participate' clearly refers to the US participation at the head of multinational operations. But 'our hopes for the new world order' are more ambiguous: they are not merely US hopes, although they include such hopes, but they are also the hopes of all reasonable people. These hopes – and the world order itself – rest upon 'us', the Americans, the reasonable people of the world. Through unremarkable cliché and a syntax which does not draw attention to itself, the unity of all 'our' hopes and 'our' American world is economically depicted.

These ambiguities were apparent in the speeches made by President Bush during the Gulf War. As he announced that the US, together with its coalition partners, was attacking Iraqi forces, the blurring of 'we' was apparent. Sometimes, 'we' were clearly American: "our sons and daughters" were going to war; and Bush was careful to mention the damage which Hussein had done to "our economy", or our interests. Sometimes 'we' were the coalition: "we will not fail". Sometimes it was a universal 'we', which could have been either the nation or the coalition or both: "when we are successful . . . we will have a real chance at this new world order" (speech delivered 16 January 1991, text in Sifry and Cerf, 1991, pp. 311f.). At times, 'we' seemed to be equated with 'the world'. Bush mentioned particular American soldiers: "Tonight, America and the world are deeply grateful to them and their families." 'The world', of course, did not include Iraq.

'Our' enemies do not merely oppose 'us', in 'our' particularity, but they can be said to oppose the very moral order which 'we' claim to represent. Accordingly, 'they' are demonized as more than just a foreign 'them' (Edelman, 1977). Nation-states may commit far more violence than terrorists, but the figure of the international terrorist is used to represent a threat to moral order and reasonableness itself (Reich, 1990). Each terrorist act threatens more than individual lives: it challenges the monopoly of violence, claimed by nation-states. Similarly, nations and their leaders can be placed outside this order of nations. Saddam Hussein stood beyond the moral order, which Bush was depicting and laying claim to lead. According to Bush, "while the world waited", Saddam Hussein raped and plundered a tiny nation; "while the world waited" Saddam added chemical weapons to his arsenal; "while the world waited", Saddam did damage to our and the world's economy (Sifry and Cerf, 1991, pp. 312–13). Repetitively, Bush placed his enemy outside the world, accomplishing rhetorically what Gillray had depicted graphically: the enemy was not of the world, but was playing with the world.

This rhetoric suggests that those nations that oppose 'us' are more than parochial competitors: they can be transformed into enemies of international morality. Thus, Libya and Iraq, in US rhetoric, are not merely rivals or strange foreigners with different folkways. Like the Soviets before them, they are demonized as threats to the moral order of the world itself (Silverstein and Flamenbaum, 1989). This order is explicitly a world of nations. Its enemies – nations themselves, as well as 'terrorists' – are the obverse of 'the universal audience': they are depicted as the universal enemy.

In the rhetoric of the new world order, the theoretical consciousness of nationalism is reproduced in the banal, commonplace cliché of the contemporary politician. This consciousness includes assumptions about how a nation should behave; how 'we' should behave; and the world, or the whole 'international community', should behave. Debate on these matters of behaviour is narrowed into the framework of nationhood. There is another theme. A nation that seeks international hegemony must deny that it is nationalist. It must claim to speak with the voice of universality, whilst protecting its own particular interests. Thus, the familiar syntax of hegemony slides together 'our' different identities. In this sense, the politics of international hegemony, as well as the politics of national hegemony, is a form of identity politics. Its rhetoric habitually assumes that there is an identity of identities.

# 5

# Flagging the Homeland Daily

The question still has not been answered directly: why do 'we', in established, democratic nations, not forget 'our' national identity? The short answer is that 'we' are constantly reminded that 'we' live in nations: 'our' identity is continually being flagged. Yet, this flagging cannot merely be a matter of the flag hanging outside the public building, or the national emblem, whether bald eagle or furry marten, on the coinage of the realm, as discussed in Chapter 3. The previous chapter suggested that 'national identity' is a short-hand for a whole series of familiar assumptions about nationhood, the world and 'our' place in that world. The limp, unwaved flag and the embossed eagle are not sufficient to keep these assumptions in their place as habits of thought. These assumptions have to be flagged discursively. And for that, banal words, jingling in the ears of the citizens, or passing before their eyes, are required.

The thesis of banal nationalism suggests that nationhood is near the surface of contemporary life. If this is correct, then routinely familiar habits of language will be continually acting as reminders of nationhood. In this way, the world of nations will be reproduced as *the* world, the natural environment of today. As has been argued, nationalism is not confined to the florid language of blood-myths. Banal nationalism operates with prosaic, routine words, which take nations for granted, and which, in so doing, enhabit them. Small words, rather than grand memorable phrases, offer constant, but barely conscious, reminders of the homeland, making 'our' national identity unforgettable. This chapter will begin by examining the language used by politicians in contemporary, established democracies. Unmemorable clichés and habits of political discourse are worth attention because of, not despite, their rhetorical dullness.

Some observers have claimed that ideology is declining in the late twentieth century, especially in democratic states. Most notably, Francis Fukuyama (1992) writes of a world-wide liberal revolution, in which the idea of democracy is emerging victorious. There is now no ideology in a position to challenge liberal democracy and there "is no legitimate principle other than sovereignty of the people" (p. 45). Nationalism, argues Fukuyama, is one of those old ideologies which are disappearing in the new liberal world order. In common with many other analysts, Fukuyama equates nationalism with its 'hot' varieties. The banal variety slips from the category and the absence of ideology is proclaimed.

There is, however, another possibility. The spread of democracy, far from eradicating nationalism, consolidates its banal, but not necessarily benign, forms. The very conditions of democracy, as envisaged in the twentieth century, are those which are based upon the nation-state, and which routinely embody a mysticism of place and people. The very phrase, 'sovereignty of the people', which Fukuyama used, contains this possibility within its comfortable sonority. The 'people' is not 'the people' of the whole world: it is the people of the particular democratic state. As Hall and Held (1989) have argued, in modern democratic politics 'the people' is a discursive formation, which is used synonymously with the nation. The world, in which 'the sovereignty of the people' is to be politically realized, is a world of different nations: it is a world which has institutionalized 'them' and 'us'.

To explore such matters, it is necessary to examine familiar habits of language. This means paying attention to words such as 'people' (or 'society'), drawing out the nationalist assumptions within their conventional usage. It, also, means becoming linguistically microscopic. The crucial words of banal nationalism are often the smallest: 'we', 'this' and 'here', which are the words of linguistic 'deixis'. Fukuyama's own phrase, 'sovereignty of the people', illustrates how easy it is to overlook the little word. If 'the people' is a significant 'discursive formation', then it comprises two words, one of which draws attention to the other, but not to itself. The 'the' of 'the people' is not mere decoration. It will be argued that, in English, the definite article is continually playing its quiet part in a routine 'deixis', which banally points out 'the' homeland.

If banal nationalism were only to be found in the words of politicians, it would hardly be embedded in the ordinary lives of those millions of people who treat the genus of politicians with cynical disdain. The flagging has other locations, as the mass media daily bring the flags home to the citizenry. A case study, which examines one nation's newspapers on one day, shows that the deixis of homeland is embedded in the very fabric of the newspapers. Beyond conscious awareness, like the hum of distant traffic, this deixis of little words makes the world of nations familiar, even homely.

As has been argued previously, nationalism is all too easily bracketed off as something extreme and irrational. For us, living in established nations of the West, there is the temptation to locate nationalist discourse in the sort of vocabulary which 'we', the educated citizens of the new global order, would disdain to use. Nationalism, for example, could be projected on to the tabloid press; 'we' can assure 'ourselves' that 'we' do not use the jingoist language with which the tabloids divert their working-class readership. If nationalism is a pervasive ideology, we should not distance ourselves so readily. When nations have fought their wars in the twentieth century, the middle and intellectual classes have not been found lagging in their support, nor in the roll call of victims.

Many of the examples of banal flagging examined in this chapter are taken from 'our' papers, the left-of-centre sophisticated press. In particular, examples come from the *Guardian*, the paper which I personally choose to read regularly. This paper, in common with others of its type, does not stand outside the ideology of banal nationalism. Built into its very structures of presentation is a complex deixis of homeland. For these reasons, an investigation into the ideology of banal nationalism should not be conducted in comfortable tones of accusation, which mock the thoughtless flag waving of 'others'. If the banal depths of nationalist consciousness are to be understood, a confessional tone is also required. In crucial respects, nationalism is 'here', close at home.

## Plebiscites, States and Nationalism

In a famous phrase, Ernest Renan declared a "nation's existence" to be "a daily plebiscite". By his metaphor of a plebiscite, Renan was drawing attention to the psychological dimension of nationalism. Nations do not have an absolute existence, but without a "clearly expressed desire to continue a common life", the nation disappears into history (1990, p. 19). The notion of a daily plebiscite suggests a psychology of the conscious will, rather as Benedict Anderson's later idea of an imagined community implies a psychology of imagination. In this respect, Renan's metaphor is somewhat misleading for, literally, there is no conscious daily choice. The citizens of an established nation do not, day by day, consciously decide that their nation should continue. On the other hand, the reproduction of a nation does not occur magically. Banal practices, rather than conscious choice or collective acts of imagination, are required. Just as a language will die rather for want of regular users, so a nation must be put to daily use.

The notion of a plebiscite also draws attention to the relations between nationalism and democracy. The nation, according to Renan, is chosen, rather than imposed: if the members of the nation reject the idea of nationhood, then the whole business of national community collapses. There is, therefore, an inherently popular, if not formally democratic, aspect of nationalism. In democratic states, the national electorate has its chance every few years to express its collective choice in formal plebiscites. In between times, the sort of daily plebiscite which Renan had in mind solidifies into habitual routines. These routines include habits of discourse, enabling 'the people' to identify themselves, and thereby reproduce themselves, as 'the people'. As 'the people', the electorates in liberal democracies at election times choose 'their' leaders and set the political course of 'their' national destiny.

John Shotter (1993a), in a perceptive insight, describes nationalism "as a tradition of argumentation" (p. 200). By this, Shotter means that nations have traditions of arguing about who 'we' are. Rival politicians and opposing factions present their different visions of the nation to their national electorates. In order for the political argument to take place within the nation, there must be elements which are beyond argument. Different factions may argue about how 'we' should think of 'ourselves' and what is to be 'our' national destiny. In so doing they will take for granted the reality of 'us', the people in its national place. In classical rhetorical theory, the *topos*, or rhetorical place, referred to the topic of argument. In the rhetoric of established nationalism, there is a *topos* beyond argument. The argument is generally placed within a place – a homeland – and the process of argumentation itself rhetorically reaffirms this national *topos*. As will be seen, this rhetorical reaffirmation of the national topography is routinely achieved through little, banal words, flagging the *topos* as the homeland.

Political discourse is important in the daily reproduction of nations, but not because politicians are necessarily figures of great influence. In fact, according to many commentators, national politicians have declining importance: key economic decisions are said to be taken supranationally (Giddens, 1990; Held, 1989). Politicians are important because, in the electronic age, they are familiar figures. Their faces regularly appear in the papers and on the television screens. The media treat political speeches as newsworthy, giving space to the words of presidents and prime ministers (Van Dijk, 1988a, 1988b). Previously, politicians were remote figures, seen by only a tiny fraction of the population. Thomas Jefferson even avoided speaking in Congress, delivering written messages to be read by a clerk (Meyrowitz, 1986, p. 279). As Kathleen Jamieson (1988) has pointed out, contemporary politicians, unlike their nineteenth-century forebears, do not have to shout to audiences of hundreds in drafty public places. First through radio, and now by courtesy of television, they can speak softly to millions, using an intimate rhetoric quite new to political oratory. This rhetoric fits its times, for, as Bakhtin wrote, "modern man does not proclaim; he speaks" (1986, p. 132). Whatever the rhetorical means, the end is unquestioned. The words of politicians daily reach millions; contemporary life has witnessed, to use Neil Postman's phrase, the emergence of the "politician-as-celebrity" (1987, p. 136).

If the politician is a celebrity, then fame is principally achieved through the medium of national politics. State sovereignty has become the constitutive principle of modern political life, as politics throughout the world, and especially in Western democratic nations, has become "state-centric" (Held, 1992; Magnusson, 1990; Walker, 1990). Anthony Giddens, in distinguishing between the political and economic orders of power in the world, claims that "nation-states are the principal 'actors' within the global political [order]" (1990, p. 71). The individuals acting within the economic order tend to be shadowy figures, as compared with the celebrities of the political order, who tend to achieve international fame through national fame.

In 1844 the young Benjamin Disraeli spoke openly of his motives, while appealing to the electors of Shrewsbury. With the innocence of youth and the enthusiasm of new times, he declared: "I love fame; I love public reputation; I love to live in the eye of the country" (quoted by Riddell, 1993, p. 14). Here was the prototype of what would become a familiar figure: the career politician, who relished the business of courting the electorate in the name of conservatism. Disraeli well realized that the politician, ambitious to cut a dash, must reach beyond the confines of market town or local shire. The real prizes were to be grasped in the eye of the whole country, not in the streets of provincial Shrewsbury. National fame was his target; Shrewsbury, he hoped, would provide the means.

The clichés of modern political discourse have, by and large, been adapted for the national stage. There is no special rhetoric for hailing the citizens of Shrewsbury or those of Hope, Arkansas. Disraeli could not have begun his speeches 'Fellow Shrewsburians', not merely because, as an outsider, he was no fellow, but because the term jars. As was discussed in Chapter 4, President-elect Clinton could start his first victorious address 'Fellow Americans'; but locally, could it ever possibly be 'Fellow Hopefuls'? For most locations within nations, there are no ready semantic equivalences of place and people, as there are on a national level.

Even where a new state is apparently emerging, the conventional semantics, unifying national people and place, can provide a serviceable rhetorical matrix. Nelson Mandela, on his night of electoral victory, following the first democratic election in South Africa after years of racist oligarchy, began his victory address in a conventional style: "My fellow South Africans – the people of South Africa" (*Guardian*, 3 May 1994). He went on to describe the new South Africa – "the type of South Africa we can build". The country had a unique, identifiable and addressable people: "We might have our differences, but, we are one people with a common destiny in our rich variety of culture, race and tradition."

The speech was not appealing to chauvinistic sentiments, yet it appealed to 'us', the people, the country, the nation. A common, national identity was being invoked. The utterance of such words may have marked an extraordinary moment, but the words themselves were reassuringly banal. The radical had joined the world system; he was speaking presidentially, like other presidents addressing their peoples, speaking in the serious clichés of nationhood. If democracy and nationhood were simultaneously being celebrated, then this was no coincidence. In the world of nations, democracy is nationally structured; its organization follows national boundaries; nations, or their 'people', are the democratic actors, who are conventionally said to make their choices, and who are to be represented democratically. It is as if democracy today knows no other home, no other grounding, except national homelands.

A further aspect of the politician addressing the nation can be noted. Convention dictates that the politician follows Aristotle's recommendation to "praise Athenians to Athenians" (*Rhetorica*, I, ix, 30; Aristotle, 1909 edn). The nation, in being hailed, should be rhetorically complimented. Speakers should identify themselves with the praised audience, using what Kenneth Burke (1969) called the rhetoric of identification to suggest an overall 'we'. Outgoing president Bush and incoming Clinton, as was seen in Chapter 4, praised the American nation, the greatest on earth. Mandela had his praise for "you the people who are our true heroes". An early *Punch* cartoon depicted the ambitious Disraeli as a tailor, measuring the shabbily dressed British lion for a finer suit of clothes (*Punch*, 7 July 1849). Politicians not only live in the eye of the country, but they represent the nation to itself. In addressing the imagined national audience, they dress it in rhetorical finery and, then, these speakers-as-outfitter hold a mirror so the nation can admire itself.

If the nation-state constitutes the grounding for political discourse, then politicians, seeking to represent the nation, must follow Disraeli in attempting to stand in the nation's eye. The notion of representation, in this context, is not straightforward. Two meanings can be distinguished in theory, but these are intertwined in political practice. First, there is 'representation' in the sense of 'standing for' or 'speaking for'. This sense of representation is implied when governments claim to represent 'the nation' or 'the people', speaking, acting and sometimes waving flags on its behalf. Disraeli was seeking to be the official representative of the electors of Shrewsbury at Westminster. He would, or so he hoped, represent their interests, acting as their metonymic embodiment, speaking for them in the parliamentary chamber.

The second meaning of representation is 'depiction', in the sense that a picture may be a representation of a scene. In contemporary political practice, the two forms of representation are closely connected. In order to claim to speak *for* the nation/people, the politician must also speak *to* that nation/people. The nation, in being addressed in the business of being represented ('stood for'), will also be represented ('depicted') in the business of being addressed. At its simplest level, the politician, who claims or campaigns to speak for the interests of the nation, will evoke the nation. The speaker who explicitly addresses 'us', claiming to know 'our' interests, simultaneously depicts 'us', whether or not elaborate, laudatory descriptions are used. In this context, the two meanings of 'represent' are not haphazard, as if a confusing accident of language had united two distinctly different activities. The rhetoric of hegemony, which elides the general and particular interest, elides the two types of representation. The particular party, or political figure, representing (speaking for) the general (national) interest, must represent (depict) in speech what is to be represented (spoken for).

In consequence, political discourse, which is grounded in the national context, set in the metaphorical eye of the nation, and employed in the practice of representation, will typically flag nationhood. Such flagging is part of the 'normal', habitual condition of contemporary state politics. It patterns the verbal muzak, incessantly produced by 'our' open-larynxed celebrity politicians.

## Playing the Patriotic Card

If flagging is the general condition of contemporary, democratic politics, then, as Nigel Harris has written, "nationalism provides the framework and language for almost all political discussion" (1990, p. 269). On this reckoning, nationalism is not a particular political strategy, but is the condition for conventional strategies, whatever the particular politics. This means that nationalism should not be equated with the particular strategies of populist right-wing parties, for this would underestimate the scope of nationalist assumptions.

Certainly there are strategies and rhetorics, which are conventionally identified as playing upon nationalist, or patriotic sentiments. These strategies have their own recognizable rhetoric. The previous chapter discussed a speech delivered by the British Prime Minister, John Major, addressing the Conservative Party in October 1982. He proclaimed that he would never let Britain's distinctive identity be lost. Woe betide anyone who dreamt of hauling down the Union Jack, he declared. This was a politician, responding to party difficulties, by doing the political business of patriotism. Anti-European elements on the Conservative right were threatening to rebel, so the party leader was making patriotic noises, assuring his party that he would never betray British sovereignty. The strategy was recognizable, especially to critics. *The Times*, which traditionally supports the Conservatives, had been losing patience with Major's leadership. The morning following Major's speech, the paper carried the headline: "Major wins time with the patriotism card" (10 October 1992). The *Guardian*, which had never supported the Conservatives, responded similarly: "Major plays the patriot card" was its headline.

John Major opened the Conservatives' campaign for the 1994 European Parliamentary elections with a speech which one paper described in familiar terms: "John Major last night moved to wrap the flag around the Conservatives' European strategy" (*Guardian*, 24 May 1994). In the rhetorical eye of the nation, Major asked his audience: "Will the party you are thinking of supporting put British interests first in any debate in Europe? We shall." The syntax of hegemony was being used. 'We' was the party and 'you' was the national audience: an identity of identities was being suggested. The loudest applause was reported to have come when the speaker praised the nation to itself:

> I positively believe that this is still the best country in the world in which to live. I have seen 60 countries in four years and there isn't one in which I would swap to live for a weekend.

'This country' was the place of all of 'us', represented by 'we' the Conservative Party, which represented 'our' British interests. If this was an inclusive 'we', the inclusion stopped at national boundaries, in order to exclude the outside world. 'Ours' was the most preferred of places; 'theirs' – the unspecified world of foreignness and others – was not worth a weekend's consideration. 'This' was home – this blessed plot, this earth, this realm.

The patriotic card is commonly played by right-wing parties, who might openly praise the virtues of patriotism. In September 1993 the German ruling coalition of Christian Democrats and the Christian Social Union announced that patriotism would figure largely in the campaign to retain power the following year. The leader of the parliamentary group, Wolfgang Schauble, a man widely tipped to be the next chancellor, declared:

> We must become more secure and certain again in a feeling of national belonging . . . Patriotism is not old-fashioned. Our fatherland could do with far more patriotism. (*Guardian*, 15 September 1993)

The message of the patriotic fatherland was carried to an audience, sitting on their sofas and upholstered armchairs, across the country. In today's political universe, the homeland card can be dealt straight into the homeland's homes.

During the 1980s such messages were common in the populist rhetoric of Reagan and Thatcher. Reagan often mixed his patriotic calls for duty with down-home folksiness, religious imagery, and the claim that the United States spoke for universal goodness. A case in point was the President's address to the nation in February 1988, when he was urging support for action against the Nicaraguan *Contras* (Ó Tuathail and Agnew, 1992). Reagan employed the imagery of America as the promised land: "I have often expressed my belief that the Almighty had a reason for placing this great and good land, the 'New World', here between two vast oceans." 'We' have enjoyed the benefits of peace and now 'we' must support those "who struggle for the same freedoms we hold dear". 'We' must do this for the sake of ourselves, 'our' children and all the peoples of the world: "We will be demonstrating that America is still a beacon of hope, still a light unto the nations." The rhetorical outfitter was holding the mirror to the nation, inviting it to imagine that the whole world admired its striped and starred coat of three colours.

Britain's Margaret Thatcher, during her premiership, was constantly reaching for the same mirror. During and after the Falklands War, she had but to open her mouth and the patriotic rhetoric would stream forth. In the previous chapter she was quoted, declaring that the Falklands campaign had shown that Britain still possessed sterling qualities. We have not changed, she declared: "We British are as we have always been – competent, courageous and resolute" (text included in Barnett, 1982, p. 150). And to a journalist, she declared: "There was a feeling of colossal pride, of relief we could still do the things for which we were renowned."

She went on: "We have ceased to be a nation in retreat. We have instead a new-found confidence, born of economic battles at home and tested and found true 8,000 miles away" (quoted in Young, 1993, pp. 280–1).

In all these examples, there is praise for the nation, as 'we' are represented as worthy of representation – at least, so long as 'you' support the recommended policies. Reagan directly praises America as a light for the nations; Thatcher is proud of the colossal pride which the nation is claimed to feel under her leadership. Major praises the British spirit, which will never be bullied, and, in so praising it, he claims that spirit for himself. Schauble urges patriotism for the fatherland, and, thereby, he implies that the fatherland deserves the patriotic loyalty.

There is a further element in these versions of contemporary rightist populism. They all evoke the past, claiming to regain, or not lose, historic glories. In this way, they are all suffused with the fear of loss. Major's 1992 speech cited a thousand years of British history and spirit, which was under threat but which Major promised to protect. When he praised the country as being the best in the world, he used the little word 'still': it was *still* the best place, as if forces were being mobilized to topple the nation from its favoured spot. Schauble's claim was that patriotism was not out-dated, but must be recaptured *again*. As for Reagan, America needed to show that it was *still* the light unto nations. And Thatcher triumphs in the claim that confidence is regained: 'we' have shown that this nation *still* has those sterling qualities; 'we' can *still* do the things for which 'we' were renowned. The past is to be regained. The enemies, who would separate 'us' from 'our' glorious destiny and 'our' unchanging identity, must be defeated.

Thomas Scheff points out that a sense of shame lurks forcefully around the rhetoric of nationalism (Scheff, 1995). All the examples evoke an implicit sense of shame: if 'we' fail the past – if 'we' abandon our precious national essence – then 'we' would be shamed: 'we' would no longer do the things for which 'we' were once renowned; 'we' would discard 'our' thousand year heritage; 'we' would not be the light unto the nations. Shame easily turns to anger (Retzinger, 1991; Scheff, 1990). The rhetoric of the patriotic card evokes anger against those who would cause 'us' to abandon 'our' heritage, 'our' duty, 'our' destiny. There are enemies abroad, who threaten to extinguish the light unto the nations and who taunt 'us', believing 'us' incapable today of performing the heroic deeds for which 'we' were once renowned. And, most ominously, there is anger against the enemies within – those who will abandon 'our' heritage, those who will bring shame upon 'us'. These internal enemies are not fit to be 'us'. Thus, Thatcher turned her patriotic rhetoric of the Falklands against striking miners at home: miners, who refused to strike, were those "we are proud to call the best of British" (quoted in Reicher, 1993). During the Gulf War, the US press depicted those, who did not support the president as the unpatriotic enemy within (Hackett and Zhao, 1994).

A dangerous anger hovers within the self-praise. Yet, the self-praise can appear harmlessly familiar. Familiar stereotypes are used within the patriotic representation, so that speaker and audience can claim to recognize and regain themselves ('ourselves'). 'Competent, courageous and resolute': 'we' see ourselves in the rhetorical mirror. With the use of stereotypes, especially in the rhetorical clichés of political discourse, comes an amalgam of imagination and its absence, as the homeland is unimaginatively imagined.

John Major, in a speech given shortly after delivering his patriotic card at the Conservative Party conference, declared that Britain would survive in 50 years time "in its unamendable essentials". Again, he was presenting himself as preserving the unique national past, reassuring the nation against the threat of loss. He listed the essential characteristics, which somehow, mystically represented the national totality. Britain would continue, he claimed, as "the country of long shadows on county grounds, warm beer, invincible green suburbs, dog lovers and pools fillers" (*Guardian*, 23 April 1993). His burst of metonymic stereotypes, in which particulars are presented to represent the whole country, combined images of persons, culture and place – 'our' people, 'our' way of life, 'our' homeland. Britain is not merely the place of dog lovers and cricketers; it is also a home of a greenery and long shadows. As with all such metonymic stereotyping, the representation involves exclusion. Major's descriptions are very English: the lack of county cricket in Scotland merits no mention. His exemplars are masculine: he evokes beer and cricket, not sweet sherry and needlepoint, thus corroborating Stuart Hall's (1991b) comment that the national type is always an English*man*, never an English*woman*. Major mentions the suburb, but not the inner city; the cricket ground, but not the football stadium; the dog lover but not the unemployed. This evoked nation is empty of motorways, mine-shafts and mosques. An artfully partial, and selectively idealized, Britain stands for the whole. The particulars represent the essence which is to be carried unamendably into the future. Throughout, there is the implication that these essential particularities (*this* greenery, *this* temperature of beer, *our* game of cricket) are unique: the essentials of 'our' nation, 'our' country' are to be found nowhere else.

In speaking thus, the politician is using the skills of political imagination to convey a representation. The imagination is not entirely original, as Major borrows heavily and unironically from the more ironic writings of George Orwell. The deliberate political strategy behind the act of rhetorical imagination serves to identify the speech as a playing of the 'patriotic card'. However, the use of stereotypes means that the imagination is not unfettered, for stereotyping involves a repetition. As Barthes (1983a) wrote, within each sign sleeps that monster, the stereotype, which is itself a repetition. Familiar particularities are employed to represent a commonly understood sense of 'us'; and, because they are familiar, the representation is a repetition, which involves an imaginative act of unimagination. Speech writers may have laboured long into the night, weighing the cadences of the images, testing the evocations against opinion poll data. Their busy imagination, nevertheless, works in the cause of the unimaginatively familiar.

If the homeland is being rhetorically represented, then, as such, it is literally being presented again (or re-presented). The familiar patterns of the patriotic flag are being waved. Flagging, in this respect, is always a reminding, a re-presenting and, thus, a constricting of the imagination. More than this, the patriotic card suggests that what is reassuringly familiar is under threat. The repetition will not be repeatable – the familiar will become unfamiliar – the praised people will no longer be praiseworthy – should 'we' not stand firm against those, within and beyond the national borders, seeking to destroy 'us'. Thus, the repetition is no mere repetition. It has, amongst its rhetorical potentialities, that familiar monster: the self-righteous call to national anger.

## Beyond the Patriotic Card

The patriotic card represents a particular political strategy, but it does not constitute the whole genus of nationalism within contemporary democratic politics. Sometimes populist right-wingers, such as Margaret Thatcher, claim that their politics, and theirs alone, has the nation's interests at heart. Not all flags, however, are waved in the same vigorous manner. If Harris is correct in suggesting that nationalism provides the very framework for contemporary political discourse, then there is no degree-zero, from which nationalism has been eradicated. A nationalist-free politics would not automatically be achieved should right-wingers stop playing the patriotic card. Even when the flags are not being waved, they are still hoisted upon the low poles of unremarkable cliché.

The players of the patriotic card, in calling upon familiar stereotypes, do not create their rhetoric anew. They are participating within, not invent-ing, nationalism's tradition of argumentation. They may advocate a particular vision of who 'we' are, and what 'we' should be like; but they are not creating the 'we', nor the homeland in which 'we' locate 'ourselves'. It is no coincidence that the post-election speeches of both Clinton and Bush represented the United States in almost identical terms. Both candidates, throughout the campaign, had spoken to crowds who had waved identically patterned flags. Clinton would prove to have a foreign policy scarcely distinguishable from Bush's; in Britain the Labour Party supported Thatcher's policy over the Falklands and, when in power, it had also administered exclusionary immigration policies.

Campaigning politicians, whether or not 'playing the patriotic card', can be heard to utter similar platitudes about 'our' country/nation/people. Rodolphe Ghiglione (1993) analysed the content of statements made during meetings of the left-wing PASOK party during the Greek general election. Nearly 50 per cent of the statements concerned 'us' – either 'us, the party', or 'us, the country'. Another 25 per cent dealt with 'the people',

typically assumed to be 'the Greeks' or 'you, the Greeks'. A similar pattern
was found when Ghiglione looked at speeches made by the French right-
wing politician Jacques Chirac in his unsuccessful campaign for the
presidency.

A few further examples of the nationalist clichés can be given. These are
taken from British newspaper reports in the last part of 1993; but almost
any speech, from any major politician, in any country, could be instanced.
In October 1993, the spokesman for the victorious PASOK party
announced that "a new era begins and it will be one of new horizons for
Greece and Hellenism" (*Guardian*, 11 October 1993). The Prime Minister
of New Zealand, in his campaign, was citing "the Kiwi spirit", claiming
that "there's a new mood, new optimism and New Zealanders are
confident of their ability and of their country's future" (*Guardian*, 5
November 1993). The Prime Minister of Canada, in her desperately
doomed campaign, was claiming that her opponent "would break the
Canadian spirit" (*Guardian*, 12 December 1993). None of these reports
claimed that the politicians were playing the patriotic card. They were all
relaying the standard, utterly forgettable stereotypes that politicians are
expected to say about themselves and their nations.

Populist patriots may be found predominantly on the political right, but,
because the nation-state is the forum for electoral politics, the left, too,
aspires to represent the nation. Left-wingers often appeal to what Antonio
Gramsci's called "the national-popular collective will" (1971, pp. 131ff.;
see Fiori, 1990). Gramsci's formula itself illustrates the extent to which
socialism's vision has been nationalized during the present century. For the
'popular will' to maintain itself as 'national', it must preserve its sense of
nationhood. Accordingly, the practical and enhabited mysticism of nationhood is assumed uncritically in Gramsci's phrase.

While John Major was playing his patriotic card before party and nation,
his opponents in the Labour Party were also seeking to stand in the eye of
the country. When the late John Smith addressed the Labour conference as
leader in the autumn of 1993, he contrasted an image of 'Conservative
Britain' with a 'Labour Britain': "In Tory Britain, an angry and disillu-
sioned people are in danger of losing faith in our future." On the other
hand, "Labour's Britain will be a confident society that opens doors wide
to new opportunities; a society that looks to the future" (*Guardian*, 29
September 1993). Nationhood and 'us' were being flagged in conventional
ways; and 'society' was being equated with nation.

The following year the Labour Party conference was addressed by its
new leader, Tony Blair. At the time of the conference, Labour was
publishing advertisements in national newspapers, inviting supporters to
contribute to the party. These advertisements carried a message of seven
sentences from Blair. Three mentioned 'Britain': "Labour's vision for
Britain . . . a Labour Government will create a Britain . . . if you share
this commitment to rebuilding Britain . . .". A fourth sentence referred to
'our country': "we will rebuild our country . . .".

As Blair spoke, he stood before a backdrop which displayed the party's slogan for the conference: 'New Labour, New Britain'. Blair's speech was not described by the press as an exercise in flag-waving. More attention was paid to his declarations about socialism and to his ideas of 'community'. Time and again, 'community' and 'nation' were elided rhetorically, as the rhetoric, together with the iconography of the podium, suggested an identity of identities. All the elements of national representation were there, for nationhood underwrote the message. 'We', 'our country', Britain, 'the British people', 'the nation' were being addressed and evoked. "The Labour Party" declared the leader, "is once again able to represent all the British people" (text of speech, distributed by Labour Party, 4 October 1994).

The mirror of narcissus was held up to the evoked national audience, which was to be represented. "The British people are a great people", he declared, "we are a nation of tolerance, innovation and creativity." And "we have a great history and culture". There was even an echo of biological nationalism: "We have an innate sense of fair play." However, 'we' are not quite perfect: "If we have a fault, it is that unless roused, we tend to let things be." Of course, it was now time to be roused. "I want to build a nation with pride in itself", said the leader, rousing his audience to the finale: "Our party: New Labour. Our mission: New Britain. New labour. New Britain." Applause. Applause.

So nationhood was flagged, as it is continually in the rhetoric of contemporary politics. Again and again, the celebrity politicians – whether from right or left on the democratic spectrum – drape the national name across their sentences, paragraphs and stage-managed backdrops. There the national name can hang as sign, context and potentiality. These familiar words are like flags hanging in the cool air. A change in atmosphere easily sets them in movement. The slightest breeze of anger, and they begin to rustle, wave and agitate.

## Homeland Deixis

The flagging within political discourse is important, not least because the words of politicians are continually transmitted to mass audiences. In this process, the boundaries of classical oratory are transcended. Audiences are no longer confined to those who are physically present to hear the speaker. Goffman (1981) distinguished between the 'ratified audience' and those who overhear what is spoken to the ratified audience. In contemporary political discourse, distinctions between audiences are frequently blurred. Politicians still talk from platforms to audiences gathered to hear them, but they aim to be overheard by a wider audience, whom they simultaneously address. The politicians, speaking to an audience of supporters, seek applause, so that their rhetorical successes can be broadcast nationally

(Atkinson, 1984; Heritage and Greatbach, 1986). In the electronic age of remote communication, not only does the style of address change (Jamieson, 1988), but there is a complex deixis of little words. 'We' may be used to evoke an identity between speaker and audience, but it is not immediately clear who constitutes this audience. Throughout this ambiguity of deixis, the little words can flag the homeland, and, in flagging it, make the homeland homely.

Deixis is a form of rhetorical pointing, for, according to linguists, "deixis has to do with the ways which sentences are anchored to certain aspects of their contexts of utterance" (Brown and Levinson, 1987, p. 118). Words, such as 'I', 'you', 'we', 'here' or 'now', are generally used deictically (Mühlhäusler and Harré, 1990). 'Now' refers to the time of the utterance and 'here' to its place. 'I', 'you' and 'we' anchor the utterance in the immediacy of the speaker and addressee (Harré, 1991). To understand the meaning of a deictic utterance, listeners have to interpret it from the position of the speaker, putting the speaker at the centre of the interpretive universe: 'I' is the speaker and the listeners recognize themselves as 'you', with 'we' frequently being the listener and speaker, evoked together as a unity. Some linguists argue that deixis can be a complex business, involving interjections and metaphors, as well as pronouns (Wilkins, 1992). In reported speech, as a speaker recounts the words of another speaker, the deixis can become even more complicated, as 'here' and 'now' may sometimes, but not always, refer to the context of the quoted speaker, rather than that of the speaking speaker (Fleischman, 1991; Maynard, 1994). Despite the importance and frequency of deixis in conversation, it is a topic which has been "grossly under-researched" by linguists (Mühlhäusler and Harré, 1990, p. 57).

Most linguists take the face-to-face conversation as providing the primary form of deixis. In such conversations, 'I', 'you', 'we', 'now' and 'here' are usually unproblematic. It is normally obvious who is talking and being addressed, not to mention when and where the talking is occurring. The deictic words, as it were, point to something concrete: the here and now, in which the speakers are standing. In the case of contemporary political discourse, the deixis is more complex. 'We' typically are not merely the speaker and the hearers: 'we' may be the party, the nation, all reasonable people and various other combinations (Fowler, 1991; Johnson, 1994; Maitland and Wilson, 1987; Wilson, 1990). If 'we' refers to the audience, then the audience may not be physically present, but has to be 'imagined' (Hartley, 1992). The audience may not even be imagined to be those who are actually listening in their various separated locations through television or radio. Politicians, rhetorically presenting themselves as standing in the eye of the nation, evoke the whole nation as their audience, well aware that their words will actually reach only a percentage of the nation's ears and eyes and that they might be overheard by others. "We must become more secure," said Schauble: 'we' did not refer to those who might listen or read his words: 'we' referred to all those belonging to "our fatherland". Mandela declared that "we are one people", outwardly addressing his remarks to the nation evoked as a whole, aware that his audience would include an eavesdropping world (at one point, he addressed "the people of South Africa and the world who are watching").

The deixis of homeland invokes the national 'we' and places 'us' within 'our' homeland. The word 'this' is frequently used deictically to indicate place. 'This room' or 'this table" can be indicated directly in a face-to-face conversation – although, even in such cases, more is often at stake rhetorically than simple pointing (Ashmore et al., 1994). But 'this country' cannot be physically indicated: what is there to point to? The speaker, in a television studio or on formal platform, has no object to indicate. The country is the whole context, which stretches beyond the individual locations of any speaker or listener, and, therefore, it cannot be indicated as the speaker's (or listeners') own particular 'here'.

John Major claimed that "*this* is still the best country in the world", and Tony Blair promised "under my leadership I will never allow *this* country to be isolated or left behind in Europe". Bush and Clinton, on their decisive election night, rhetorically pointed in the same direction. Clinton pointed to "*this*, the greatest country in human history" and Bush to "*this*, the world's greatest nation" (emphases added). This nation/this country: in no instance is there any ambiguity about which nation/country *this* is. This 'this' is the place of the evoked unseen and unseeable audience (or at least those of the audience presumed to belong to 'our' nation). It is evoked as the national place of 'us', conceived as a community. If the vocabulary appears pointedly concrete (as in 'this table' or 'this room'), then the word points to something which cannot be apprehended in its totality and which is always more than a geographical location. This place has to be unimaginatively imagined and the assumptions of nationhood accepted, for the routine phrase to do its routine rhetorical business. Through this routine business, the nation continues to be made habitual, to be enhabited.

There is a further form of deixis which, in many respects, is even more enhabiting, and which, because it involves no metaphorical pointing, hardly even seems deictic. The definite article can be used to refer to 'this/ our' country and its inhabitants. The country need not be named to be indicated as the ground on which the figures of speech appear. "Across *the* nation", declared Tony Blair; "you, *the* people, who are our true heroes", complimented Mandela, holding up the mirror of representation; Disraeli wanted to "live in the eye of *the* country". Which country? Which people? Which nation? No specification is necessary: *the* nation is *this* nation, 'our' nation.

This deixis can do its business unobtrusively, running up the flag so discreetly that it is unnoticed even by speaker or writer. The nation does not need to be mentioned, let alone named. Pierre Achard (1993) analysed a sentence in a British newspaper: "Government pressure has forced colleges to increase dramatically the number of students." He comments that the frame of the text is the nation, without being designated as such: "Britain is the universe of the ongoing discourse", although "the term 'we' is not used, and no external point relative to this universe is designated" (p. 82). Rae and Drury (1993), in an analysis of the way the phrase 'the economy' is used in newspapers, point out that there is an implied national frame and an implied 'we': *the* economy is 'our' economy. Deixis is being accomplished without the vulgar business of pointing.

The *Guardian* began its report of John Major's European piece of flag-waving with the words: "The Prime Minister slipped into Bristol un-announced yesterday to give the first big speech of the Tories' European election campaign" (24 May 1994). The sentence rhetorically sets the scene for the main story to follow. The very first word, which rhetorically draws no attention to itself, sets a scene for the scene-setting. It slips into the sentence unannounced: *The* Prime Minister. This is not any prime minister: it is *the* prime minister of 'our country' (*the* country). However, the phrase of 'our country' is omitted; it is unnecessary. The definite article accomplishes the deixis, indicating Britain as the centre of reader's and writer's ('our') shared universe.

This form of deixis, in flagging the homeland, helps to make the homeland homely. Utterances are not merely produced by contexts, but they also renew those contexts (Heritage, 1984; Linell, 1990; Nofsinger, 1991). For example, the 'home' is more than a mere physical place. To use the well-known proverb, a house is not a home. Particular forms of conduct and discourse are necessary to translate the house into the home, making it 'homely' and marking it as a place for homely living (Csikszent-mihalyi and Rochberg-Halton, 1981; Dittmar, 1992). Because the members of the home speak in a relaxed, 'homely' way, when at home, the home is renewed as the homely place: being 'at home', thus, is a way of home-making.

It is the same for talk within the homeland. One might describe the deictic use of the definite article as 'homeland-making', for it is the equiv-alent of a homely, home-making way of speaking. Consider the utterance 'it's in the kitchen', spoken within a house by one member of the household to another. The speaker might know that, within the neighbour-hood, there are hundreds of other kitchens. There is only one kitchen – *the* kitchen – in this context. The universe has shrunk to the boundaries of the home; here, other kitchens have to be marked, specifically indicated as 'other': 'my brother's kitchen' or 'the kitchen on the cover of the magazine' are not *the* kitchen in its unqualified uniqueness. The banal utterance of 'the kitchen', (or 'the living-room' or 'the stairs') not only assumes the boundary of the home as the context of the utterance, but it also helps to renew this homely context. The phrase 'the prime minister' operates similarly.

There is a parallel between the language of home and homeland. The French philosopher Gaston Bachelard, in his *Poetics of Space*, suggested that our childhood home is "our first universe, a real cosmos in every sense of the word." Thereafter, all inhabited space "bears the essence of the notion of home" (1969, pp. 4–5). The national space most notably bears this trace, being imagined as homely space, cosy within its borders, secure against the dangerous outside world. And 'we' the nation within the homeland can so easily imagine 'ourselves' as some sort of family. If the national home is to be homely, then 'we' must make it so. 'We' cannot do this by constant, conscious endeavour. To be at home, 'we' must routinely and unconsciously use the homeland-making language. 'We' must daily inhabit the environment of this language. Small, unnoticed words of deixis are important in this respect. They help to shut the national door on the outside world. 'The' shuts the door more tightly than 'this'. Just as 'we' implies 'them', so 'this country' generally implies a contrastive 'those countries'. When Major was claiming that 'this' was still the best country in the world, he was comparing 'this' with those foreign countries in which he could not bear to pass a weekend. Blair's 'this country' was being mentioned in relation to the rest of Europe from which it might be isolated or left behind. Bush and Clinton, in 'this, the world's greatest country', were implicitly evoking a comparison with all those lesser countries. But *the* nation – with *the* president or *the* economy or, even, *the* weather – makes no such comparison. What is 'ours' is presented as if it were the objective world: *the* is so concrete, so objective, so uncontroversial. In all these respects the phrasing differs from the patriotic waving of the flag. The homeland is made both present and unnoticeable by being presented as *the* context. When the homeland-making phrases are used with regularity, 'we' are unmindfully reminded who 'we' are and where 'we' are. 'We' are identified without even being mentioned. In this way, national identity is a routine way of talking and listening; it is a form of life, which habitually closes the front door, and seals the borders.

## The Day Survey

An objection might be raised. Perhaps, the rhetorical forms of flagging and deixis, which have been outlined, are confined to the discourse of professional politicians. If citizens today are generally blasé about the words of politicians, then such flaggings may not be especially important. They would be words falling on largely unlistening ears. The objection shows the need for further evidence to show that the banal flaggings of nationhood are neither unusual, nor confined to politics. If nationalism is banally enhabited, then such flaggings should be continually made in the media, not just when the words of politicians are repeated.

To demonstrate this systematically, it would be necessary to sample the various forms of mass media and mass culture over a lengthy period in a number of countries. Of particular interest would be the quotient of flagging on 'ordinary' days, which are not days of national celebration or intense electoral campaigning. In lieu of such systematic evidence, an illustrative Day Survey is offered here. This looks at flagging in one country, in one medium, on one day: British national newspapers on 28 June 1993.

No times – indeed no places – can be called wholly 'ordinary'. Throughout the United Kingdom during the early 1990s, the issue of national identity was very much a political issue. John Major's Conservative government was continuing Margaret Thatcher's mixture of free market economics and popular, national authoritarianism (see Hall, 1988a, 1988b; Jessop et al., 1988, for analyses of Thatcherism). Quite apart from the continuing conflict in Northern Ireland, and the steady political support for the separatist Scottish Nationalist Party, Britain's uneasy relations with the European Community were dividing the Conservatives. To appease the anti-European wing, Major, as has been seen, frequently played the patriotic card, but with little effect on the wider audience. During 1993 and the following year, opinion polls showed the British government's popularity, and the personal standing of its leader, slumping to record lows. On the other hand, there is some suggestive evidence that the patriotic card – in the form of scares about immigrants and 'others' from Europe – might have helped the Conservatives to secure their fourth successive General Election victory in 1992 (Billig and Golding 1992; more generally, see Layton-Henry, 1984; Van Dijk, 1993). In a general sense, a number of issues concerning sovereignty were current within the British political context of June 1993.

Historically, Britain has the second highest newspaper readership in the world (Bairstow, 1985). According to the British National Attitudes Survey, roughly two-thirds of the population read a newspaper at least three times a week, although this has been declining (Jowell et al., 1987, 1992). As in other countries, newspapers are a main source of news for significant numbers of the population (Sparks, 1992). The morning press is basically national, although the evening papers are local. The ten major daily, national newspapers were chosen for this survey. They are conventionally divided into three market groups: the 'sensational tabloids' – *Daily Star*, *Daily Mirror* and *Sun*, aimed principally at working-class readers; the 'respectable' tabloids – *Daily Mail*, *Daily Express* and *Today*; and the 'heavies' or broadsheets – *The Times*, *Guardian*, *Daily Telegraph* and *Independent*, addressed at a middle-class audience.

The terms 'tabloid' and 'broadsheet' refer to more than the size of the newspaper's page: they refer to the paper's own sense of its readership. The distinction between tabloid and broadsheet is not a political one, for it cuts across editorial commitments. Politically, the *Mirror* has a tradition of supporting the Labour Party. *Today*, the *Guardian*, and the *Independent* can also be described as left-of-centre. The rest, which constitute the majority both in terms of the number of papers and in terms of readership, support the Conservative Party. Ownership cuts across the tabloid/broadsheet distinction. Rupert Murdoch's News International owns the tabloid *Sun* and *Today*, together with *The Times*.

According to the Audit Bureau of Circulation, the average combined sales for the ten papers at that time was approximately 12,900,000 (as reported in *Guardian*, 12 July 1993). The *Sun*, with sales figures of over three and a half million copies per day for the first six months of 1993, was the most popular paper, followed by the *Mirror*, selling just under a million less on average. The British Social Attitudes Survey, however, reveals that less people claim (or admit) to reading the *Sun* than the *Mirror* (Jowell et al., 1992). The ten papers selected for the Day Survey account for over 97 per cent of national newspaper sales in England and Wales (Monopolies and Mergers Commission, 1993). *The Financial Times*, which is the one major paper not included in the Day Survey, has a high overseas readership (Sparks and Campbell, 1987). It only has 1.3 per cent of the national newspaper sales within Britain; a further 1.3 per cent is accounted for by the combined sales of the communist *Morning Star* and of the racing press, *Sporting Life* and *Racing Post* (Monopolies and Mergers Commission, 1993).

Technically, the British press is not national in the sense that the same editions cover the whole of the United Kingdom. Some papers publish separate, editorially independent editions for Scotland. In the case of the *Mirror*, the Scottish equivalent even has its own title – the *Daily Record*. Also, Scotland has its own newspaper, *The Scotsman*, which presents itself as a national newspaper in contradistinction from Scotland's daily provincial newspapers. Northern Ireland, too, has its separate press. In this respect, the British press, in common with so many other things described as 'British', is English-based. By calling the Day Survey a national survey, while concentrating on the English editions, some of the conventional, hegemonic semantics of 'British' nationalism have already been adopted.

Choosing a day for the survey was always going to be somewhat arbitrary. The day had to be selected in advance to avoid electoral campaigns and planned national celebrations. I chose Monday 28 June 1993 for the Day Survey, fixing on that day a week in advance. No general election, international summit or royal birth was in the offing. I could not predict the topics for the major headlines of that day: whether they would report a political speech, savage crime or royal scandal. Otherwise, there was no particular justification for choosing that date, as compared with others, except, most importantly, that it was convenient for me.

## Flagging the Daily News

In the event, the main news story of the day was presented as a sudden, unforeseen event, although, taken over time, it was an event which fitted a predictable, long-established pattern. All but two of the newspapers led their front pages with the bombing of Baghdad by American war-planes, acting on the orders of President Clinton. The *Star* featured a story about pop fans wilting in the heat of an open air concert in London. The *Sun*, on the morning after the Baghdad raid, used its banner headlines to announce: 'Rock Star's Mum of 70 Has a Toyboy, 29'. The US bombing made an appearance on the fourth page of the *Sun*, following bare-chested young women who, as is customary, could be viewed on page three (see Holland, 1983, for an analysis of the *Sun*'s 'page three').

The bombing of Baghdad was a story which flagged nationhood in a direct manner. At first sight, however, some of the headlines seemed to suggest the story of a personal quarrel between Presidents Clinton and Hussein. *The Times* declared: "Clinton warns Saddam: don't try to hit us back". The *Star* had a similar headline: "Fight back and we smash you, warns Clinton". Its first sentence declared: "President Clinton last night threatened to 'finish off' evil Saddam Hussein", thereby indicating the quarrel to be one between good and bad, and signalling its own stance (see Gruber, 1993 for a discussion of the ways journalists signal their own positions). The individuals, nevertheless, are not mere individuals, for they personify nations. The pronominal plural is in evidence: 'we' smash you; don't hit 'us' back. The deixis of reported speech was being used: the national 'us' is not that of the paper and its readers but that of the quoted Clinton (Zelizer, 1989, 1990). The *Star* completed its opening sentence by locating the individual actors in a world of nations: Saddam Hussein will be finished off "if the Iraqi despot dares a revenge attack for America's missile attack on Baghdad". The attack was not merely Clinton's: it was America's. The target was not merely Baghdad or Hussein: it was Iraq, a nation: "Clinton acclaims Iraqi strike", headlined the *Independent*. The civilian casualties were unfortunate by-products of this attack on a nation: "Six dead as missiles miss Iraqi target" subheadlined the *Guardian*.

America and Iraq may have been the main characters, but the papers depicted a chorus of nations reacting to the episode. Typically, nations and their governments were presented as single actors, often metonymically represented by the capital city. "Britain, Russia and other American allies expressed firm support", stated *The Times*. "French reaction struck an equivocal note", declared the *Independent*, "Paris said it understood the reasons for the strike . . .". The style was conventional. There was much talk about what 'Washington' and other capital places were saying and doing. The semantic conventions depict a world of national actors, in which nations, courtesy of their governmental leaders, speak and act. The general pattern matches the British press's coverage of President Reagan's bombing of Libya a few years earlier, as analysed by Roger Fowler (1991).

The papers, in covering the story of the attack, gave particular prominence to British dimensions. Papers supporting the British govern-ment conveyed an image of Britain at the head of the international chorus: "John Major led international support for the raid", wrote the *Daily Mail*, perennially loyal to the Conservative Party. One particular British angle was accorded special attention: the plight of three British citizens im-prisoned in Iraq. *The Times*, on its front page, headlined this story "Hopes for prisoners dashed". *Today*, which editorially was critical of the raid, led with the story. "What hope for them now" was its headline, with "Families of jailed Brits slam Iraq raid" as the subheading. The opening paragraph stated that the "Families of Britons imprisoned by Saddam Hussein say their men have been condemned to more years in jail by the US attack on Iraq." Again, there is a mixture of personal and national actors: Saddam Hussein and the United States. But there is more. The story implies a national audience. This audience is assumed to be British, hoping for the release of fellow Britons. Moreover, this audience is also presented simultaneously as if it were a 'universal audience' (Perelman, 1979; Perelman and Olbrechts-Tyteca, 1971). The 'hopes' of the headlines are not attributed to any particular persons: they are not even 'our hopes'. They are disembodied, universal hopes, which all of 'us' – all reasonable readers – are invited to share with the paper. These (reasonable) hopes are for the future of three British men, not for the injured citizenry of Baghdad.

Perhaps it is hardly surprising that the news of the world's most powerful nation bombing the capital city of another nation should capture such attention. Nor is it surprising that the news should be presented in a framework of nationhood. If nationhood were only flagged in this particular story, then the Day Survey would have provided poor evidence for the thesis of banal nationalism. However, the headline flagging of nationhood was by no means confined to the Baghdad bombing. All the papers on that day carried other stories, whose headlines or first lines outwardly flagged Britishness: "Britain got a triple dose of good news yesterday" (*Sun*); "Britain basked in 79° temperatures yesterday" (*Sun*); "Britain's highest bungee jump" (*Star*); "Britain's latest cult heroes" (*Today*); "Brits in passport scam" (*Today*); "Is the British teenager dead or just resting a lot?" (*Today*); "A new eating fad is about to hit Britain" (*Mirror*); "Britain's Best Cartoons" (*Mirror*); "British Scrabble champion" (*Mail*); "the Blue-Print for Britain" (*Express*); "Britain's super-saviours" (*Express*); "Billions spent 'needlessly' by Britain on Black Wednesday" (*Guardian*); "worst places in Britain to be without a job" (*Guardian*); Concorde and "the British Aerospace industry" (*Independent*); "Britain's first gene transplant" (*Telegraph*); "Britain's timekeepers" and "the last minute of Wednesday, June 30" (*Telegraph*); "Martin Hoyle on a new British voice" (*Times*); and lastly, and least snappily, there was "Britain's most successful and widely publicised community-led urban renewal project" (*Times*). And these exclude the sports pages, whose vigorous flaggings will be discussed later.

There was a particularly noteworthy example of waved, celebratory flagging. Nowadays, it is unnecessary to wait for an official day of celebration in order to put out the national bunting. Heritage is a booming industry, successfully marketing the national past as a leisure commodity (Hewison, 1986). 'Wilful nostalgia', especially with a national dimension, has been said to be a distinguishing feature of contemporary, Western culture (Robertson, 1990, 1992; Turner, 1987). Certainly, patriotic themes provide the value-added selling points for many a product's marketing campaigns (Pedic, 1989, 1990). Special national celebrations can be sponsored to boost the sales of commodities, with national flags and advertising logos jointly hoisted in commercial harmony.

That Monday, the *Mirror* announced the start of "British Pub Week". The newspaper, to mark the occasion (its own occasion), produced a special supplement, *The Great British Pub*, which included advertisements from the brewing industry, declaring support for the event and for the virtues of their own products. As the week's name suggested, pubs were not being celebrated merely as commercial retail outlets for alcohol: they were presented as icons of nationhood. From the title onwards, the supplement promoted heritage themes, waving flags and the national first person plural. The pub was pronounced "the bastion of British social life", which, of course, is 'our' social life:

> As a nation, over a quarter of the adult population – 12,500,000 – visit the pub at least once a week. And we know exactly what we want from our pubs.

Foreigners were admirers, believing that "when it comes to atmosphere, British pubs can't be beaten". Pubs did their bit to flag the homeland in a homely way: "British life wouldn't be the same without pub signs".

The Great Week was introduced as a special occasion. *Mirror* readers would not have the bonus of a free "16 page guide to a splendid tradition" every Monday morning. Nevertheless, the eye of the reader, whether of tabloid or quality paper, will have seen 'Britain' draped around a variety of other stories on that day. Some of the headlines and opening sentences may have caught the attention, but this attention will, as likely as not, have been only momentary, before becoming lost in the collective forgetfulness which accompanies each daily presentation of news. The Great British Pub Week, not having the backing of an established place in the calendar, was fated also to be unmemorable. The memory of specific items is not what matters. Beyond, the specifics lies a pattern, or what Stuart Hall (1975) called a "context of awareness". The frequency of nations being mentioned suggests that, in the context of awareness, flagging plays an important part.

**Newspapers and the Deictics of Homeland-Making**

The context of awareness employs a complex deixis of 'here' and 'now'. The 'now' is to be routinely understood as the 'now' of up-to-date news. The 'here' is more complex. The papers, like the television, are giving 'us' today's news from the world. Baghdad, Washington, Paris are 'here' on the page. But where are 'we', the receivers, and where are 'we', the writers? Routinely, newspapers, like politicians, claim to stand in the eye of the country. Particularly in their opinion and editorial columns, they use the nationalized syntax of hegemony, simultaneously speaking to and for the nation, and representing the nation in both senses of 'representation'. They evoke a national 'we', which includes the 'we' of reader and writer, as well as the 'we' of the universal audience (see above, Chapter 4).

The *Sun*, in its editorial, complained that the European Community had taken "our money". 'Our' did not refer to the finances of the paper, nor to the vast resources of its proprietor. It was to be read as 'us' the nation. *Today*'s regular columnist ended his piece with a ringing declaration: "Time we changed Government. Certainly time we changed Prime Minister." The 'we' was not the 'we' of writer and *Today* readers; nor was it the 'we' of the proprietor which *Today* shares with the *Sun*. Nor was it the 'we' of the whole world. A national 'we' was being invoked, comprising the 'reasonable people' of the nation, who were being represented as the whole nation. This 'we' included non-readers of the paper, whilst the readers were being addressed as nationals.

Lest it be thought that the national 'we', with its presumed internal identity of identities, represents a style of journalism, which is confined to the popular press, the same address is used in the 'serious' papers – on their most serious of pages. The *Daily Telegraph*, in its Business News, headlined an article: "Why our taxes need never rise again". The writer suggested that "if our huge borrowing requirement can spawn even the slightest move in this direction, we will all have cause to bless £1 billion a week spewing into the financial markets". This 'we' is a national 'we', which is simultaneously identified with the readership and with the wider nation. The *Guardian* might advocate different economic policies from the *Telegraph*, but it addresses a similar 'we'. Its economics page featured a piece entitled "Turning our industrial sunset into new dawn" (sic). The headline did not specify who 'we' were: readers could be expected to recognize their national selves. In the text, sentences slipped easily between the first person plural and the name of the homeland: "Hostile to innovation and production, *Britain's* financial/corporate governance system has been the principal cause of *our* decline for most of this century"; "The revival of *Britain's* supply side is not just about techniques and reforms; it is about who and what *we* are" (emphases added). 'We' – writer and reader – are assumed to be British. Whatever perplexities 'we' might have, 'we' are assumed to know that 'we' belong to 'our' homeland, here and now.

Roger Fowler (1991), in his book *Language in the News*, has suggested that deixis does not occur commonly in newspapers, as compared with ordinary conversation. That might be true if deixis is identified overtly with the use of words like 'this', 'here' and 'us'. Editorial writers, feature-columnists and even reporters on the business pages may, from time to time, address the readers as a national 'us'. But in the news sections, 'we' are not evoked so often. Nevertheless, there are other routine forms of deixis, especially the deixis of homeland-making, which presents *the* national home as the context of utterance. *The* nation becomes *the* place, as the centre of the universe contracts to the national borders. Three examples of homeland-making deixis can be given: the nation, the weather and the home news. Detailed analysis would doubtless reveal many other instances.

## The Nation

Examples from the Day Survey suggest that the phrase 'the nation' is commonly used by journalists, as well as politicians (see also Achard, 1993). The *Mail* wrote about "one of the nation's most wanted men"; a British tennis player was "the centre of the nation's sporting focus". The *Express* discussed medium-sized companies which "contribute nearly £4 billion to the nation's wealth". The *Guardian* cited a politician referring to "the nation's interest and love of music". *Today*, using a quoted deixis, reported that "a group of backbenchers are set to tear apart defence policies claiming the Prime Minister is risking the nation's security". Britain is *the* nation; and, in the last example and elsewhere, the British Prime Minister is *the* Prime Minister.

Readers, unless informed to the contrary by headline or first paragraph, can usually assume that a story is being set in the homeland. *The Times* had a special 'focus' on the nuclear industry. The items referred to the British nuclear industry, except when they contained specific markers of foreignness. The unqualified definite article could be used to indicate the homeland: "*the* industry wants *the* government to think long-term, looking to energy needs in the 21st century" (emphases added). The stories in the *Telegraph*'s Business News likewise indicated a British scene, unless otherwise specified: "Unemployment is on course to fall further as key regions . . .": 'key regions' were to be understood as regions within Britain. By contrast a foreign scene was specified, particularly in the first sentence: "Two American software entrepreneurs . . ."; "A £500m offer of shares in French pharmaceuticals company Roussel–Uclaf . . .". In these cases, 'we' know immediately that 'we' are not 'here', in 'this', 'our' country. Otherwise, 'we' can relax at home.

## The Weather

The weather can often be a topic of news in the press. On the day of the survey, the *Star* led with a 'sizzling-heat' story about hundreds of fans collapsing at a pop concert. The opening paragraphs provided no geographic location. Without the setting being specified, readers could assume correctly that the drama had occurred 'here', in Britain. Hot weather abroad would not have been newsworthy.

The very notion of 'the weather' implies a national deixis, which is routinely repeated. The papers regularly carry small, unobtrusive weather reports, typically labelled 'Weather'. The *Mirror* has 'Today's Weather' and the *Sun*, with obscure individuality, puts its weather information beneath the sign 'Newsdesk'. The reports tend to be similar. They contain a map of Britain, which is not actually labelled as Britain: the shape of the national geography is presumed to be recognizable. The *Telegraph*, *Guardian*, *Independent* and *The Times* have a longer report, accompanied by a further map showing Europe and the north Atlantic. In these maps, the British Isles happen to be placed in a central location.

'Weather' sections routinely report the weather of Britain, typically without mentioning the national name, although sub-parts and districts (including England) may be identified. '*The* country' suffices: "Early fog patches in the southwest will clear leaving a dry, bright, sunny day across the whole country" (*Sun*); "Quite warm throughout the country" (*Mail*). Both *The Times* and the *Guardian* began their reports identically: "Fog patches may linger for a time in coastal districts of southwest England". The *Guardian* continued with the prediction that "over the rest of the country any mist or fog will rapidly clear". Although this was opening a section headed 'General Outlook', what was general was being contained within ('our') national boundaries. *The Times* completed its opening sentence: "but elsewhere any mist will rapidly clear". 'Elsewhere', of course, was to be understood as elsewhere in Britain; it was not elsewhere on the map of the north Atlantic, nor elsewhere on the list of temperatures headed 'Abroad'.

The similarity of the reports in the *Guardian* and *The Times* was no coincidence. The weather reports are derived from the same official source, which is usually acknowledged. In *The Times*, the *Mail* and the *Independent*, a small note states: "Information supplied by the Met Office". The *Guardian* more formally describes their supplier as "the Meteorological Office". None adds an adjective 'British' to the Office in question. In this universe of weather, there is only one Met(eorological) Office, *the* one.

A homeland-making move transforms meteorology into *the* weather. And *the* weather – with its 'other places', its 'elsewheres' and its 'around the country's – must be understood to have its deictic centre within the homeland. 'The weather' appears as an objective, physical category, yet it is contained within national boundaries. At the same time, it is known that the universe of weather is larger than the nation. There is 'abroad'; there is 'around the world'. These are elsewheres beyond 'our' elsewheres. The national homeland is set deictically in the central place, syntactically replicating the maps of the North Atlantic. All this is reproduced in the newspapers; and all this, in its small way, helps to reproduce the homeland as the place in which 'we' are at home, 'here' at the habitual centre of 'our' daily universe.

## The Home News

The deixis of homeland-making is not confined to the little words, such as 'the', 'this' or 'us'. There is a further element built into the organization of many newspapers, especially the broadsheets. It is a truism that, in the British press, national news predominates over international items. Fowler refers to the 'homocentrism' of the press, which is "a preoccupation with countries, societies and individuals perceived to be like oneself" (1991, p. 16). An international story, such as the bombing of Baghdad, can force its way on to the front pages of most papers, but even so, the British angle is not to be denied. The *Sun* resisted the pressure of international crises. The 'Rock star' and his 'mum', who dominated its headlines, were both British: the 'toyboy', adding spice to the story, was Spanish, and a 'jobless waiter' to boot. The *Star*'s weather story was set in Britain. The *Guardian* writer Martin Kettle wrote several days later about "the old Fleet Street slide rule for the news value of death and disaster stories – six Brits, 60 Frogs, 600 more remote aliens" (*Guardian*, 17 July 1993). He was, of course, writing about Fleet Street and British journalism, criticizing 'our' biased interest in 'ourselves'.

Perhaps one might expect higher imbalances between domestic and foreign news in the tabloids. One might expect also a greater number of flaggings of the national name. A controlled study would be needed to determine the frequency of 'Brits', 'British' and 'Britain' in the various tabloid and broadsheet papers, together with phrases such as 'the country', 'the nation' and 'we, British'. However, one should not presume that a higher frequency of the national name is necessarily an indicator of an increased level of banal nationalism. The deixis of home-making can be subtly accomplished, being ingrained in the structures of presentation, which make the particular flagging of national location unnecessary.

On the day of the survey, both the broadsheet *Times* and the tabloid *Express* reported news about the employment prospects for university graduates. The *Express* specifically set its story in Britain, mentioning at the start that a survey had been conducted of "300 leading British companies" and that "this summer 150,000 students will be awarded degrees in Britain". By contrast *The Times*, in its report, did not mention Britain at all: "University students' chance of a first class degree improved 50 per cent during the 1980s, according to a report published today." A simple census of flags might put the *Express* ahead at this point: their story had flagged the homeland, while *The Times* had not.

The *Express*, in common with most tabloids, mixes foreign and domestic items on its news pages, with domestic stories generally outnumbering the foreign ones. By contrast, the broadsheets, on their inside pages, separate foreign from domestic news, reserving different pages for each. At the top of each page is a signpost informing readers where they are. *The Times* signposts 'Home News' and 'Overseas News'; the *Telegraph* uses 'News' and 'Foreign News', as if all news is homeland news, unless otherwise specified; the *Independent* distinguishes between 'Home', 'Europe' and 'International', whilst the *Guardian* has a similar tri-partite division into 'Home News', 'European News' and 'International News'. Thus, all the broadsheets, whatever their politics, maintain a principle of news *apartheid*, keeping 'home' news and foreign news paginally separate. All, except the *Telegraph*, use the term 'home' to signpost events taking place within the national boundaries. In consequence, any regular *Times* reader, unless they were lost within their paper, would have known that the story about university students was 'home news'. It was located on a page that had already been signposted as homeland territory.

The broadsheets habitually organize their news so that nationhood operates, to use Hall's phrase, as a context for awareness. The structuring is not so much homocentric as home-centric. The signposts are not merely page headings. 'Home' indicates more than the contents of the particular page: it flags the home of the newspaper and of the assumed, addressed readers. Daily, we, the regular readers, flick our eyes over the directing signs. Without conscious awareness, we find our way around the familiar territory of our newspaper. As we do so, we are habitually at home in a textual structure, which uses the homeland's national boundaries, dividing the world into 'homeland' and 'foreign', *Heimat* and *Ausland*. Thus, we readers, find ourselves at home in the homeland and in a world of homelands.

## Masculine Arms Waving the Flags of Sport

Through the routine deictics of homeland-making, the press may flag nationhood across its pages. This does not mean, however, that those flags are waved. Some right-wing papers, like the *Mail*, *Express*, *Sun* and *Telegraph*, are known for supporting the right-wing players of patriotic cards, at least in British politics. Nevertheless, all the papers, whatever their politics, have a section in which the flag is waved with regular enthusiasm. This is the sports section. These sections are aimed at men. As Sparks and Campbell have written, "the reader inscribed in the sports pages is overwhelmingly masculine" (1987; p. 462).

Perhaps it is more than a coincidence that the other main site of overt flag-waving that day was the *Mirror*'s 'Great British Pub' supplement. That was celebrating an institution which historically has been masculine territory, permitting women entrance under specific circumstances (Clark, 1983; Golby and Purdue, 1984). Fifty years ago, the Mass Observation study *The Pub and the People* noted that over 80 per cent of customers in this great British tradition were men (Mass Observation, 1987). To this day, pubs continue to be places which, in the words of Valerie Hey, are "expressive of deeply held gender ideologies" (1986, p. 72). The *Mirror*, in praising the British pub, ignored its historical and contemporary masculinity. Far from being male territory, the pub was 'our' institution, 'our' old tradition, a home from home for all of 'us': the part was representing the whole again.

Sport is also historically a largely masculine domain, as are the pages which the British press devotes to it. Sport may have its own separate ghetto in the newspapers, but sport is never merely sport, as C.L.R. James, the profoundest analyst of the subject, repeatedly stressed. The motto prefacing his *Beyond a Boundary* asked "What do they know of cricket who only cricket know?" (1964, p. 11). Modern sport has a social and political significance, extending through the media beyond the player and the spectator. James observed of the sport, which he loved and dissected intellectually, that "far more people scan the cricket news in the morning paper" than read books (1989, p. xi). Not least of this significance is that the sporting pages repeat the commonplace stereotypes of nation, place and race, not to mention those of masculinity (O'Donnell, 1994).

On the Monday of the Survey, a swirling flurry of flags was waving for 'us', 'our victories' and 'our heroes'. That day marked the start of the second week of the annual tennis tournament at Wimbledon, in which the top professional players from around the world compete in gendered competition. The *Sun* had actually hoisted the flag for Britain, presenting, at the start of the tournament, the "*Sun* Sport's Union Jack", flying at the top of a flag-pole. The idea was to lower the flag one notch each time a British competitor was eliminated from the competition. On past form, a quick lowering of the national flag could be expected, followed by semi-ironic articles bemoaning the national plight. Against predicted expectations, a British player still remained in the competition; and the national flag still could be depicted to flutter across the *Sun*'s sporting pages, albeit not far up the pole. Under the headline 'Battler Brits' (in red type against a blue and white background), the paper proclaimed: "We've done it! *Sun* Sport's Union Jack is still with us as the second week of Wimbledon gets underway today – thanks to Andrew Foster the only surviving Brit in the singles competition." There was much more about "our new star", whom 'we', the readers and the nation, were invited to praise.

The *Sun* was not alone in celebrating British success, or, rather, British avoidance of quick defeat in the tennis. If the *Star* wrote of "Britain's new Wimbledon hero" and the *Mirror* praised "British tennis hero Andrew Foster" who carried "British tennis hopes", then the broadsheets, using wordier phrases, bore the same message. *The Times*, under the headline "Battling Britons enjoy joke at critics' expense", declared that "Brit after Brit has been brave enough to win". The *Guardian*'s tennis correspondent argued that Wimbledon's first week had been particularly "memorable" because of "the contributions made by British players against the odds and expectations". Here, the flag was being waved tastefully. 'We' were not praising 'ourselves' with brazen, outward ostentation, raising and lowering iconographic flags. The celebration was objectified: the event simply was 'memorable', as if being memorable were an objective characteristic. The particular collective memory – 'our memory' – was elided with an implied universal memory. Everyone, or all reasonable people, would remember the British avoidance of defeat.

The right-wing press, which generally supports the flag-waving politicians, specifically mentioned patriotism as an appropriate reaction. The *Mail*, praising "the great British devotion to this most hallowed of our summer institutions", claimed that "a little patriotism goes a long way".

The *Telegraph*, complaining that "the last surviving British player" had not been scheduled to appear on the most prestigious court, declared that "other considerations, such as rankings, should have come second to patriotic and public feeling". 'Public feeling' in this context was to be understood as indicating 'our' feeling; the 'patriotic considerations' were 'ours'; other countries and other patriotisms did not come into this. 'Our' world and 'our' patriotism were deictically on centre court.

That day offered a whole range of sporting options for flag-waving. The European athletics championship had finished the previous day in Rome. Headlines, whether in tabloids or broadsheets, told how the brave British (men) had achieved a battling second place by virtue of their performance in the final relay event. "That's Relay Great, Lads" headlined the *Sun*. The text declared that "Britain staged an epic last-gasp cavalry charge . . . our athletes began looking for a miracle", and so on. The *Mirror* headlined: "British heroes are pipped". And there was more stuff about "the brave Brits". Who pipped the battling Brits was of less account than the deeds of 'our' heroes. The victorious Russian teams (men and women) were scarcely news, not being heroes. The broadsheets were little different. The *Independent*'s main athletics headline was "Jackson's flying start provides the life for Britain". The *Guardian*'s was "Britain make a bold effort to rebuild Rome in a day". The subheading was: "John Rodda sees the men's team finish second, only four points behind Russia with a spirited recovery in the Olympic Stadium". As far as presentation goes, the Russians finish many points behind *the* men ('our', British men). British women were even further behind in terms of 'our' interest. Russian women were all but invisible.

There were other British heroes to admire on that day. The British rugby union team had beaten the New Zealand team in Wellington. In a series of three matches, this was to prove the sole British victory, interspersed between two defeats. The reactions to this solitary win were not understated: "Mirror Sport Salutes Britain's Rugby Heroes" (*Mirror*); "Pride of Lions points towards place in history" (*The Times*). The *Guardian* declared that "it would be difficult to overestimate the importance of the Wellington win". The match was a 'win', not a 'defeat'. The choice of words assumes that the reader will take the British (not New Zealand, nor neutral) perspective. This was the unmarked, and thereby 'natural', option.

The *Guardian* deserves careful attention. Its politics are the most liberal of the British quality press, as it presents itself as a voice of enlightenment and fairness. It frequently distances itself from the vulgar chauvinism of the tabloids, while worrying whether "we are witnessing the tabloiding of Britain" (*Guardian*, 15 February 1994). As was shown in Chapter 3, the paper follows the common-sense practice of associating nationalism with extreme 'others'. Yet, its sports pages reproduce the typical British focus, inviting readers to celebrate 'our' victories and to salute 'our' heroes. The 'Wellington win' was displayed prominently, whilst only brief mention was given to the rugby match between South Africa and France, which took place at the same time. The *Guardian*'s rowing correspondent discussed "Britain's hopes" in the Henley regatta. The *Guardian* even introduced a nationalist dimension into its racing report: "Hopes of a British success in the group two Sea World International Stakes were dashed . . .". The reporter does not mention any other national hopes. Only British hopes are presented, just as newspapers that day had carried on their front pages stories about 'hopes' for the jailed British men in Iraq. These hopes are disembodied: no one is identified as doing the hoping. The hopes are presented as if existing in some universalized and objectified space against the foreshortened horizon of 'our' universe.

It might be objected that the Day Survey was not conducted on a typical day, as far as sporting flags were concerned. After all, it was summertime, when many sporting activities, such as the Wimbledon tennis fortnight, are scheduled. Also, the day was a Monday, when newspapers can report on a weekend of sport. In addition, Britain is a country in which sport has been culturally important in the past 150 years; indeed, many of the major, organized sports of today's world originated in nineteenth-century Britain. If, as C.L.R. James points out, sport is part of cultural and political history, then the specific sorts of flag-wavings to be found in the British national press cannot be presumed to be world-wide. On the other hand, the general ethos of international sporting tournaments, by definition, crosses national boundaries: Olympic Games, World Cups, Wimbledons and so on, are global events, part of a global culture.

Perhaps, other places, at other times of the year and times of the week, might have produced only the merest hint of flag-waving on the sporting pages, although the evidence suggests that is unlikely (O'Donnell, 1994). Detailed monitoring would resolve the issue. On the other hand, it should be said that there are always international sporting events taking place, about to take place or having just taken place. Sport is not something peripheral to the contemporary world; there are regular, heavily sponsored and commercialized sporting tournaments the world over. As Elias and Dunning (1986) have argued, leisure and pastimes have been deeply affected by the development of sport in the modern age. The sports pages in newspapers are not optional extras, which are included only on Mondays or on other days when there are major tournaments to report. There are always sports pages, and these are never left empty. Every day, the world over, millions upon millions of men scan these pages, sharing in defeats and victories, feeling at home in this world of waved flags.

### Sport, War and Masculinity

One has to ask what is the significance of the daily flag-waving, such as that revealed in the Day Survey? The issue of masculinity is clearly important. The sports pages are men's pages, although they are not presented as such. They appear as pages for all the nation, like the British pub was presented as an institution for all the British. On foreign fields, the men win their trophies, or lose their honour, doing battle on the nation's behalf. The readers, mainly men, are invited to see these male exploits in terms of the whole homeland, and, thus, men's concerns are presented as if defining the whole national honour.

The parallel between sport and warfare seems obvious, yet it is difficult to specify precisely the nature of the connection. At first sight, it might appear that sport is a benign reproduction of war. It is easy – all too easy – to see the regular circuses of international sport as substitutes for warfare. Where nations once fought for real, now they sublimate their aggressive energies into struggles for ascendancy on the playing field (Eriksen, 1993, p. 111). The sports pages, in inviting us readers to wave flags, echo the language of warfare. Frequently, the metaphors of weaponry (firing, shooting, attacking) are employed (Sherrard, 1993). If sport is a sublimation, then the flag-waving is a safety-valve, draining away masculine, aggressive energies and making the world a more peaceable place.

However, one should be sceptical of such a comforting thought. The voluminous evidence about television and violence does not suggest that 'aggressive energies' operate in such a way (Berkowitz, 1993; Cumberbatch and Howitt, 1989). Moreover, the links between sports and politics ensure that the former is not merely a symbolic replacement for the latter. Umberto Eco, with due irony, suggests that "sports debate (I mean the sports shows, the talk about it, the talk about the journalists who talk about it) is the easiest substitute for political debate" (1987, p. 170). But, sport does not confine itself to the playing field and its marked territory in the newspapers. It intrudes upon political discourse. Politicians frequently use sporting metaphors, including those which echo warfare (Shapiro, 1990). Nixon was particularly fond of boxing analogies (Beattie, 1988). Margaret Thatcher preferred the language of cricket, often declaring that she was "batting for Britain", and claiming during the last days of her premiership that she "was still at the crease, though the bowling has been pretty hostile of late" (Young, 1993; see also *Guardian*, Editorial, 26 July 1994). The US President traditionally opens the baseball season, throwing the first pitch.

Politicians can, when waving the national flag, advocate sporting policies, so that the flag-waving of sport itself becomes another flag to be waved. John Major, addressing his party's conference in 1994, announced a policy to put competitive sport "back at the heart of school life": he declared sport to be "part of the British instinct, part of our character" (p. 7, text of speech issued by Conservative Central Office, 14 October 1994). Also, as Eco implied, sport can replace political debate within politics, thereby contributing to a dangerous politics of 'us' and 'them', which seems beyond the scope of debate. In Italy, Silvio Berlusconi, the media entrepreneur and owner of Italy's most successful professional football side, campaigned successfully for the presidency, using the symbols associated with support for the national football team. His television commercials culminated in the football chant 'Forza Italia'.

Having triumphed in the election, the new president introduced fascists into his coalition government.

Sport does not merely echo warfare, but it can provide the symbolic models for the understanding of war. When the British troops returned victoriously from the Falklands War, they were met at the harbour by crowds, swaying, chanting and waving flags, as if they were celebrating a football team returning with a silver trophy. During the war, cartoonists had frequently depicted the contest as a football match (Aulich, 1992). Those engaged in fighting, such as the US pilots in the Vietnamese War, often use the metaphors of the playing field to make sense of their experiences (Rosenberg, 1993). In this way, war is understood in terms of something more familiar.

Of course, the issue of gender cannot be ignored. It is men who largely read the daily flag-waving accounts of the sports pages. Although the creation of the nation-state may have brought women into political life on a scale hitherto unknown (Colley, 1992, chapter 6), citizenship still is often gendered in the details of its entitlements and duties (Lister, 1994; Williams, 1987; Yuval-Davies, 1993, 1994). Above all, it is men who are expected to answer the state's ultimate call to arms; they are the ones who will pursue the conduct of the war, shooting and being shot, raping, but not being raped, in the cause of the homeland (Jones, 1994). As Jane Bethke Elshtain argues, the compelling theme driving young men to the battlefield is sacrifice, rather than aggression: "The young man goes to war not so much to kill as to die, to forfeit his particular body for that of the larger body, the body politic" (1993, p. 160).

The political crisis which leads to the war can be quickly created, but the willingness to sacrifice cannot be. There must be prior rehearsals and reminders so that, when the fateful occasion arises, men, and women, know how they are expected to behave. Daily, there is a banal preparation. On the sporting pages, as men scan for the results of the favoured team, they read of the deeds of other men doing battle, in the cause of that larger body, the team. And often the team is the nation, battling for honour against foreigners. Then, an unspecifiable added value of honour is at stake.

In the Day Survey, personal sacrifice in the cause of the nation was applauded on the sports pages. An athlete (described as a "reluctant hero", and male, of course) is reported as saying "when your country needs you . . . how can you say No" (*Mail*). The same paper reported the rugby hero, who, despite pain and injury, carried on to fight for the cause of national honour against New Zealand. The "Anglicised Welshman at the heart of the Wellington campaign" (a description which itself echoes military history), appeared afterwards with "one eye blackened, one knee strapped, hand and cheekbone swollen". He declared: "This was a do-or-die situation. The tour had to be saved."

Scanning the cricket, football or baseball results is not like reading the speech of a finance minister or of 'Tokyo's reaction' to a raid on Baghdad.

No sense of duty attends the reading of sports reports. The sporting pages are, to adapt a phrase from Barthes (1975), texts of pleasure. Day after day, millions of men seek their pleasures on these pages, admiring heroism in the national cause, enjoying prose which intertextually echoes warfare. Such pleasures cannot be innocent. If nationhood is being flagged, then the routine reminders might also be rehearsals; the echoes of the past cannot be discounted as preparations for future time. Perhaps we – or our sons, nephews or grandsons – might respond one day, with ready enthusiasm, or with dutiful regret, on hearing that our country needs us to do-or-die. The call will already be familiar; the obligations have been primed; their words have long been installed in the territory of our pleasure.

**Concluding Confession**

At the start of the chapter, I wrote that, such is the spread of banal nationalism, the analysis requires a confessional tone. Traces of nationalism and flag-waving are not merely to be found in others. Analysts, too, should confess. The language of confession demands a switch from the plural to the singular. I read the sporting pages, turning to them more quickly than is appropriate, given the news of suffering on other pages. Regularly I answer the invitation to celebrate national sporting triumphs. If a citizen from the homeland runs quicker or jumps higher than foreigners, I feel pleasure. Why, I do not know. I want the national team to beat the teams of other countries, scoring more goals, runs or whatever. International matches seem so much more important than domestic ones: there is an extra thrill of competition, with something indefinable at stake. Daily, I scan the papers for yet more scores, thoughtless of the future to which this routine activity might be pointing. I do not ask myself why I do it. I just do it, habitually.

In one sense, the confessional is not fully personal. It is offered in the knowledge that the confessional 'I' could be multiplied many millionfold: the guilt, not being mine alone, hardly seems like guilt. Benedict Anderson (1983) suggested that a feeling of national community is produced by the knowledge that all over the nation people are performing the daily ritual of reading the same newspaper. But it cannot be that simple. Men know (should they wish to be aware of the information) that other men are reading the same sporting results. However, the ritual can reproduce division, rather than an overall sense of sporting community.

Anderson is surely correct in stressing the importance of newspapers in the reproduction of nationality. They operate directly, through their messages, stereotypes and deictics, rather than by setting up the possibility of what Freud called 'secondary identification', or a perceived feeling of similarity. In this respect, the pleasure of waving the sporting flag is not the sole matter to be admitted. Another personal confession, which is also impersonal, is in order: I read the 'home' news with greater interest; I do not object to its greater coverage; I expect it habitually. These faults I share with others, both male and female.

The flagging is not confined to the sporting pages, just as the nation does not disappear between moments of collective celebration. The national ground extends into other sections of the news. Nor is the sport confined to the sporting pages. The Wimbledon tennis tournament is virtually unique among major British sporting occasions in attracting equal, if not greater, interest from women as from men. Significantly, the new battling British hero, who managed to avoid early defeat, was much in evidence in the inside pages, photographed in a variety of handsome, non-sporting poses. "Girl fans court Andy the Wimbledon hunk", announced the *Mirror* on a news page; the British players were being "besieged by women who love the way they've shaped up in the tournament". If men are encouraged to emulate the national heroes, women are invited to love them.

I personally find my way around a paper that addresses its readers (male and female) as members of the homeland; even 'the women's page' does so. We, the readers, readily accept the deixis of homeland, and the apartheid of news into 'home' and foreign. We feel at home in a paper which gives more attention to news located within the homeland's borders. This is important, because, however patriarchal the nation-state and however much the actual business of the battle-field is masculine, national-ism is not confined to males. Men may be called upon to sacrifice their bodies, but women are to prepare themselves to sacrifice their sons and husbands; and in the First World War, the sacrifice of the older brother took on special significance and grief (Woollacott, 1993). As Elshtain (1987, 1993) has emphasized, wars could not be fought without the contributions of women as patriotic mothers and carers – without women answering the call to love the masculine warriors.

During the Gulf War, opinion polls revealed high levels of support from American women, who often showed their care for 'our boys' by outwardly displaying yellow ribbons (Boose, 1993). As Conover and Sapiro (1993) report from their study of the polls, there was little difference between men and women's support for the War, nor, more generally, in their support for US military spending. Most strikingly, the authors report that "feminists were as likely to support the war effort as non-feminists" (p. 1095). If women, including those with feminist attitudes, give such support in moments of national crisis, they, too, must be primed to live in a world of national loyalties. The banal reminders of the homeliness of the homeland are not just addressed to, and tacitly absorbed by, men. The daily deixis of the homeland crosses the divides of gender. 'We' all are daily reminded that 'we' are 'here', living at home in 'our' precious homeland.

Nationhood is not something remote in contemporary life, but it is present in 'our' little words, in homely discourses which we take for granted. Liberals, socialists and feminists, whatever ideals for the future are entertained, cannot pretend to a present absent-mindedness which forgets which is 'their' nation. We, too, inhabit this world of nations. We, too, are being primed – or rather we participate in the priming of ourselves. Our words, also, reflect the conditions of their utterance. Newspapers are not to be blamed as the sole transmitters of 'home-centrism'. The banality of nationalism extends into analysis. This chapter has looked at the press of the author's homeland. There has only been passing reference to what happens elsewhere. The analysis has been grounded in a homeland, even as a universal audience is presumably addressed.

The constant flaggings ensure that, whatever else is forgotten in a world of information overload, we do not forget our homelands. The plebiscite, whether through habitual deixis or sporting cheers, reproduces the nation-state. If we are being routinely primed for the dangers of the future, then this is not a priming which tops up a reservoir of aggressive energy. It is a form of reading and watching, of understanding and of taking for granted. It is a form of life in which 'we' are constantly invited to relax, at home, within the homeland's borders. This form of life is the national identity, which is being renewed continually, with its dangerous potentials appearing so harmlessly homely.

# 6

# Postmodernity and Identity

The extent of the banal flagging, described in the previous chapter, may come as a surprise. Increasingly, it is becoming commonplace to hear that the nation-state is in decline. Many commentators are arguing that the contemporary world is postmodern rather than modern. Nation-states, they argue, were a product of the modern era and are now becoming outmoded. If nationalism and national identity are both adjuncts of the nation-state, then they too belong to the fast disappearing world of modernity. This change from modernity to postmodernity has, so it is claimed, important political consequences. The old politics of nationhood are giving way to new politics of identity. The nationalist consciousness with its emphasis on boundaries and the homeland is supposedly passé. Banal flagging of nationhood, therefore, is not something that is to be expected in this postmodern world.

The thesis of postmodernism represents an important analysis of contemporary times. It proposes that a matrix of economic, cultural and psychological changes is occurring in the world. As will be argued in this chapter, the thesis, however, overlooks the banality of nationalism. In discussing nationalism and postmodernity, it is necessary to refocus attention. When the previous chapter documented the banality of national identity, it did so by concentrating its Day Survey on British newspapers. Britain may not provide the best register of portents for the postmodern future. As a nation-state, Britain's world role belongs to the earlier age of modernity. Geopolitically, Britain has become a bit player, flapping about indecisively on the edge of the European Union. The nation on whose sphere of influence the sun never sets is now the United States.

Many of the ideas about postmodernism are currently being developed in the United States. However, it is arguable whether the thesis of postmodernity has come to terms with US nationalism. Part of the problem, as with orthodox sociology, is the tendency to equate nationalism with its 'hot', rather than banal, varieties. But it is not just a matter of definitions. Perhaps one of the most interesting questions to ask about postmodernist analyses is 'how can nationhood appear so invisible within the world's strongest nation – a nation, which continues to display and salute its flag?'

In attempting to throw light upon this question, an earlier argument should be borne in mind. Chapter 4 suggested that international themes have always been part of the nationalist consciousness. It is misleading to think that nationalist and internationalist habits of thought are necessarily in opposition to each other. They can be, and frequently are, intermixed. One could expect this intermixture to be especially marked in the case of a nation bidding for global hegemony. What appears to be international will also be national and vice versa. This is an important consideration for the thesis of postmodernity. Part of the thesis maintains that a global, transnational culture is developing. If this culture has a national provenance, then what appears to be global may not be quite so transnational. The global culture, bearing the marks of its national heritage, may be flagging 'America'. An identity of identities – national and global – will be claimed. 'America' may not be flagged as a particular place: it will be universalized as the world. As will be suggested, in postmodern times the national flags have not been hauled down, or transmuted into a pastiche of ironic decorations. Today, the United States flags its presence so often and so globally that it almost seems invisible.

## The Thesis of Postmodernism and the Global Culture

In the past 15 years, there has been an outpouring of words within the social sciences on the topic of postmodernity. Writers from a variety of academic disciplines and theoretical standpoints have taken a bewildering range of stances. There are those who have welcomed the postmodern spirit; and there are those who condemn it.

Postmodernism has been variously described as conservative, radical, conservatively radical and radically conservative. There is uncertainty when the age of modernity is supposed to have ended and postmodernity begun (see, Murdock, 1993, for a critique). Some analysts pronounce postmodernity to be a decisive rupture with previous times; others claim that modernity has gradually dribbled into its post-phase. Jean-François Lyotard (1984), in a major work which popularized the concept of 'postmodernity', even suggested that modernity was always postmodern. Despite all the differences of interpretation, theorists, who claim that there is a vital difference between the age of modernity and that of postmodernity, share several broad areas of agreement. They tend to agree that by the end of the twentieth century there has been a series of economic, cultural and psychological changes which are associated with a growing 'globalization' (Lash, 1990). As the twentieth century dawned, the climate of the times was still largely modernist. It was then possible to have faith in progress, and to believe that science would produce a bright, new world of unambiguous truth. Now, by the end of the century, the hopes of the modern movement seem naive; doubts and ambiguities abound.

Roland Robertson, who has written extensively on globalization and postmodernity, claims that the heyday of the nation-state was from 1880 to 1920 (for example, Robertson, 1990, 1992). Many of the states that were to enjoy sovereignty during that period had been created in the previous hundred or so years. A modernist spirit had attended their creation. One of the essential characteristics of modernity was vital to state-making: the intolerance of difference. The new states were to be centralized polities, which flattened traditional regional, cultural, linguistic and ethnic differences. As Bauman has claimed, "nationalism was a programme of unification, and a postulate of homogeneity" (1992b, p. 683). Unity within the bordered territory was the state's goal. Official languages were imposed upon a mosaic of speech patterns (see above, Chapter 2). Citizens, with their way of thinking moulded by a common education, would use the same currency, travel on the state's highways and be expected to show unequivocal loyalty to the nation.

The result was not a uniform world, but a world of limited, independent uniformities. The quest for uniformity involves the imposition of firm boundaries, whether these are boundaries between truth and error, science and nonsense, rationality and irrationality. The world of nation-states, being constructed in the modernist mood, is a world of boundaries. States, following a general uniform pattern, were divided one from another, as nationals and foreigners were clearly and legally demarcated. Psychologically, the modernist world of the nation-state resembles the state of mind described by Henri Tajfel's (1981) theory of categorical judgement: differences between members of categories are minimized and differences between categories are exaggerated. This boundary-consciousness represents, according to the thesis of postmodernity, a decidedly modern cast of mind and modern form of life.

In the days of modernity, or so it is argued, nations were economically and politically independent. Industries and capital were nationally based, and, in consequence, governments were able to exert direct influence over the economic life of nations. Classical sociology, as was argued in Chapter 3, contains a vision of the world as containing separate, bounded 'societies'. This image, according to Wallerstein (1987), describes the world-system of the late nineteenth century. Since then, however, there has been a vast internationalization of capital. Multinational corporations, which transfer monies and products around the globe, have grown. As financial transactions have become increasingly internationalized, so the economies of nation-states have become globally interrelated. Since the 1940s, nation-states, as Nigel Harris observes, have been obliged "to unwind much of the structure of economic nationalism and to free capital", in order to create economic growth (1990, p. 250). The development of global communication systems has accelerated this internationalization of capital (Schiller, 1993). The flow of information across electronic networks knows of no national boundaries. Capital can be transferred across the globe through the keying of computers in Tokyo or New York (Harvey, 1989). If finance is transferred globally, then so is labour, albeit with more physical and psychological difficulty. Nevertheless, the global economy is characterized by massive migration across national boundaries (Castles and Kosack, 1985; Cohen, 1992).

All these factors have combined, so it is argued, to diminish the autonomy and stability of the nation-state. It is no wonder that states are combining to form supra-national economic and political organizations, such as the European Union or even the United Nations. Held suggests that one of the chief aspects of "the contemporary global system lies in the vast array of international regimes and organisations (of which Nato is only one type) which have been established to manage whole areas of trans-national activity (trade, the oceans, space and so on)" (1989, p. 196). In 1905 there were 176 international, non-governmental organizations; by 1984 there were 4,615, according to Held's calculations. Some of these organizations make direct demands upon sovereign nations. The International Monetary Fund, in loaning funds to hard-pressed governments, will often insist that those governments reduce public expenditure on welfare programmes and devalue their currency. Nation-states may still exist in this global world but their sovereignty is compromised.

A number of theorists contend that the economic conditions of late capitalism are producing postmodern, rather than modernist, forms of sensibility, which are very different from the old boundary-consciousness of modernism (Hall, 1991a, 1991b; Harvey, 1989; Jameson, 1991). Grand 'meta-narratives', which aim to establish clear boundaries between truth and falsity belong to the modernist past, as does confidence in the benefits of science and the inevitability of progress (Lyotard, 1984). According to Jean Baudrillard, the very possibilities for 'truth' and 'reality' have been undermined; the contemporary world is marked by the electronic relay of images, which are simulacra of other images, rather than representations of an external 'reality' (Baudrillard, 1983). In a world where information circulates through 'cool' electronic transfers, there is only 'hyperreality', not truth and falsity. This hyperreality looks the same in Los Angeles and Tokyo, London and New York. The vast distances of previous ages have disappeared, as information incessantly pulsates across the globe in nano-seconds.

On one level, the logic of late capitalism is dictating a homogenized culture. No longer is the world a patchwork of bounded, national cultures, which claim to be uniquely different. George Orwell, writing during the Second World War, could believe that anyone returning to England from a foreign country would have "immediately the sensation of breathing a different air". So much would be noticeably different even in the first few minutes: "The beer is bitterer, the coins heavier, the grass greener, the advertisements more blatant" (1962, p. 64). Orwell's England, now, seems to belong to another world: Today, the traveller is likely to land at an international airport resembling the one just left. The cafeterias will sell 'continental lager'; the advertisements will proclaim their international products; and the coinage has shrunk to standardized dimensions. Britain is only one place where this homogenization has occurred. McDonald's and Coca-Cola are internationally available; so are Nintendo games and the iconic representations of international stars. Across the 'global village', there is a similarity of experience. The world becomes nightly available on the television screen:

> The whole world can watch the Olympic Games, the World Cup, the fall of a dictator, a political summit, a deadly tragedy . . . while mass tourism, films made in spectacular locations, make a wide range of simulated or vicarious experiences of what the world contains available to many people. (Harvey, 1989, p. 293)

The thesis of postmodernism suggests that life in the contemporary world is marked by a banal globalism. Daily the 'global village' is flagged, and this banal globalism is supplanting the conditions of banal nationalism.

## The Declining, Fragmenting Nation-State

There is another important theme in the thesis of postmodernism. The forces of globalization are not producing cultural homogeneity in an absolute manner. They may be eroding differences between national cultures, but they are also multiplying differences within nations. Theorists of the postmodern emphasize the importance of consumption in the postmodern experience (Featherstone, 1990, 1991; Sherry, 1991). The consumer is expected to buy a variety of products; these express so many styles that boundaries are constantly traversed. The consumer, especially in the rich countries of the West, can eat Chinese food on one day, followed by French or Malayan the next. Meals can combine different national cuisines, just as clothing can mix 'ethnic' styles. An English family can decide to have 'traditional English roast beef', in exactly the same way that they can decide upon any other marketed exotica.

Patterns of consumption are not strictly national. Consumers can no longer imagine themselves as part of a national community, all purchasing the same type of article, which is marketed within the nation's borders and which represents a distinctive national culture. Instead, there is the development of niche-marketing, aimed at particular groups of consumers, often defined in terms of 'life-style', rather than class. Consumers can create their own identities through their changing patterns of consumption. Moreover, these identities cross boundaries of state. 'Yuppies', 'punks', 'thirty-somethings' can be found throughout Europe, north America, Australia and, even, Japan. In the communications industries, 'narrow-casting' is replacing 'broad-casting'. Television programmes are not aimed at a general national audience, but at specialized segments, whose particular patterns of consumption are targeted by advertisers; at the same time globalized, satellite broadcasting is developing so that programmes are shown internationally (Morley, 1992; Schlesinger, 1991). In consequence, the nationally imagined identity is diminishing in importance, as compared with imagined 'life-style' groups of consumers. The result is that the processes of globalization, which are diminishing differences and spaces between nations, are also fragmenting the imagined unity within those nations.

The state, declining in its powers, is no longer able to impose a uniform sense of identity. With the pressure for national uniformity removed, a variety of other forces is released. Within the national territory, multiple narratives and new identities are emerging. Local, ethnic and gender identities have become the site for postmodern politics (Roosens, 1989). It is as if the nation-state is being fatally assailed from above and below. The hurricanes of globalization swirl in the skies above, whilst from below, the national soil is fissured by seismic faults. The two disasters are linked:

> In effect nationalism, the tendency towards centralization that accompanied the state formation process, in which attempts were made to eliminate differences in order to create a unified integrating culture for the nation, has given way to de-centralization and the acknowledgement of local, regional and subcultural differences in the Western world. (Featherstone, 1991, p. 142)

The result is that the sovereignty of the nation-state is collapsing under pressure from global and local forces. Economic necessities are compelling states to surrender parts of their sovereignty to supra-national organizations. The European Union is a good example: no longer do the parliaments of the member states have the powers which they formally had. National identity no longer enjoys its preeminence as the psychological identity that claims the ultimate loyalty of the individual. Instead, it must compete with other identities on a free market of identities.

In addition to supra-national identities, there are sub-national identities to challenge the state's claims. The very differences and attachments which the state sought to erase in its modernist quest for uniformity are now being revived. Some of these newly revived identities are constructed in the image of nationhood. Smaller homelands within the territory of the existing state are being imagined. Separatist movements, whether in Quebec, Scotland or the Balkans, are attaining the sort of support in the 1980s and 1990s which they never attracted 30 years earlier. There is evidence that a sense of place is important as a component of separatist support: adherents define the nation which is to be created as a place (a homeland), rather than as a network of 'primordial ties' (Linz, 1985). These homelands tend to be of ever-decreasing size, for each new homeland is being carved out of a portion of an existing homeland.

If new, smaller nations succeed in gaining their independence, they do not enjoy the sovereignty which nations were said to possess in the heyday of nationalism. These new states must seek admittance to supranational organizations. In addition, they are threatened by the very sub-national processes which permitted their own birth. Having come into existence through processes of national fragmentation, they are liable to be threatened by the imagining of other identities, claiming their own even smaller homeland space. The USSR embodied Russian hegemony over the other 14 legally constituted republics, with over a hundred 'nationalities' also legally recognized (Breuilly, 1992). Just as the republics have moved for national independence, so some of the 'nationalities' now move against the newly independent republics. Ukrainians find Tartar minorities, claiming the right to a Crimean Tartar Republic. Russia, now constituted as a nation-state, faces separatist movements in Chechenia, Tatarstan, Tuva and Bashkortostan. Czechoslovakia, after a brief period of autonomy from the Soviet influence, has split into two. And as for Yugoslavia, it is unclear how many of the new small states will fragment further, as minorities claim their right to self-determination. Even before independence is achieved, signs of fragmentation can be apparent. The Quebecqois in Canada see their own arguments for national independence being turned against themselves by the Cree (Ignatieff, 1993).

It is as if the whole business of nationhood is being unravelled. At each turn, it seems that a group separates from a state, to declare a new state in its own name and then minority groups within the new state claim national status. An infinite regress beckons, with states fragmenting into infinitely smaller units. These units, in their turn, cannot be culturally isolated entities. They are plugged into the vast networks of information, which respect no natural, political, or linguistic boundaries. Thus, the thesis of postmodernism proclaims a vision of a future world. In this world, no longer is the national territory *the* place from which identities, attachments and patterns of life spring. The order of the national world gives way to a new mediaevalism. The binary language of electronics is like a new Latin, binding together the knowledgeable across political kingdoms. In place of the bordered, national state, a multiplicity of *terrae* are emerging. And those, who see their identities in terms of gender or sexual orientation, are, like monks before them, bound by no earthly *terra*, restricted by no mere sense of place. Thus, a new sensibility – a new psychology – emerges in global times.

### Depthless and Depth Psychology

The postmodern image is a beguiling one. It seems to describe trends which are apparent in the contemporary world and it appears to give a historic significance to these trends. Given the popularity of the thesis, it is little wonder that the decline of the nation-state is being treated as a truism, an obvious fact in a postmodern world of few facts. The thesis proclaims the world of postmodernity to be marked by new modes of apprehension and forms of identity. Unfortunately, many analysts of contemporary culture use a very abstract sort of psychology. Few actually get round to talking to ordinary people to see how so-called subjects of postmodernity actually think and feel (Brunt, 1992; Morley, 1992). This is a pity, because the thesis of postmodernity rests upon important psychological assumptions.

Two very different psychological themes are discernible in the broad thesis of globalization. On the one hand, there are claims about a new postmodern psyche, which differs from the old modern psyche. This postmodern psyche is at home playing with the free market of identities. In contrast, there is the not-so-new (and not-so-cool) psyche of 'hot', nationalism. Globalism is said to be producing nationalist reactions, in which there is little spirit of playful irony. As was discussed in Chapter 3, a number of observers, surveying ethnic conflicts and the rise of neo-fascism, have the sense of the repressed returning: an older, fiercer psychology of identity is being unleashed.

Sometimes there is a reluctance to call these unleashed identities 'nationalist'. The left-wing British 'think-tank', Demos, produced a widely publicized report, claiming that "after the Cold War, a new politics is emerging". This new politics is gaining ground across the world: "The surface may be different – language, colour, tribe, caste, clan or region – but the subterranean source is the same: an assertion of cultural identity." The report specifically declared that "tribalism holds sway in the Balkans, Belgium, Burundi and Belfast" (Vincent Cable, 'Insiders and Outsiders', *Independent on Sunday*, 24 January 1994). Although mentioning the identities of 'tribe', caste, religion etc., the report does not mention the identities of nation. The nation is presumed to be in decline, withering towards its point-zero: tribalism, rather than nationalism, is returning.

The two psychological themes relate directly to the claim that the nation-state is in decline. There is the global psychology, which strikes the nation from above, withering loyalties with a free play of identities. And, then, there is the hot psychology of caste or tribe, which hits at the soft underbelly of the state with a powerfully intolerant commitment and emotional ferocity. How these two psychologies are related is unsure. But taken together, they seem to leave little room for the sort of banal national loyalties which were seen to be daily flagged in the previous chapter.

To begin with, the global psychology can be considered. The thesis of postmodernity suggests the new postmodern culture signifies a change in psychic tone. Frederic Jameson argues that the culture of late capitalism possesses a constant "depthlessness", for, today, "depth is replaced by surface". Postmodernism often achieves this depthlessness through pastiche, which is "one of the most significant features or practices in postmodernism today" (1991, p. 12). Pastiche is not parody, according to Jameson, because it does not have an ulterior motive, or an underlying programme of truth. Instead, postmodernist products – whether of art, clothing or cuisine – mix styles in a constantly altering pastiche. The result is a culture which is without fixed points or uniform truths and which speaks with a multiplicity of voices (Bauman, 1992a). Given that this culture erodes boundaries, there is a loss of sense of place (Giddens, 1990; Meyrowitz, 1986).

The depthlessness of culture is accompanied by a psychological lack of depth. Psychological attachments have become weaker. Jameson, for example, writes of the "waning of affect" (1991, p. 10). In place of an autonomous ego, which invests 'truths' and 'fixed identities' with an emotional force, there is a shifting sense of depthless selves – a continual 'cognitive mapping' rather than a deep emotional attachment to a few fixed points (Jameson, 1991). If, as has been claimed, "our identity has become synonymous with patterns of consumption" (Miller, 1986, p. 165), then individuals no longer have a firm, centred sense of their self, but the postmodern consumer is liable to buy whole series of identities. As fashions change, and as different styles of clothing are worn – or as new products enter the market and old ones are replaced – so the ego takes on yet another identity (Tseelon, 1991). The autonomous ego belongs to the past: the individual in the postmodern world, like the cultural climate of the times, "is now fragmented, dispersed and decentered" (Michael, 1994, p. 384; see also Lather, 1992, 1994).

Kenneth Gergen's *The Saturated Self* provides a deeply sensitive and insightful account of the psychology of the de-centred, postmodern self. According to Gergen, the cultural conditions of postmodernity are repro-duced psychologically. People in the postmodern world are saturated with information and relationships. They have no clear sense of self, for the self is filled with the voices of others. Gergen refers to this as 'multiphrenia', or "the splitting of the individual into a multiplicity of self-investments" (1991, pp. 73–4). For Gergen, the condition is filled with possibilities: "As the moorings of the substantial self are slowly left behind and one begins to experience the raptures of pastiche personality, the dominant indulgence becomes the persona – the image as presented" (p. 156).

The pastiche personality differs from the patriotic psyche of former times. No particular identity is to be accorded a special psychic investment, in the way that the patriot invested the homeland with a depth of emotional feeling. Any such investment would disrupt the ever-changing carnival of pastiche. Indeed, the cosmopolitan individual is thought to inhabit an electronic, global world, rather than a single homeland. In consequence, the conditions for national loyalty have been undermined. Accordingly, writes Gergen, in the postmodern world "the very idea of independent or sovereign nations is thrown into question" (p. 254).

Not everyone, however, is able to enjoy the raptures of the pastiche personality. The ironic detachment and the shifting depthlessness of the de-centred ego ill describe the fascist thug or the ethnic cleanser, both of whom are being washed up on the beach of 'tribalism' in the postmodern world. A number of writers have suggested that some people feel lost in the fluid conditions of the postmodern world: such people retreat psycholo-gically from the possibilities offered by postmodernism. The collapse of old boundaries, the loss of certainty and the blurring of a sense of place have caused what Giddens (1990) terms 'ontological insecurity'. Melucci (1989) believes that such insecurity is built into the contemporary condition, for the person today is a 'nomad of the mind', living with a sense of homelessness. As Bauman (1992b) suggests, the postmodern citizen is a nomad wandering between unconnected places.

The dispossessed and insecure cannot bear this nomadic condition of homelessness: for them there is no rapture in ambiguity. They are driven to seek secure identities, often regressing to an earlier stage of development.

Myths of nation, tribe and religion seem to hold out the hope of psychological wholeness, offering the fragmented, disorientated person the promise of psychic security. As Julia Kristeva writes, "the values crisis and the fragmentation of individuals have reached the point where we no longer know what we are and take shelter, to preserve a token of personality, under the most massive, regressive common denominators: national origins and the faith of our forebears" (1993, p. 2).

Anthony Giddens (1985, 1987) makes a similar point about regressive reactions to the ontological insecurity of contemporary times. As was mentioned in Chapter 3, Giddens suggests that people often react against ontological insecurity with 'regressive forms of object-identification'. They identify with, and invest great emotional energy in, the symbols of nationhood and the promise of strong leadership. Giddens' argument, and, indeed, that of Kristeva, resemble Erich Fromm's classic, psychological explanation of fascism. In *Fear of Freedom*, Fromm (1942) claimed that capitalism has destroyed the fixed identities of traditional societies. People have been freed to create their own identities in ways which were impossible hitherto. Some people are scared by this freedom. Turning away from the uncertainties of the present, they regressively yearn for the security of a solid identity. So, they are drawn towards the simplicities of nationalist and fascist propaganda.

Two psychological portraits are contained in such visions of the post-modern world: the portrait of the depthless psyche, bobbing along on the postmodern tide; and the regressive psyche, struggling against the flow. In many respects, these two portraits represent polar opposites. Although theorists of postmodernism tend not to detail exactly what a 'decentred ego' is, their image of the postmodern psyche appears as an almost exact mirror reversal of a well-known psychological type: the authoritarian personality, as described by Adorno et al. (1950). In fact, Adorno and his co-workers built upon Fromm's insights about the psychological origins of fascism. Unable to handle ambivalence, authoritarians need unambiguous truths and clearly demarcated hierarchies. They seek the security of a clear world-view in which evil 'others' can be hated and a pure 'us' loved. Recently, there is evidence that supporters of fundamentalist Christian sects in north America and members of the fascist Front National in France show the characteristics of authoritarianism (Altemeyer, 1981, 1988; Orfali, 1990).

On practically every count, the decentred, postmodern self, as repre-sented in writings of postmodern theorists, can be contrasted with the portrait of the authoritarian personality.

1   Authoritarians were said to need a serious sense of order and hierarchy; by contrast, postmodernists subvert distinctions and they play with the idea of 'liminality' (Gergen, 1991; Michael, 1992).
2   The authoritarian's psyche is marked by a brittle, emotional intensity; the postmodernist has an ironic, playful detachment.

3  The authoritarian is driven by affect, which dominates cognition, causing the authoritarian to apprehend the world through rigid stereotypes; the postmodernist possesses a shallower psyche, in which affect has waned and cognition (or what Jameson calls 'cognitive mapping') predominates.
4  The authoritarian fixates on a single identity, particularly that of race or nation; by contrast, "postmoderns have no 'investment' in particular groups or identities", but, instead, "the investment is in the turnover of identities" (Michael, 1991, p. 215).
5  The authoritarian's commitment to the beloved ingroup is marked by a deep rejection of outgroups, who are felt to be different from the self; the postmodern person experiences no such divisions for "as consciousness of interdependence expands, so withers the distinction between self and other, mine and yours" (Gergen, 1991, p. 254).

At first sight, the psychological dimensions seem to be falling into place in the thesis of postmodernism. Two contrasting psychologies are indicated: one is making the assault on nationhood from above and the other from below. These psychological assaults match economic ones. The middle is being excluded by an extreme either/or: *either* there are the playful uncertainties of the decentred ego, *or* there are the fierce furies of an ego centred upon a single identity. The banal identity of nationhood is presumed to be withering away along with the nation-state.

And yet, it all appears too neat. The middle has not disappeared. As was argued in the previous chapter, political celebrities in the established democracies continue to address the nation as the nation. Daily the citizens encounter the flagged signs of nationhood. Discourses of national sacrifice still appear as commonplace. An example of their continuing ordinariness can be given. An English father was talking with his family about the British Royal Family. He was the only anti-royalist in his family: he enjoyed arguing with his wife and children on the issue, as he took the shockingly radical stance. Suddenly, in the middle of the conversation, as if to counter an unspoken accusation, this Robespierre of the suburbs declared himself to be "very patriotic". Just because he did not like royalty, don't think, he said, that he would not "fight for my country"; yes, he would "fight to the end for Britain" (for details, see Billig, 1989b, 1992). No one in his family seemed amazed by his outburst. Neither wife nor teenage daughter told him to stop being silly. His utterance was treated as perfectly unexceptionable. How is this possible? How can a man, in the comfort of his suburban sitting-room, and himself with no military record of service, declare a willingness to sacrifice all for his country in an unspecified cause? And how can his family consider the utterance as appropriate? Surely nationhood cannot have withered into insignificance.

Not all identities should be considered as equivalent and interchangeable. Perhaps the postmodern consumer can purchase a bewildering range of identity-styles. Certainly, the commercial structures are in place for the economically comfortable to change styles in the Western world. However, national identity cannot be exchanged like last year's clothes. The anti-royalist father was declaring his national identity *primus inter pares*: he was declaring a commitment over time. One can eat Chinese tomorrow and Turkish the day after; one can even dress in Chinese or Turkish styles. But *being* Chinese or Turkish are not commercially available options. Cosmo-politans and authoritarians alike are constrained by the permanence of national identity.

Another question can be asked: what is the relation between the two psychologies, which supposedly are assaulting the nation-state from their differing directions? Surely, they are not totally separated consciousnesses, belonging to two totally different species of individual. The passions of 'hot' nationalism do not merely indicate that particular homelands continue to have a hold upon the political imagination; they indicate that the universal principle of nationalism – the abstractly expressed right to possess a homeland – also maintains its hold. It is surely too simple to believe that this principle is confined to those who imagine themselves to be dispossessed. Perhaps those, who live in established nations and who take the reproduction of their homeland for granted, assume the principle to be set in place. In this case, the so-called postmodern cast of mind may not be so disdainful of boundaries and place: it may be taking much for granted.

There is a sense of 'as-if' in some versions of the postmodern thesis. It is as if the nation-state had already withered away; as if people's national commitments have been flattened to the level of a consumer choice; as if millions of children in the world's most powerful nation do not daily salute one, and only one, style of flag; as if, at this moment around the globe, vast armies are not practising their battle manoeuvres beneath national colours.

**The State in Global Times**

One major problem with the thesis of postmodernism is that the elements of nationalist consciousness appear to be persisting. As the previous chapter's Day Survey indicated, the sense of the importance of a bounded homeland, together with the distinction between 'us' and 'foreigners', have not disappeared. Moreover, these habits of thinking persist, not as vestiges of a past age, having outlived their function; they are rooted to forms of life, in an era in which the state may be changing, but has not yet withered away. After all, nations still maintain their massive armouries. As Giddens (1990) has commented, there is no Third World with respect to weaponry. And this weaponry remains the property of nations, not individuals nor corporations.

The thesis of postmodernism suggests that nationalism has changed its function. No longer is nationalism a force which creates and reproduces nation-states: it is one of the forces which is destroying nations. Thus, there is a paradox: the more that 'hot' nationalists commit themselves to the ideal of nationhood in the struggles to establish their own particular homelands, the more they hasten the end of nationhood. Because of this position, some theorists seem uneasy about describing today's movements for national independence as genuinely nationalist. As was seen in the British think-tank's report, the very word itself can be avoided. Sometimes the term 'nationalism' is used, but authors imply that this is not proper nationalism. Hobsbawm, predicting the end of nationalism, writes that the world of the next century "will be largely supranational and infranational, but even infranationality, whether or not it dresses itself up in the costume of some mini-nationalism, will reflect the decline of the old nation-state as an operational entity" (1992, p. 191). Even when nationalism appears, it is only 'infranationalism' dressed up: it is not really nationalist. Stuart Hall and David Held claim that "everywhere the nation state . . . is eroded and challenged". Not only is globalization eroding the state from above, but "the rise of regional and local 'nationalisms' are beginning to erode it from below" (1989, p. 183). The authors put nationalism between apostrophes, as if to signal its current forms to be inauthentic.

Zygmunt Bauman, one of the most important and scholarly of sociologists charting postmodernity, argues that the nations being created in the contemporary postmodern world differ so much from the nations created by nationalism in the age of modernity, that the term nation should not properly be applied: "Exit the nation-state, enter the tribe", declares Bauman (1993, p. 141). The new so-called nations lack "viability", because national viability has been generally undermined in the present world; they are too small to be sovereign, and, in any case, state sovereignty is disappearing (1992b, 1993). The rhetoric implies that France and the United States, having been established in the heyday of nationhood, were (and perhaps still are) 'real' nations. But Slovenia and Byelorus are *arrivistes*, seeking entrance after all the tickets to genuine nationhood have been sold.

It may be too easy to dismiss nationalism in this way. After all, the movements of national independence seek bounded, homeland states; their political imagination is constrained within the limits of the national ideal, which continues to be valued above life. And, as Linz's evidence implies, the movements tend to define themselves in terms of territory, rather than 'tribal' or 'primordial' loyalties. Moreover, not all social trends point towards the fragmentation and division of states. The two parts of Germany have been united. Irish nationalists in Northern Ireland are struggling for a united Ireland; Yuri Meshkov's Russian nationalist party is campaigning for secession from the newly seceded Ukraine, in order to re-unite with Russia. There is little evidence that the bulk of states in Africa are unravelling (Brown, 1989). In addition, there is no law of sociology to specify that the new states must inevitably fragment beyond some hypo-thetical point of viability.

As for the argument that the new states are too small for viability, then it must be said that the world of nations has always contained micro-states, existing in the shadow of super-powers, who have tried to run the world internationally. It is a myth to think that during the peak of modernity the world comprised states which were sovereignly independent both *de jure* and *de facto*. Many small states, such as Nepal, Andorra and Guatemala, not only defied the sensible logic of 'viability' to survive, but they never possessed the free autonomy of larger, more powerful states. Even during the nation-state's supposed heyday, states like Serbia and Montenegro could disappear because their sovereignty got in the way of the powerful national players. Hinsley is surely correct to caution against confusing national sovereignty with the freedom of a nation-state to act independently of a superior power: the latter is historically "the situation to which many states may have often aspired, but have never in fact enjoyed" (1986, p. 226).

One reason why Bauman and others claim that the new states are not proper nation-states is that they face pressures to absorb themselves in supra-national organizations. The European Union is often seen to be the model of the supra-national organization, which is eroding statehood. However, it is not at all clear that, in the European Union, the ideal of nationhood is being replaced by a new image of community (Smith, 1990). Within the EU there is controversy about the nature of the organization. The argument is not conducted between those who cling to nationhood and those who wish to move towards a radically different image of community. Some envisage the EU developing into a federal state – a United States of Europe built on the model of a United States of America. Already some of the symbols of common statehood have been adopted. The EU has its own flag and anthem. It boasts a 'parliament'. Proponents of federalism are attempting to construct, or imagine, a form of community. For example, Jacques Delors, when chairman of the European Commission, suggested that Europeans unite behind the label of 'Christian European Civilization' (Hagendoorn, 1993b). The label indicates an amorphous otherness: a non-Christian, non-European lack of civilization massing beyond the boundaries.

The federal plan is resisted by those who seek a looser amalgamation of sovereign member states. As was quoted in Chapter 4, British premier John Major declared that he would oppose all attempts to haul down the Union Jack and replace it by the star-spangled banner of a United States of Europe. In this vision, the EU becomes like some sort of permanent alliance and trading agreement between states, which jealously preserve their historical independence. Both visions – federalist and anti-federalist – perpetuate the notion of nationhood. The federalist vision transfers nationhood to a wider entity, as states combine to form a super-state. The non-federalist image defines membership of the community in terms of existing nationhood and national boundaries.

Most importantly, the notion of boundary continues to be important in both visions: the European Union will continue to be clearly bounded, with its perimeter being defined in terms of existing national boundaries.

Thus, Europe will be imagined as a totality, either as a homeland itself or as a homeland of homelands. Either way, the ideological traditions of nationhood, including its boundary-consciousness, are not transcended.

Within the European Union, national boundaries may be eroded, as a free transfer of labour, goods and money is encouraged within the community. But as internal boundaries have been eroded, so the outer perimeter has been strengthened. Immigration (or rather its prevention) has been a central concern in EU policy. 'Fortress Europe' is being constructed in order to keep at bay what in Delors' image becomes the non-Christian, non-European and non-civilized world. It has been revealed that in 1991 immigration ministers of member countries approved in principle a document called "the External Frontiers Convention which sought to erect a wall around the EC high enough to allow the internal borders to be dismantled" (reported in *Guardian*, 27 May 1993).

The issue of immigration, more than any other, shows that the state has not withered away in the age of late capitalism. There is no free market of labour in the world, for all states seek to regulate the human flow across their borders. As Harris (1990) argues, states retain control over immigration and the definition of citizenship. These most important functions of state show little sign of erosion. Two points can be briefly made. First, there is little reason to suppose that the migration of populations across state boundaries in itself signifies the erosion of states (although right-wing politicians often claim that it does). Historically, the great era of European state-making was preceded by unparalleled movements of population both within Europe and from Europe (Bailyn, 1988). Secondly, concern about immigration is today almost invariably expressed within nationalist ways of talking, as speakers wonder what is happening to 'our' country, 'our' homeland.

This way of talking is not confined to the extreme margins of right-wing politics. There is a banal discourse of borders and migration. Indeed, there must be: each state has its own legislative apparatus to restrict the market of labour and to define citizenship. In Chapter 4 examples were given of such discourse. A German minister was justifying exclusion of immigrants in order to protect 'our' society and 'our' fairness. Across Europe similar rhetorics can be heard (Van Dijk, 1991, 1993). This is not merely a European issue. The world over, governments, faced with migrants or refugees, strengthen legislation, whilst citing the value of their own (threatened) national essence. For example, the government of the Bahamas mentioned in its election manifesto the problems of illegal immigration and promised a "strengthening of the Bahamianisation process" (*Guardian*, 3 January 1994). Malaysia's Prime Minister, Dr Mahathir Mohamad, claims that Malays have a "primary right" to Malaysia and that Indian and Chinese immigrants should be required to absorb Malay culture (quoted in *Independent*, 5 December 1993). Even within the United States, supposedly the historic land of immigration, anti-immigration rhetoric is to be heard – against Mexicans, against Chinese and, in 1993 from a bi-partisan group of 75 members of Congress, against Iraqis. Sometimes the themes of borders, 'us' and foreigners become intermingled with the emotionally evocative themes of purity and dirt. Fascist propagandists, in particular, make this connection (Hainsworth, 1992; Orfali, 1990). But the theme of the 'pure' nation and the pollutants from abroad cannot be confined to the margins. It has its own more familiar, even banal, versions. In Sweden, for example, mainstream politicians can be heard regularly to argue for the strengthening of borders to keep out drugs, which are presumed to be alien to 'us' and 'our' identity and which pollute the nation (see Gould, 1993; Tham 1993). Across the globe, there are votes to be gathered from such ways of talking.

There is a further factor to take into account, when considering the thesis of postmodernism. The thesis asserts that nationhood is unravelling. Small nations no longer can assert their own independent sovereignty. However, the issue does not hang merely on the 'viability' of a Slovenia or Moldova. The thesis is being proposed at a moment when one nation, above all others, is bidding to lead a world order of nations. There would be a stronger case for declaring the end of the nation-state if this nation were showing signs of unravelling – either by disintegrating into sub-regions, or by dissolving its sovereignty into a United States of All the Americas. With the exception of the small Ka Lahui Hawai'i movement in the strangely positioned state of Hawaii, the United States is free from separatist movements. Even states like Texas, which once were indepen-dent states, have no populist movements, which aim to recreate the former independence. If the world's most powerful nation, whose cultural and political influence stretches across the so-called 'global village', is not unravelling in this way, then surely it is too premature to declare the exit of the nation-state from the world's stage. Given the global power of the United States, one might, indeed, wonder what such a declaration is forgetting.

**Around the Country**

The United States occupies a central place in the analyses of postmodern culture. To put the matter crudely, the States is believed to be the place where the future can be observed most clearly. Jean Baudrillard, for example, sees Disneyland as the microcosm of the whole West, exemplify-ing perfectly the orders of hyperreal simulation, which represent the near future for the world (Baudrillard, 1983, 1988). A banal nationalism must be reproducing the USA as the USA, place of the future. If the future is American, and if the United States is escaping the fissiparous forces which are fracturing less powerful nation-states, then it might be too early to book nationalism into the retirement home of ageing ideologies.

It appears easy to overlook the nationalist factors in the equation. As was discussed in Chapter 3, forgetting is part of the operation of banal nationalism. The nation is flagged, but the flagging itself is forgotten as the nation is mindlessly remembered. The previous chapter showed how a daily deixis of little words can point out the homeland, reproducing it as the homeland in banally forgettable ways. This constant deixis shows the continuing presence of the homeland, and the ease with which it can be taken for granted. An illustration can be given to show how important, pervasive and forgettable this deixis is: the texts of postmodernism themselves often use the homeland-making deixis. Even as writers seek to describe the cosmopolitan, global world of today, they can take for granted the place of the United States, using a familiar, yet banal, deixis.

Joshua Meyrowitz's *No Sense of Place* (1986) articulates themes which are close to the heart of the postmodern thesis. Although Meyrowitz himself does not use the term 'postmodernism', *No Sense of Place* has been interpreted as depicting a "postmodern geography" (Morley, 1992, p. 279) and as describing a postmodern phenomenology (Michael, 1994). In a superbly imaginative analysis, Meyrowitz suggests that physically bounded space is becoming less important in the age of electronic information. Television has eroded traditional boundaries, both social and physical, so that many social spheres, which were once distinct, now overlap each other. This is seen in "the blurring of conceptions of childhood and adulthood, the merging of notions of masculinity and femininity, and the lowering of political heroes to the level of average citizens" (1986, p. 5). The depths of traditional allegiances are being replaced by a sensibility which flattens differences. In short, according to Meyrowitz, there is 'no sense of place'.

Despite this repeated theme, there is a constant, but largely unacknowledged, sense of place throughout *No Sense of Place*. The text, and what it describes, are located within a place – the United States of America. There is a sense of 'us', who are American. In the preface, Meyrowitz states that "electronic media are present in nearly all physical settings in our country". The context makes it clear which country is 'ours': "almost every American home has at least one telephone and television set" (p. viii). The main text of the book is full of such examples of the national first person plural: "all *our* recent Presidents have been plagued with problems of 'credibility' " (p. 268); "television has encouraged *us* to nominate candidates who like Jimmy Carter, Ronald Reagan and Walter Mondale avoid acting like 'great leaders' " (p. 304, emphases added).

Meyrowitz even suggests that the sense of America may be enhanced by the very electronic media which are supposedly destroying place. For example, he writes that "through television, Americans may gain a strange sort of communion with each other" (p. 90). Thus, the argument contains its own paradox. Meyrowitz claims that there is no sense of place, and he specifies the place where this absence of place is taking place. This place is a nation – America. His text signals its own sense of belonging to this place.

Another example of such deixis is provided by Gergen's *The Saturated Self*. In presenting a vivid account of the life led by the decentred, postmodern self, Gergen speaks personally of his own life. The opening sentence of the book sets the scene: "I had just returned to Swarthmore from a two-day conference in Washington, which had brought together fifty scholars from around the country" (1991, p. 1). On returning, there is "an urgent fax from Spain"; Gergen's secretary has "a sheaf of telephone messages and some accumulated mail, including an IRS notice of a tax audit"; there are calls from a London publisher, a message about a summer trip to Holland and so on. The picture is one of brief, depthless, global interconnections.

But the text also tells its readers that the writer is at home in America. The very first sentence uses the definite article in a piece of homeland-making deixis: 'Around the country' – *the* country is the nation-state of the writer, the 50 scholars and Washington. Immediately, America as a whole – as an entire homeland – has been flagged, but not named as such. Reader and writer are expected to take for granted a world in which people live in countries and pay their taxes to the national state. Gergen does not feel it necessary to explain the initials of the Inland Revenue Service (or to describe which 'inland' this refers to). Without such shared understanding, the text would be puzzling. As it is, the text conveys its subtext smoothly. The phrase 'around the country' slips into the book's opening sentence, while the author is doing something else – while his creative imagination is depicting a world from which nations are supposedly disappearing.

All this gives a depth to the depicted world. It is a banal depth, for the deeper surfaces are neither hidden nor unknown. The powers of the United States' government, to which taxes are paid, and the military, which is funded by those taxes, are not concealed secrets: they are publicly known. They are centrally part of the forms of life which the words of the text evoke. The words, however, do not dwell on the national forms: they dwell in them, forgetfully.

**Identities and Politics**

The examples from Gergen and Meyrowitz illustrate how easily the national context can be taken for granted. There is a broader point and this relates to the sorts of new politics which supposedly threaten nationhood. Even when subnational forms of politics appear to be eroding the nation-state, these forms may actually be taking the state for granted, deictically situating themselves within the homeland. This possibility needs to be seriously considered, given that 'identity politics' is being claimed both as the politics of the future and as a politics which is eroding the nation-state. The case of the United States, as the special place of placelessness, needs particular attention.

Some writers assume that the politics of identity in the United States – such as the movements for Hispanic, gay or women's interests – are equivalent to the 'subnational' rumblings of separatism elsewhere (see, for example, Friedman, 1988). However, identities should not be treated as identical, as if all are merely fulfilling an identical psychological substrate of 'identity-needs' (Bhavnani and Phoenix, 1994; Sampson, 1993). 'Identity politics' is politics and the political dimension is crucial (Roosens, 1989). As far as nationalism is concerned, a distinction should be made between those social movements which are mobilizing 'identities' in the cause of securing homeland territory and those which are mobilizing 'identities' within an existing polity.

Identity politics in the United States is not directed towards creating separate national homelands. In fact, identity politics appears, at first sight, to transcend place. Feminists, gays, Hispanics and so on are not localized within the United States. To be sure, there are ethnic and racial ghettoes within cities; but there is no African-American or Italian-American state, with its own bordered territory and with its claims for national independence. On the contrary, the politics of identity, unlike that of nationalist movements, gathers together those who are geographically scattered into an imagined unity of identification: a placeless community of interests is to be imagined.

Some have argued that this ethnic identification contains a typically postmodern element of 'consumer choice' or "voluntary identification" (Levine, 1993). Sollors (1986) gives the example of two brothers in the United States with the same complex ancestry, one choosing to call himself 'Franco-American', whilst the other identifies himself as 'German-American'. According to Sollors, this sort of ethnicity is not a matter of compulsion: one can select from the shelves of ancestors the identity-product conforming to taste. It is hard, however, to see how deprived blacks in the United States, confined to all-black, deprived neighbourhoods, have chosen their ethnic destiny. Sollors argues that the chosen identities are depthless, for they do not come with whole cultural ways of life attached: "American ethnicity . . . is a matter not of content, but of the importance that individuals ascribe to it" (Sollors, 1986, p. 35; see also, Fitzgerald, 1992). The placeless quality of such identity is underlined if two persons, from the same family, living in the same city, can claim different ethnic identities and different places of origin.

The question is whether identity politics and the importance attached to ethnic identification are undermining the nation-state. Some critics are enthusiastic about the radical possibilities of identity politics. Henry Giroux (1993) maintains that identity politics is "the struggle to construct counter-narratives and create new critical spaces and social practices" (p. 3). On the other hand, conservatives may feel that the new narratives are destroying old patriotic ones. Both sides, however, may be exaggerating, for the new politics, and its narratives, typically take the nation-state for granted. What is often at stake is not an argument against nationhood, but an argument about the nature of the nation and who should be taken as representing the nation. There is nothing remarkable in this: the creation of a nation "is a recurrent activity", which involves "ceaseless reinterpretations, rediscoveries and reconstructions" (Smith, 1986, p. 106). These processes of reinterpretation are typically processes of controversy and argument. As was mentioned in the previous chapter, nationalism is, to quote John Shotter, a 'tradition of argument'.

There is no doubt that identity politics is challenging old ways of defining the nation. Those who have been excluded from the power to make definitions are now claiming the right to re-imagine the community. During his lifetime, the painter Norman Rockwell was much praised for supposedly depicting the American people and the American way of life. In Rockwell's America, the people are 'naturally' presented with white, Anglo-Saxon faces. Blacks and Hispanics are as rare as recognizably Jewish faces. At best, they appear as special subjects. In 'The Problem We all Live With' a little black girl is escorted to school by big, protective, white, male bodies, bearing the ensigns of 'US Marshall'. Now the bias in the depiction of America is contested by those faces who have long been excluded from the national definition. Pictures such as Rockwell's can no longer be innocently painted. More faces are to be painted in. But if they are, it is still an America which is being painted.

Charge, counter-charge and background acceptance can be briefly illustrated by an article originally published in the *Washington Post* (and reproduced in the *Guardian*, 10 March 1994). It exemplifies the sort of contemporary controversy about ethnic identity in the United States. The reporter, Mary Jordan, was describing the growing trend for American college students to live in ethnically separated residences. An Ivy League school had just opened a new dormitory for African-Americans. The new Harambee House overlooked Hispanic House, French House, Slavic House and so on. Educators, so it was reported, were becoming increasingly worried: "The separatist movement is a hot issue nationwide." The report quoted the President of the University of Pennsylvania:

> We are moving into a very, very hyphenated world. It's Asian-American, African-American. It's so contrary to everything I grew up with – when everyone fought just to be American.

The semantics are revealing. 'Separatism' is used, but these separatists do not seek an independent, national territory. They imagine no new homeland. They want separate dormitories within institutions across the nation. The national context is given – the issue is controversial 'nationwide'. The worried opponent of this separatism voices the fears of a threatened hegemony. From her position in an old elite university, she speaks for 'everyone'. For her, the whole American identity itself – just being American – is threatened by the dangerous hyphens.

What she does not mention is that all the hyphenated identities flag the nation, as surely as if they bore portable flag-poles. To claim to be African-American or Hispanic-American is to claim be American. Of course, the rhetoric of identity-claims, when made within the nation, often leaves the flags unwaved, unsaluted, unnoticed. In Iowa or Denver, where there are few African-Africans to speak of, to be 'African-American' may indicate a difference from others assumed to be American; in Nairobi or Lagos, it carries a different rhetoric (Eriksen, 1993; Fitzgerald, 1992). Nevertheless, this hyphenated world continually flags the national territory in which it dwells.

If identity politics is based on the vision of the 'multicultural society', this politics takes for granted that there is a 'society', which is to be multicultural and which is to be represented by a greater variety of faces than on a Rockwell canvas. When the multicultural ideal is tied to the notion of a nation, then 'identity politics' is situated within the nation's tradition of argument: identities within the nation are contested, but not the identity of the nation itself. An apparent radicalism can become constrained within national borders. For example, Sneja Gunew (1990) criticizes the narrow definitions of Australian culture, based upon white, Anglo-Saxon, male narratives. She advocates an alternative "narrative of a national culture", representing multicultural narratives (p. 100). The result is a re-imagined Australia: the culture is still 'national' and still located within the same territorial homeland. 'Australia' as an entity is still to be reproduced.

Although multiculturalism might threaten old hegemonies, which claimed to speak for the whole nation, and although it might promise an equality of identities, it still typically is constrained within the notion of nationhood. As such, it implicitly inherits a tradition of 'us' and 'them', the 'nation' and 'foreignness', not to mention the acceptance of the world of nations in which nationhood is accepted as important and worth defining. As Paul Gilroy forcefully argues, there are aspects of multicultural orthodoxy "which can be shown to replicate in many ways the *volkish* new right sense of the relationship between race, nation and culture" (1992a, p. 57). Unless identity politics can transcend the nation, escaping the bounds of the homeland, the radicalism of the challenge to old images and narratives is critically constrained within the assumptions of nationalism (see also Gilroy, 1992b).

There is a further theme. The national element in the hyphenated America is flagged and typically forgotten. The President of the Ivy League university, in talking of America, says that the 'world' is becoming hyphenated. It was just a turn of phrase, scarcely significant in itself. But the lack of significance shows the banality of the phrase, and the habit of identifying the particular with the universal. This matches certain features of identity politics in the United States. The nation appears as a global village, in which the identities transcend differences of space: and social scientists are quick to read these signs as portents for everywhere. It is as if the United States contains the whole world: Hispanics, Africans, French, Slavs are all 'here'. The prefix predominates, as the suffix, identifying the particular nationality, slips from attention. The campus, with its dormitories, is like the World Showcase in Disney World: the whole world is contained within a part of America. The new world order can be ordered 'here at home', in the homeland. Within the nation's parade of different identities, a wider, more subtle identity of identities is suggested.

## Globalization and the United States

It is easy to suppose that what is global cannot be national and vice versa, just as it is easy to suppose that nationalism is the direct opposite of cosmopolitan universalism. However, nationalism contains its universal features. As was argued in the previous chapter, American political nationalism often presents itself as the universal voice of reason, addressing a universal audience. Similarly, the 'global culture', which supposedly is threatening traditional national cultures, is not itself disconnected from all sense of national place. It does not represent a free flow of information, circulating effortlessly across the synapses of a self-enclosed electronic network. Stuart Hall acutely comments that globalization is not an abstract force, but that the global, transnational culture is predominantly American, presenting "what is essentially an American conception of the world" (1991b, p. 28; see, also, Hall, 1991a; Schiller, 1993).

Clearly, the global transmission of American culture is a vast topic. Levis and baseball caps have become universal apparel as Coke and McDonald's have become universal foods: and all have become universal symbols. Hollywood stars are not generally '*American* stars', in the way that a Depardieu or a Loren always remains a *French* or an *Italian* star: a Costner or a Streep drops the confines of nationality and is simply a 'star', a 'mega-star', a universal icon. A small illustrative example of the mega-star in the global world can be given. Barry Manilow's press agent is talking with enthusiasm about the singer's tour of the Philippines:

> Every time we turned on the radio it was a Manilow song . . . He played to 48,000 people every night for five nights . . . these people, they're so repressed, so poor that they *worshipped* Barry. Knew all the songs. Knew all the words to all the songs. (Quoted in Heller, 1993, emphasis in original)

People in the Philippines worship the American singer; they take the English words to their hearts. In its turn, the American public has no Philippino star to worship, no Philippino words to memorize.

The image of the global culture as a self-sufficient electronic circuit – an image to be found, for example, in Baudrillard's writings – seems misplaced: it dispels geography and ignores hegemony. The global culture is like water, pouring and trickling from higher ground, deluging valley and plane. The flow has the irreversibility of a Niagara. On the lower ground, embankments can only be built with great effort, and then, the water, as if in insulted anger, rushes with increased ferocity against the ramparts, seeking the parched markets beyond. Parts of the Islamic world turn against the Western Satan and its culture. Levi jeans are branded anti-Islamic, their tight fitting is said to inhibit prostrated prayer (Ahmed, 1992). The ramparts against Hollywood and McDonald's are not easily constructed in Iran; the political pressure from outside is constant; the resistors, in turning against the modern world, find themselves building their ramparts with materials that come from modern nationalism (Zubaida, 1993).

The products of the global culture bear the marks of the higher ground, which itself is no mere physical geography: the higher ground is a national place, indeed *the* national place. There has been no detailed study of the quantity and quality of the ways in which Hollywood films and American-made, globally distributed television programmes flag the United States. Not only would the number of flaggings per visual hour need to be counted, but, most crucially, a taxonomy of flaggings would be necessary. Waved and unwaved flags would need to be distinguished from each other, and the taxonomy would also reveal the various ways in which flaggings can be unwaved. There are, for example, flaggings of scene, which allow the audience to recognize, often before the opening titles have finished rolling, that the action, telling its universalized story, is to be set in the United States. And for most films, this is the flagging of the unmarked place – the normal, familiar place. This is the place of the sky-scrapered skyline, or the white-boarded suburban house or the cowboy gulch, none of which needs to advertise itself self-consciously as *America*. Such scenic flaggings, like the phrase 'around the country', deictically allow the audience (including those who have never seen America) to recognize immediately that 'we' are 'here' in America. Then, this familiar America might unselfconsciously flag its Americanness. Stars and Stripes might hang from the depicted public buildings or be sewn on to the sleeves of law enforcement officers. The marshall will be a '*US* Marshall'. These flaggings, produced in the name of realism, will be just out of the reach of conscious awareness.

There will be the flaggings which rustle the flag slightly, as characters draw attention to their Americanness. There will be flaggings which combine the particular and the universal, as the peculiarly American dilemmas, which confront the central characters, are presented as if universal dilemmas. Further along the taxonomy will be the wavings and salutings, as Americanness is praised, even as it is presented in universal guises. Jane Bethke Elshtain (1987) provides a brief but incisive analysis of the popular films *Private Benjamin* and *An Officer and a Gentleman*. Both films developed the general themes (and stereotypes) of the masculine warrior and the gentle, female soul. These universal themes were given the precise location of the modern US army. Flags were waved and saluted on screen, as raw recruits faced the demanding tests of initiation. The happy endings, which audiences saluted with cheers or tears according to gender, saw the recruits passing successfully beneath the flag to take their place in the US military. Audiences around the world shared these crescendoes of happiness.

There is a further form of flagging to be scored. This is a flagging of hegemony, where the identity of the particular is presented as a universal identity. If, as C.L.R. James pointed out, sport possesses a cultural and political significance, then the special nature of US sports bears attention.

The United States is peculiarly isolated from the ethos of international team contests. The major team sports of the United States – baseball and football – are local. The 'United States' does not compete against other nations; the possibility of embarrassing defeats by minor nations has been eliminated. However, the local appears as if global. In baseball, the winners of the National and American Leagues compete annually for the 'World Series'. The symbols of baseball, together with their Hollywood representations, are transmitted globally. It is a cultural pattern which well fits a nation seeking world hegemony.

Themes that might seem to be mythically universal are co-opted by a nationalism which has its own particular universality or globalism. Again, a brief illustration, or mini case-study, can illustrate a point, which deserves far greater analysis. One of the classic pieces of modern cultural analysis is Roland Barthes' 'The world of wrestling', first published in 1952. His essay was an affectionate celebration of professional wrestling as a moral pantomime. Good and Bad confront each other in grandiloquently theatrical displays, staged in seedy Parisian halls. It is a working-class art-form, which bears traces of early theatre. In an aside, Barthes commented that French wrestling differed from American. In France, the performance was one of pure, even innocent, ethics. In American wrestling, politics intrudes, with "the 'bad' wrestler always supposed to be a Red" (1983c, p. 28).

Two generations on, such a comparison, suggesting two equal cultural traditions of wrestling, is not possible. The seedy halls cannot compete with the slickly marketed, multi-million dollar business of American wrestling. The stars perform on the grand stages of cable and satellite television. Their fame is international. Their plastic replicas, made in China, are bought by children (mostly boys) across the West, to play in toy rings, supplied with suitable sound effects and displayable American flag. The occasional French or British wrestler makes it on to the American circuit: it is a sign of their fame. Strictly speaking, it is a mistake to call this *American* wrestling. It proclaims itself to be world wrestling, whether conducted under the aegis of the World Wrestling Federation or its rival business World Championship Wrestling. Its title and its operations are global, but its heart, both commercially and thematically, remains in the United States.

'World wrestling', as befits its commercial ownership and adminis-tration, depicts the world as an American morality tale of masculine display. The element of pantomime persists, with the bodies pumped to muscular proportions unseen by Barthes in the back-street venues. Lincoln (1989), in an essay which aimed to bring Barthes up to date, comments that in most matches it was "those individuals most palpably 'American', not those most virtuous, who emerged triumphant" (p. 156). Lincoln picked the figure of Sergeant Slaughter as representing the most "hyperbolically" American patriot (p. 157). Times have since moved on. In true post-modern style, the pastiche characters of this wrestling world are not just undimensional but are exchangeable. During the Gulf War, Sergeant Slaughter had become the hyperbolic traitor. He carried the Iraqi flag; his manager, speaking mock Arabic, sported the military fatigues and black moustache of Saddam Hussein. At the final of that year's Wrestle Mania (broadcast live across the States on pay-per-view channels), Slaughter was opposed by the mature, suitably blond, heroic Hulk Hogan. Head wrapped in a Stars and Stripes bandana, Hogan waved his American flag as he strode into the ring, the sporting but tough patriot determined to withstand whatever foul moves the enemy had in mind. Never before could have Good and Evil been so clearly signified in a wrestling ring. Or just beyond the ring. Thank goodness for the cameras in the dressing-room: we could witness the cowardly Slaughter appearing to blind Hogan with a flame-thrower, as if aiming his personal Scud missile into the face of the good American. Hogan was not merely defending the honour of America, but that of World Wrestling, the world itself. A few weeks after the battles and bombings in the Gulf, this was pantomime paralleling war.

The world of wrestling does not restrict its flag-waving to times of war. The global goodness of America is constantly to be defended. In December 1993, *WWF*, the official magazine, advertising a Thanksgiving Eve event, showed two pictures. The first depicted "the Thanksgiving Tradition foreign fanatics wait for". Non-American wrestlers, ugly and snarling, were menacing an American turkey, draped with the Stars and Stripes. The second showed "the Thanksgiving Tradition all Americans wait for": smiling, good-natured American wrestlers tuck into a turkey adorned with a Japanese flag. The themes travel well. The World Wrestling Federation came to Britain's National Indoor Arena in September 1993. The well-recognized figures were cheered and booed by a full crowd, which, as usual, contained a much higher proportion of women and family groups than is customary at 'proper' sporting events. The top match pitted Yokozuna (enormous, brooding and very Japanese) against Hacksaw Jim Duggan (cheerful, smaller, red-necked American). The crowd read the symbols of Good and Evil appropriately. Yokozuna, with his manager bearing the flag of Japan, was booed into the ring. Duggan, waving his Stars and Stripes and delivering his back-woodsman's whoops, conducted the audience in the happy chant 'Yoo-Ess-Ay'.

As for Hogan, after his wrestling triumphs he has progressed to Hollywood. His films tend towards the higher flagging quotient. In *Mr Nanny*, the hero mixes his muscular masculinity with the job of nanny. Looking after children is not the sole occupation of the hero. The film sees Hogan battling to recover a crucial micro-chip for an anti-missile missile, so that "they" will never declare war on "us" again. 'They' is left unspecified, but the enemy characters speak with heavy, Germanic accents. 'Us' is obvious: and 'we', as always, are the potential victims of cowardly attack, never the aggressors.

No longer does the world of wrestling have the seedy naivety which attracted Barthes. The excesses and the depthless unreality of today's top professional wrestling make it a pre-eminently postmodern spectacle. If this is so, then wrestling also illustrates the ideological limits of postmodernism's free-flow of imagery. Not all combinations are possible. It is unthinkable for US audiences to boo the heroic bearers of the US flag, for Americanness is here a semantic sign of goodness itself. The toy rings come equipped, the world over, with the American flag: no other flag is supplied. Could audiences in the USA chant 'Ja-Pan', as foreign audiences can 'Yoo-Ess-Ay'? How could the world of world wrestling have at its centre any other nation? And how could this world of worlds be devoid of nationhood in its depiction of hyper-morality?

Of course, professional wrestling is just pastiche: it lacks the intensity of 'real' sports; it is understood as display, as fun. But that is the point. The flags and the flow of loyalties are not innocent. If the product is globalized (international audiences, spin-off products made in China, images transmitted supra-terrestrially), then so is the message. This is not the world of American wrestling: it is the American world of wrestling displayed as the whole world of wrestling. As Barthes realized, the world of wrestling can only work if its meanings, amplified to the point of parody, are already familiar. The world of world wrestling plays with familiar themes: it does not create its aggressive hyper-masculinity, nor its nationalism. And as it amplifies the familiar, so it illustrates just how banal and how global is this American world of worlds. In this way, the pantomime bears a wider message, or rather a clue, about the globalized nationalism which is so familiar today.

# 7

# Philosophy as a Flag for the *Pax Americana*

Banal nationalism possesses a low key, understated tone. In routine practices and everyday discourses, especially those in the mass media, the idea of nationhood is regularly flagged. Even the daily weather forecast can do this. Through such flagging, established nations are reproduced as nations, with their citizenry being unmindfully reminded of their national identity. This banal flagging provides the home-making groundwork, turning ground into homeland. A constant deixis keeps 'us' nationally playing at home. Accordingly, the playing pitch is watered and mulched, in constant readiness for quickly declared, intermittent contests of passionate attack and defence. At the same time, as was suggested in the previous chapter, the global nationalism of the United States is flagged across the world. Perhaps it might sometimes take the grossly hyperbolic forms of professional wrestling, but there is, too, a constant, lower key deixis placing the United States centre stage in a world of nations.

A question may be asked: do these sorts of flaggings constitute what could be called an 'ideology'? Surely, so it might be objected, they are merely habits of thought and disjointed clichés of discourse. By contrast, ideologies have their intellectual dimensions: they contain theories as well as reflexes. Critical analysts, who have sought to lay bare the operations of ideology, have historically paid great attention to the role of philosophy. In *The German Ideology*, the first work to use the term 'ideology' in its modern critical sense, Marx and Engels declared, in a much quoted phrase, that "the ideas of the ruling class are in every epoch the ruling ideas" (1970, p. 64). The ideas to which Marx and Engels were referring were not the ideas to be found in newspaper editorials or on sporting handbills; they were certainly not the poses of professional wrestlers. Marx and Engels had in mind the ideas of philosophy. At great length, they argued that the limitations of Hegelianism fitted the social conditions from which that philosophy sprang and which, in turn, it implicitly justified. In so arguing, Marx and Engels indicated that philosophy performs an ideological task: it formulates abstract, universal principles which, in fact, express, and mask, the particular interests of ruling groups.

At first sight, the great traditions of philosophy seem to have no place in banal nationalism. Indeed, one might question whether banal nationalism could possibly possess a philosophical aspect: its distinguishing mark is a banality which would seem to be a denial of a theoretical consciousness.

Banal nationalism is found in the weather reports, on the sporting pages and hanging limply in the flags on the filling-station forecourts. Bùt it does not end there. Nationalism also appears banally in the words of politicians, speaking to 'us' in their clichés about 'the nation' and about 'society'. Their words have intellectual echoes. If politicians regularly elide 'nation' and 'society', talking as if there were no imaginable form of community outside the nation, then this has been paralleled in classical sociological theorizing. As previous chapters have shown, on this point high social theory has coincided with the banal language of politics and journalism. Such coincidences do not by themselves show that banal nationalism has a continuing intellectual tradition. The question to be asked is whether philosophies, suited for the times of banal nationalism, are being developed: to be more precise, whether there is a nationalist philosophy for the new world order, in which one nation bids for political and cultural hegemony?

If the times are not producing any such a philosophy, then this absence may be significant. Analysts of ideology have often treated philosophy as a weather-vane, theoretically pointing in the direction of future practice. Proponents of the thesis of postmodernity might argue that absence of any philosophy of banal nationalism might indicate that the conditions for producing nationalism and nationalist ideas have passed. In this case, the meteorological omens might be indicating a postmodern future, in which nations and nation-states have all but declined. All that are left today are the habits and reflexes of banal nationalism. Once nationalism becomes banal, then this is a sign that history is moving in other directions, which are already being prefigured philosophically.

Postmodern theorists have declared the death of philosophy in its old garb. No longer are the grand meta-narratives and the old systems of truth possible: a playful world of multi-narratives beckons. Some critics claim to identify ideological interests in this play. They detect, between the lines of the anti-philosophical philosophies, the particular conditions of the West, being expressed as a general, global thesis. Such critics charge that the thesis of postmodernism assumes a pattern of social development: from pre-industrialization to modernism and, then, to postmodernism. This pattern, in the view of the critics, describes the path taken by the rich nations of the West (see, for example, the critiques of Bhabha, 1992; Franco, 1988; Slater, 1994; Spivak, 1988). Such critics point out that a celebration of postmodernism, and its supposed culture of diversìty, is *de facto* a celebration of the West and its supposed cultural sophistication. Parts of the world, such as the impoverished South, which fail to show postmodern features, are deemed to be lagging behind. Thus, postmodernist theory, despite its outward celebration of diversity, tends to brand non-Western voices as second-best.

It is necessary to go further in order to identify nationalist elements in postmodern theorizing. The question is whether one or other of the anti-philosophies of postmodern philosophy possesses a nationalist dimension, one which echoes the banal nationalism of everyday routines. If any philosophy is to be so identified, it should possess the following four characteristics.

1   It should welcome or justify the so-called new, global order, whether or not this order is called 'postmodern'. Thus, it should not be the sort of romantic, conservative philosophy which looks back to a past age of 'real' nations', and which, by implication, criticizes the present era of declining nations.

2   Such a philosophy should include the notion of nationhood, without necessarily justifying it overtly. In keeping with the banal mood of nationalism, nationhood could be taken for granted rather than celebrated. Thus, the assumptions of nationhood should cling to such a philosophy, just as they do to the banal speeches of politicians and daily words of newspapers. By taking nationhood for granted, rather than by justifying its principles, such a philosophy can disclaim its own nationalism. Such a philosophy might claim to belong to a globalized, postmodern world, while tacitly accepting the existence of nations in this world and not making proposals to change this aspect of the world.

3   Having taken nationhood for granted, the philosophy should not treat all nations equivalently. If the philosophy is to echo the current times, then one national voice should be heard more loudly than others. The United States should be accorded special space philosophically, just as the United States claims a special global position in the new order. However, ambivalence should accompany the according of a special place to the USA. In the politics of hegemony, the particular and the universal are elided, as US leaders, in representing the interests of the nation, claim to represent universal interests and vice versa. The ambivalences of an anti-philosophical philosophy might provide the ideal uniform for an ideology which needs to deny both its universalism and its particularism.

4   If the philosophy is one for the current times, then it should not be obscure. Gramsci noted that "every philosophy has a tendency to become the common sense of a fairly limited environment (that of all the intellectuals)" (1971, p. 330n.). He also noted that hegemonic philosophies express an ethics which reaches beyond the narrow world of philosophy into the wider world of common sense. In the contemporary conditions of fame, in which the politician is a celebrity, the philosopher, who expresses the current mood, should not be expressing views which can only find published expression in abstruse journals, read by a handful of professional colleagues. At the minimum, such a philosopher should have a wider audience of intellectuals and should occasionally, through the mass media, reach beyond the intellectuals.

It will be suggested that the philosophy of Richard Rorty fulfils these criteria. His philosophy is attuned to current times; it uncritically accepts the notion of nationhood; the United States is placed at the deictic centre of its textual and philosophic universe; and, last but not least, Rorty enjoys the sort of fame to make his fellow academics jealous.

## Sage for a Faithless Age

Richard Rorty is fast attaining the sort of eminence normally reserved for French *philosophes*. He is one of the few English-language thinkers whom defenders of postmodernism feel able to cite alongside the continental icons of Foucault, Derrida and Baudrillard. He has been described, for example, as "one of the major US philosophers of the postmodern movement" (Harvey, 1989, p. 52) and his work as "by far the most symptomatic expression of the current intellectual re-orientation" (Bauman, 1992a, p. 82). More sardonically, Christopher Norris has commented that "Rorty is undoubtedly swimming with the cultural tide despite his fondness . . . for making the same point over and again, as if against a massive and well-nigh unbudgeable weight of received opinion" (1993, p. 285). Rorty's fame spreads beyond the narrow world of professional philosophy. When he visited Britain in 1993 the *Guardian* newspaper devoted a special article to him. The writer claimed that Rorty "may turn out to be the most perfect *fin-de-siècle* philosopher, for those of us in an age that has lost faith in God, in scientific progress, or in any of the great Truths". The piece was headlined "Sage for a faithless age" (*Guardian*, 26 February 1993).

In this and in other tributes Rorty is hailed as more than an individual academic; he becomes a representative of his, and 'our', times. Critics, too, have treated Rorty in this way, seeing his philosophy as encapsulating ideological trends. Roy Bhaskar in *Philosophy and the Idea of Freedom* asks "Why Rorty?", having devoted the bulk of his book to criticizing the American philosopher. Bhaskar answers his own question by claiming that Rorty's philosophy, with its anti-realism and its celebration of irony, "provides an ideology for intellectual yuppies for a leisured elite – intellectual yuppies – neither racked by pain nor immersed in toil" (1992, p. 134). Terry Eagleton, in similar vein, claims that in Rorty's ideal society "the intellectuals will be 'ironists', practising a suitably cavalier, laid-back attitude to their beliefs, while the masses . . . will continue to salute the flag and take life seriously" (1991, p. 11). Shotter (1993a) refers to the "irritation and disdain" with which Rorty's writings are viewed on the left (p. 41). Feminist critics, such as Nancy Fraser (1989), have accused Rorty of failing to acknowledge patriarchal assumptions. Richard Bernstein (1987) suggested that Rorty was a Cold War theorist, and Burrows (1990) accuses Rorty of being too "prone to see red" (p. 337). Rorty himself writes that "the left's favourite word for me is 'complacent', just as the right's is 'irresponsible' " (1993a, p. 43).

It will be suggested that Rorty is very much a figure for his times, but not quite in the way that some critics have suggested. If Rorty were offering a remodelled version of Cold War ideology, then his importance would be declining. With the collapse of the Soviet Empire, US foreign policy no longer needs to be based upon an unrelenting anti-Marxism. Fear of communism gave Cold War politicians, such as Reagan or Bush, a moral certainty. Now, a new era – with a younger face in the White House – offers a more open-spirited rhetoric, in which a sense of reasoned doubt is combined with further possibilities for a global *Pax Americana*.

Rorty's philosophy captures this mood with its ironic iconoclasm and its rejection of old strident certainties. Yet, it also contains hegemonic themes, well suited to these so-called post-Marxist, post-ideological, post-modern times. The key lies in nationalism of a particular banal, low-keyed variety, which none the less is deeply nationalist. In this respect, Eagleton's image of Rorty is misleading. Not only the masses are encouraged to salute the flag: so, for all their irony and sophistication, are the cosmopolitan intellectuals. Indeed, the philosophical texts themselves can be seen as a sort of flag. The fact that sophisticated critics, while seeing Rorty's philosophy as an ideological reflection of the age, can overlook the nationalist dimension, itself is significant. It illustrates how elusively familiar nationalism can be: at once, nationalism is obvious but invisible because of its obviousness. All this, it will be argued, can be seen in Rorty's work. His postmodernist, anti-philosophical philosophizing does not so much reflect the path of Minerva's owl, flying out wisely in the evening of nationalism. Rather it is the flight path of Uncle Sam's bald-headed eagle, flying across the globe at any time of its choosing.

### A Call For Patriotism

To begin with, an article in an American newspaper. On 13 February 1994, the *New York Times* carried a short piece on its inside pages calling for increased patriotism. It was not an especially auspicious item, but, in its detail, it reveals that philosophy is not confined to the technical journals. It can be used to request the intellectuals to raise their arms in patriotic tribute to the Stars and Stripes.

The opening sentence of the article declared that "most of us, despite the outrage we may feel about governmental cowardice or corruption, and despite our despair over what is being done to the weakest and poorest among us, still identify with our country". The next sentence moved from identification to pride: "We take pride in being citizens of a self-invented, self-reforming, enduring constitutional democracy." The final sentence of the opening paragraph introduced the name of the country, which most of 'us' were said to identify with: "We think of the United States as having glorious – if tarnished – national traditions." The title of the piece was 'The Unpatriotic Academy', accompanied by a bold sub-heading, which declared: 'We need our national identity'. There was no deictic confusion: 'we' are Americans, 'here' in America, 'our' homeland. An American writer was addressing the readers as fellow Americans.

As the heading indicated, the point of the article was to criticize the unpatriotic elements of 'our' nation. The particular target was the intellectual left, to be found "in colleges and universities, in the academic departments that have become sanctuaries for left-wing political views". What concerned the writer was that "there is a problem with this left: it is unpatriotic". The writer was following a path well-trod by those who criticize the left from a position of right-wing patriotic virtue. In this case, however, the writer was not claiming to speak for the patriotic right; nor was he playing the patriotic card in their characteristic style.

By his opening words about governmental cowardice and the poor, the writer had put himself within the liberal camp. He was claiming to speak as a friend of the left, praising the left's concern for those "who have gotten a raw deal in our society". By such concern, the left helps "to make our country much more decent, more tolerant and more civilized". The first person plural is not only to be understood as a national 'us'; 'we' are also the caring, liberal part of the national 'us'. 'We' are the ones who care about the weak and the poor; and 'we' (the writer's 'we') claim to speak for all 'us' patriotic Americans. In this way, the writer, having distanced himself rhetorically from the patriotic right, and having displayed his liberal credentials, gathers rhetorical support for his advance on the target – the unpatriotic left.

The text proudly and patriotically hoists the national flag in the name of decency, tolerance and reform. Left-wingers should realize that "a nation cannot reform itself unless it takes pride in itself". Multiculturalism, including the sort of identity politics, which was discussed in the previous chapter, should not divide the nation for "there is no incompatibility between respect for cultural differences and American patriotism". The left shows no such patriotism because "it repudiates the idea of a national identity and the emotion of national pride".

The argument's rhetoric invokes a patriotic common sense against dangerous, none-too-sensible intellectuals. Commonplaces, rather than documentation, suffice for persuasion. In the concluding paragraph, the writer asserts: "an unpatriotic left has never achieved anything". The sentiments are presented as if readers will recognize their obvious truth: evidence is unnecessary. And so, the author moves to the final assertion: "A left that refuses to take pride in its country will have no impact on that country's politics, and will eventually become an object of contempt." The rhetoric has subtly shifted. It is no longer merely 'our' country, the USA, which is at stake. The conclusion is stated as a universal law, applying to any country and any left. Everywhere – in all nations – patriotism is required. This is advanced as if it were a law of common sense.

The writer is making points which have been made many times before, sometimes with a fiercer political edge and sometimes with a similar tone of pained concern. The rhetoric contains a number of features which are familiarly banal. For example, the naturalness of nations is assumed. 'Society', 'nation' and 'country' are used as synonyms. "Our society" might give a raw deal to some, but the left, by campaigning against this, is helping to reform "our country". 'We' should take pride in being citizens of a democracy, and should identify with America's traditions: in such statements, the nation state is assumed to provide the ground for democracy. There is also an implicit distinction between 'patriotism' and 'nationalism'. Patriotism is the good which is desired: in describing this good, the word 'nationalism' is avoided. The author, however, acknowledges that patriotic pride can be taken to unpleasant extremes. Then, the word 'nationalism' makes its first and only textual appearance: "such pride sometimes takes the form of arrogant, bellicose nationalism". This distinction between nationalism and patriotism, which, as was seen in Chapter 3, typifies much social scientific writing, appears here as if it were common-sensically obvious. Moreover, the word 'nationalism' seems 'naturally' to attract those adjectives of criticism ('arrogant', 'bellicose') which 'patriotism' avoids. The author does not justify the distinction between 'patriotism' and 'nationalism', but uses it almost off-handedly, thereby treating it as if it were common sense.

So far there is nothing specifically philosophical about the article. However, there are additional features. The writer, in presenting the American traditions which 'we' should identify with, specifies the predictable figure of Martin Luther King. He also mentions less obvious heroes: the philosophers John Dewey and Ralph Waldo Emerson. The text, thus, invites intellectuals to take pride in the American tradition of philosophy.

The philosophical theme is hardly surprising, given that the author was Richard Rorty. Here in the pages of the *New York Times*, the philosopher – the heralded sage of 'our' age – was waving his national flag. And, in the name of patriotism, he was also waving the flag of American philosophy. Given the intrusion of philosophy into Rorty's argument, the suspicion is that the patriotic call is not a private obsession, kept apart from professional concerns. It is not something which impels Rorty, the individual citizen, to write in newspapers, while another Rorty, the philosopher, struggles with a different set of problems in journals such as *Review of Metaphysics* or *The Proceedings of the Aristotelian Society*. The suspicion is that the two are of a piece: that there might be a harmony between his philosophy of detached, postmodern irony and the call for a greater patriotism of the American way. If the former is seen by some observers as the philosophy for current times, and if its key themes encompass nationalism, then this, in itself, is a commentary on the unacknowledged strength of American nationalism.

**A Complex Nationalism**

If Rorty is to be seen as a nationalist for the *Pax Americana*, then this is not the nationalism which is conventionally recognized to be 'extreme'. Rorty is no romantic conservative, reconstructing a heroic national past. Nor, by any stretch of the imagination, is Rorty an 'ethnic cleanser', glorifying the 'pure' race. His views do not belong to the sort of nationalism which his *New York Times* piece implicitly differentiated from 'patriotism'. His is the sort of banal nationalism which denies its own nationalism but urges loyalty to the nation-state, to 'our' nation. It is a nationalism which imagines 'our' nation to be tolerant and non-nationalist: 'others' are the bigots and the ethnic cleansers. As previous chapters have argued, these themes are commonplace in contemporary Western democracies. The denial of 'our' nationalism is nationalist, for it is part of the common-sense imagining of 'us', the democratic, tolerant and reasonable nation, rightfully inhabiting 'our' homeland.

There is another reason why the specific nationalism of the *Pax Americana* might have a complex rhetoric. The nation, which aspires to lead the other nations of the world, cannot appear merely to speak for itself – it must speak for all the world. If flags are to be waved internationally, they must be waved for 'all of us'. A complex rhetoric of hegemony can be expected: the cause of a nation, which imagines itself to be non-nationalist and which bids to be the voice of the world, must appear to transcend narrow nationalism. The particular and the universal will be combined, as they were in the *New York Times*, which switched seamlessly – almost unconsciously – from 'our' particular patriotism to the universal desirability of patriotism.

Rorty's philosophical texts can be seen as flags for the nationalism of the *Pax Americana* in the new global order. Two aspects can be mentioned, as a summary of the argument which is to follow. And a third point can be made as a prelude to the main argumentative business.

1  **Acceptance of the world of nations**. Rorty has strongly criticized the universalist tendencies of Enlightenment philosophy, especially in his book *Contingency, Irony and Solidarity* (1989). He argues that morality and politics should not be based upon ideas about 'common humanity', but should start from specific communities or societies. In the contemporary age, this means keeping nationhood in its place. Abandoning the Enlightenment dream of a common humanity implies, in Rorty's work, an acceptance of the presently divided world of nations.

2  **Promoting the American way**. A global American hegemony is rhetorically constructed in Rorty's texts, as he suggests that the pragmatic, non-ideological voice of America should be the voice of 'us all'. There are 'ideological dilemmas' at the heart of this nationalism (Billig et al., 1988). It cannot appear too nationalist, yet it cannot be too universalist, for it must defend 'us' and 'our' way of life. In consequence, there is a rhetorical ambiguity, even evasion, about the issue of nation in Rorty's open-minded, liberal philosophy.

3  **Intellectual creativity**. To pursue such arguments is not to gainsay Rorty's creativity as a philosopher. Nor is it to deny that his philosophy contains many attractive features. Rorty's sense of humane concern,

the clarity of his writing and his willingness to address serious political
issues all deserve high praise. Indeed, it is precisely because of the
depth and originality of his thinking, and because his writing does not
retreat behind textual barricades of self-serving jargon, that Rorty's
work has the importance that it does. It strikes chords which produce a
wider echo: if it did not, Rorty would not have been heralded as a sage
for the times.


## Starting From Where We Are

Classic nationalist theories do not start from the Cartesian 'I', which could
be the ego of any human being. Instead, they are philosophies of the first
person plural. They start from the group, and, in surveying the history of
groups, one particular group (nation or culture) is made to stand out from
the rest: 'ours'. Rorty, too, formulates a philosophy of the first person
plural. In *Contingency, Irony and Solidarity* he asserts that "*we* have to
start from where *we* are" (1989, p. 198, emphases in original).

Rorty's own rhetoric conveys this basic message: the first person plural
constantly appears in his texts. Rorty's conception of 'us' is directly related
to his anti-realism, which was most comprehensively worked out in
*Philosophy and the Mirror of Nature* (1979). There is no absolute
knowledge, Rorty argues: truth is not out there waiting to be discovered.
Through 'our' contingent use of language, 'we' construct statements, which
'we' claim to be true. Always, there has to be a 'we', for knowledge is
contingently related to some community. As Rorty suggests, "there is
nothing to be said about either truth or rationality apart from descriptions
of the familiar procedures of justification, which a given society – *ours* –
uses in one or another area of inquiry" (Rorty, 1987a, p. 42, emphasis in
original).

Morality is also socially constructed. Rorty argues that there are no
absolute standards, such as 'liberty, equality and fraternity', which can be
proclaimed as universally appropriate for all humanity. He advises that
"we try *not* to want something which stands beyond history and institutions" (1989, p. 189, emphasis in original). Moral judgements make sense
in relation to the customs of specific communities: "the core meaning of
'immoral action' is 'the sort of thing *we* don't do' " (1989, p. 59, emphasis
in original). Again, Rorty's rhetoric can be noted: the first person plural is
not only used, but it is emphasized.

A sense of communal identity, or a sense of 'us' being 'us', is a
prerequisite for morality and for reason. As Rorty (1990) puts it: "What
counts as rational or as fanatical is relative to the group to which we think it
necessary to justify ourselves – to the body of shared belief that determines
the reference of the word 'we' " (p. 281). In this way, the community is
prior to specific moral, political or scientific judgements. Communal
solidarity is an end in itself. It cannot be justified in terms of other moral

principles, because that would posit some form of universal morality existing outside of 'our' community. Therefore, 'our' society is not in need of its own legitimation, for it is the source of legitimation. Rorty has suggested that liberals, such as himself, should seek to "convince our society that loyalty to itself is morality enough and that such loyalty no longer needs an ahistorical backup" (1991, p. 199).

A philosophy of the first person plural, which disclaims that 'we' covers all humanity, is also, by implication, a philosophy of the third person plural. If there is an 'us', there must also be a 'them', from which 'we' distinguish ourselves. According to Rorty, every group has distinctive features "which it uses to construct its self-image through contrasts with other groups" (1991, p. 200). Nations are prime examples, he adds, along with churches and social movements. Through such 'contrast effects', dignity is claimed. Thus, "persons have dignity not as an interior luminescence, but because they share in such contrast effects" (p. 200). In this way, Rorty depicts a world of different societies, each claiming the loyalties of its members, each asserting its own moralities, and each distinguishing itself from others. If 'we' have to start from where 'we' are, then this world of distinctive groups is 'our' world.

In articulating this, Rorty's own rhetoric shifts. As in the *New York Times* piece, Rorty moves from the particular to the general. From talking about 'us', in 'our' particular society or nation, he moves to groups in general. In effect, he is articulating a universal social psychology of groups, which is rather similar to the Social Identity Theory discussed in Chapter 4. Rorty invokes psychological assumptions as he makes his points about loyalties, self-images and group identity in general. Thus, 'our' particular sense of 'ourselves' as distinct from 'others' is depicted as an instance of something universal, even as 'we' are denying the validity of universal statements.

## Defending Ethnocentrism

Nineteenth-century nationalists would recognize Rorty's depiction of a world comprising different groups. They would share Rorty's impatience with Enlightenment ideals, which try to wish away differences by appealing to a common humanity. Indeed, classic nationalists would find the notion of a 'common humanity' as much a fiction as does Rorty. They would nod at the implication that 'we' must give loyalty to 'our' own society and that other duties are subservient to the creation of communal solidarity. And, indeed, they would applaud Rorty for describing his outlook as 'ethnocentric', as he does in his essay 'On ethnocentrism: a reply to Clifford Geertz', which is reprinted in *Objectivity, Relativism and Truth* (1991).

The old-style nationalists would, nevertheless, be perplexed by the way in which Rorty sticks up for his 'us'. He appears to advocate a restricted, rather defensive form of ethnocentrism: "In my sense of ethnocentrism, to be ethnocentric is simply to work by our own lights" (1987a, p. 43). Rorty stresses that 'we' should resist the temptations of cultural relativism. 'We' should not feel embarrassed to condemn the moral views of others as "irredeemably crazy, stupid, base or sinful" (1991, p. 203). It is right that 'we' tend to see the enemies of constitutional democracy as "crazy": "They are crazy because the limits of sanity are set by what *we* can take seriously" (1990, p. 288, emphasis in original). If "we begin to lose any capacity for moral indignation, any capacity to feel contempt", then "our sense of selfhood dissolves" (1991, p. 203). 'We' would no longer be confident in thinking of 'ourselves' as 'us': 'our' sense of morality and rationality would, then, crumble.

Rorty notes that a liberal, who defends ethnocentrism, faces a particular problem: liberalism is supposed to oppose ethnocentric bigotry. In calling 'others' mad or bad, aren't 'we' displaying the very ethnocentrism which 'we' deplore in 'others'? There is a paradox: "We would rather die than be ethnocentric, but ethnocentrism is precisely the conviction that one would rather die than share certain beliefs" (1991, p. 203).

Rorty's answer to the paradox is that 'we' have to start from 'ourselves'. 'Our' ethnocentrism is different, principally because 'we' can recognize it as ethnocentrism. Whilst others are convinced of the absolute truthfulness of their beliefs, 'we' recognize the cultural contingency of 'ours'. When Rorty introduces the term 'ethnocentrism' to describe his (or, rather, 'our') beliefs, he uses a careful semantics: a more extreme ethnocentrism (one which 'we' oppose) is indicated. For instance, he claims that "to say that we must be ethnocentric may sound suspicious, but this will only happen if we identify ethnocentrism with pig-headed refusal to talk to representatives of other communities" (1987a, p. 43). 'Our' culture encourages tolerance and "among the enemies it diabolizes are the people who attempt to diminish this capacity, the vicious ethnocentrics" (1991, p. 204).

Rorty's admission of 'our' ethnocentrism rhetorically accomplishes three things. First, he suggests that ethnocentrism is inevitable: 'we' (everyone, all humans) have to start from 'our' particular group, 'our' own lights. In declaring that 'we' are all ethnocentric, Rorty is making just the sort of claim about a common human nature which he criticizes Enlightenment philosophers for making. Whereas such philosophers assumed a perfectible human nature, Rorty assumes 'our' imperfectibility as a 'fact'. Their belief in universal perfectibility is a problem for Rorty, but not his own belief in universal imperfectibility. Secondly, Rorty bolsters 'our' (Western) claims to tolerance, for 'our' ethnocentrism is broad-minded: 'we' recognize 'our' limitations; 'we' are the people who distrust pig-headed ethnocentrism etc. Thirdly, in stating this, Rorty is contrasting 'us' favourably with 'others'.

In this way, the admitted ethnocentrism (which simultaneously is a subtly denied ethnocentrism) enables 'us' to praise 'ourselves', and to condemn 'others'. Given that 'we' all have to be ethnocentric, then 'we' are the best of ethnocentrics. On the final page of *Contingency, Irony and Solidarity*, Rorty declares the need for 'us' to show solidarity with 'our' community. If this is ethnocentrism, then what "takes the curse off this ethnocentrism" is that 'we' are "the people who have been brought up to distrust ethnocentrism" (1989, p. 198). The distinction between 'our' reasonable ethnocentrism and 'their' pig-headed ethnocentrism can be re-cast as the difference between 'patriotism' and 'nationalism', or between 'necessary pride' and 'surplus pride'. 'Our' pride, of course, is both patriotic and necessary. As such, 'we' can be proud of 'our' pride. 'We' can boast "the signal glory of our liberal society" and 'we' can take "pride in being bourgeois liberals, in being a part of a great tradition, a citizen of no mean culture" (1991, pp. 206 and 203). 'We' can be proud of 'ourselves', because 'we' are not the sort of people to be proud of 'ourselves'.

For all its elegant sophistication, Rorty's argument parallels those voices of common-sense nationalism which imagine the tolerant 'us', beset by intolerant hordes. Of course, no one's perfect, but 'we' can be proud that 'we're' not as bad as the rest. After all, 'we' know 'our' limitations. Unlike the mad and the bad, massing beyond 'our' boundaries. Yes, it's time 'we' stuck up for 'ourselves'. Despite what all those clever-clever lefties say. And while we're on the subject: it's time they showed a bit of decent respect for the flag.

### 'We' and the Syntax of Hegemony

Although Rorty discusses 'us' at length, it is unclear exactly who 'we' are. In keeping with his view that language is contingent and that universal claims are empty, Rorty argues that the first person plural should not be used in a general way. Instead, philosophers should "give 'we' as concrete and historically specific sense as possible" (1989, p. 196). Rorty himself parades a whole variety of 'we's in his writings. A few examples can be given, although practically any page of Rorty's is likely to yield up more 'we-descriptions'. He has a whole collection of specialized liberal flags: "we liberals" (1990, p. 289); "we Western liberals" (1987a, p. 51); "we twentieth century liberals" (1989, p. 196); "we bourgeois liberals" (1991, p. 206); "we postmodern bourgeois liberals" (1991, p. 208); "we decent, liberal, humanitarian types" (1993a, p. 44) etc. and etc. There are a host of other 'we's: "we pragmatists"; "we fuzzies" (1987a, p. 41); "we new fuzzies" (1987a, p. 48); "we heirs of the Enlightenment" (1990, p. 287); "we post-Kuhnians", "we anti-essentialists" (1991, pp. 96 and 106); "we philosophers"; "we philosophy professors" (1993a, pp. 45 and 49); "we Deweyans", "us twentieth century Western social democrats", "we Anglo-Saxons" (1991, pp. 212, 214 and 221); and, also, "we Americans" (1991, p. 76).

As one critic has noted, in Rorty's writings " 'we' contracts or expands . . . to fit any available space" (Comay, 1986, p. 69; see also Bernstein, 1987, pp. 547f.; Bhaskar, 1992, pp. 93ff.). Sometimes, 'we' are a philoso-phical school, sometimes a whole political culture; sometimes 'we' are bounded by time and place; sometimes 'we' are Western, sometimes postmodern, and sometimes merely Anglo-Saxon. On other occasions, 'we' are left free to roam unfettered across the whole human race: "The world does not speak. Only we do" (Rorty, 1989, p. 6). All human beings, all of 'us' – not merely the Deweyans, the bourgeois and the Anglo-Saxons – speak. Here 'we' are speaking for all of 'us'.

One might ask what is going on in Rorty's texts? What is this rhetoric of the first person plural accomplishing? In the first place, the multiplicity of 'we's can be interpreted as suggesting a postmodernist multiplicity of selves, which 'we' possess today (e.g., Heller, 1991). There is, however, a further point, which can be made. 'We' is an important feature of the syntax of hegemony, for it can provide a handy rhetorical device for presenting sectional interests as if they were universal ones. 'We', the sectional interest, invoke an 'all of us', for whom 'we' claim to speak. Hegemonic discourse is marked by such elisions of 'we's. As was seen in previous chapters, the syntax of hegemony can be used to suggest an identity of identities. Political speakers routinely elide first person plurals: we the speaker and audience, we the party, we the government, we the nation, we the right-thinking people, we the Western world, we the universal audience – they all slide together. The boundaries between one 'we' and another one are routinely and rhetorically entangled, as speakers skilfully portray a harmonious world, in which all 'we's speak with one voice – the speaker's own voice. In this way, 'we' are integrated and directed by a pronoun which semantically integrates and directs (see, for example, Mühlhäusler and Harré, 1990).

Something similar occurs in Rorty's texts. 'We' never keeps still: it keeps popping up with new adjectival costumes. Even a single sentence can alternate particular and universal 'we's. 'We', the pragmatists, the fuzzies or the Deweyans, have understood how 'we', all humans, use language. 'Our' anti-realist message does not refer just to 'us' but to 'all of us'. Rorty claims that there is no reality to which philosophers can appeal "save the way *we* live now, what *we* do now, how *we* talk now – anything beyond *our* own little moment of world history" (1991, p. 158, emphases in original). He is not saying that only 'we' (perhaps Westerners, Americans, liberals), in this little moment of world history, are limited in this way. He is not making the critical point that 'our' contemporary society has destroyed the possibility of 'our' being in contact with reality (indeed, Rorty, 1990, specifically criticizes theorists like Adorno for attempting to make such claims). In such passages, Rorty's 'we' is not historically contingent. It is a universal 'we': all 'we's, whatever their own little moments of history, are limited by those little moments. In this way, Rorty's 'we' expands from the local 'we' to an imagined 'universal we', and, in so doing he rhetorically addresses himself to a 'universal audience', placing himself in the community of all reasonable people, who might understand what 'we' are saying (Perelman and Olbrechts-Tyteca, 1971).

This shifting of 'we's does not make the texts hard to follow, any more than the routine pronominal ambiguities of political speeches leave audiences perplexed. The syntax of hegemony is rhetorically familiar. Through its use, Rorty can claim to be more than Rorty, the writer. 'We pragmatists' or 'we Deweyans' are more than a minor movement in contemporary philosophy: 'we' speak for 'us' liberals, democrats, citizens of the West, and for humanity.

## Return of the Repressed Nationhood

There is one identity largely absent in Rorty's philosophical 'we's, but hugely foregrounded in his *New York Times* article: a national identity. 'We Americans' is not one of his major philosophical flags, although it is occasionally hoisted. In his philosophical texts, Rorty tends to write of 'our society' rather than 'our nation'. In the passage quoted earlier from *Objectivity, Relativity and Truth*, Rorty asserts that loyalty to 'our society' (rather than 'nation') is an end in itself. Rorty writes as if the notion of 'society' is unproblematic: he advocates loyalty to 'our society' without specifying what a 'society' is. Most importantly, he does not say how this society ('ours') distinguishes itself from other 'societies' in a world of distinctive 'societies' and 'contrast-effects'.

Although Rorty argues for the need to situate 'us' in a concrete, historical context, he tends to gloss over the fact that the nation-state is the contingent form of what is understood by 'society' in the contemporary world. The textual elision of 'nation' into 'society' permits nationhood to remain uncriticized; it is the taken-for-granted grounding, while the text (together with its writer, its readers and its constructed community of 'us') appears non-nationalist, assuming the reality of 'societies'. Rorty's own syntax indicates that nationhood stands behind 'societies'. Sometimes this is directly expressed, especially when Rorty is writing of the United States. For instance, he comments: "I think that our country . . . is an example of the best kind of society so far invented" (1993a, p. 33). Thus, 'the best sort of society' is a nation-state, considered by its citizens as 'our country' – and it is one to which 'we' should show patriotic loyalty. The same sentiment, and elision between society and nation, occurred in the *New York Times* piece. Sometimes the assumption of nationhood is expressed more indirectly. For instance, Rorty suggests that 'we postmodern bourgeois liberals' should attempt "to defend the institutions and practices of the rich North Atlantic democracies" (1991, p. 198). The use of the plural – 'democracies' – is significant. This plurality does not refer to a multiplicity of democratic forms, but to a multiplicity of independent 'societies' in which democratic institutions are situated. What the text does not specify – nor could it without going into the issue of nationhood – is why there should be a plurality of 'societies', and, thus, a plurality of 'we's, who will be making contrasts between themselves and the other 'we's.

Again, the phrase 'the institutions of democracy' (which Rorty often uses) omits something crucial. In the modern age, democratic institutions developed within the nation-state, and, therefore, nationhood can be seen as one of the institutions of democracy (Harris, 1990). If so, then Rorty's argument has an unstated theme: to protect democracies and their institutions, one ('we') must protect the 'societies' in which they are situated. Unless otherwise stated, this means protecting the institutions of nationhood ('our' nationhood). To protect a nation is to protect a national identity, which, as Rorty recognizes, distinguishes that community from other communities. In the context of nations, this means preserving the nationalist myths by which nations depict themselves as unique 'imagined communities' – as 'our country' with its mystically assumed associations with a delimited territory. In this way, Rorty's argument contains within itself an implicit defence of the world of nations, and, thus, a world of nationalisms.

Using, and glossing over, the word 'society' pushes the uncomfortable implications of this argument to the textual margins. These can be brought out by the simple textual device of replacing 'society' by 'nation'. The replacement can be justified by Rorty's own recommendation to be as historically specific as possible, for 'nation' is more historically bound than the universal term 'society'. Using a quotation already cited, an example of such a textual replacement can be given:

> I hope thereby to suggest how such liberals might convince our nation that loyalty to itself is morality enough.

If this has an uncomfortable echo, then the echo itself is contained in Rorty's own work. His abandonment of universal dreams, combined with his defence of ethnocentrism and 'our' own contingently existing institutions, provide no stance for criticizing nationalism. Instead, his views are adjusted to this world of nations.

## The Philosophy of the *Pax Americana*

Many of Rorty's phrases suggest that 'we' belong to 'the rich North Atlantic democracies' as a whole, rather than to a single nation. The syntax of hegemony suggests that 'we pragmatists' are not just speaking on behalf of 'our society', but for an alliance of 'societies'. There are a number of themes in this evocation of hegemony. Three aspects can be briefly mentioned: (a) the unity within America; (b) the rhetorical construction of the alliance of the West; and (c) the relations between 'our' bloc and the rest of the world.

### American Society

When Rorty describes what makes 'our country' the best sort of society, he writes as a liberal. His more academic writings, in this regard, are at one with the *New York Times* article. He sees "the 'progressivists' as defining the only America I care about" (1993a, p. 46). The conservative right, he argues, threatens this America. Rorty's political rhetoric is far more Clinton than Bush. Indeed, Rorty has declared in a newspaper interview that he supported Clinton for the presidency and that "Reagan and Bush were a disaster for the country" (*Guardian*, 26 February 1993).

There is also a strong anti-Marxist element in this 'progressivism': the *New York Times* attack on the leftist, unpatriotic academy has an intellectual background. Generally, Rorty situates himself in the "anti-ideological liberalism" which is pragmatic and anti-theoretical. In his view, pragmatism is "the most valuable tradition of American intellectual life" (1991, p. 64). The anti-Marxist element of this tradition is evident in Rorty's tribute to the philosopher Sydney Hook. According to Rorty, it was Hook's later dedication to the cause of anti-Marxism which prevented American intellectual leftists as a whole from being "buffaloed by the Marxists" (p. 49). Rorty praises Hook's attack on 'knee-jerk liberalism', especially that which blames "anything bad that happens on American ruling circles" (1991, p. 76). Rorty also distances himself from the McCarthyism which Hook came to represent. Rorty uses a softer rhetoric, and he specifically criticizes Hook's tactics, if not his principles.

Rorty, in outlining his liberal position, uses the rhetoric of union rather than that of division. He wishes to develop feelings of communal solidarity, rather than divide the community. He deplores the exclusion of marginal groups from 'our' society, and he advocates a politics of incorporation. The rhetoric of national identity can be useful for developing a liberal community. In *Contingency, Irony and Solidarity* he asks how "American liberals" should talk to young, urban blacks (the text assumes that the latter are American, and that the liberals are white). More effective than addressing "these people" as 'fellow human beings' would be to talk to them as "our fellow *Americans* – to insist that it is outrageous that an *American* should live without hope" (1989, p. 191, emphases in original).

There is a curious rhetorical reversal in the same paragraph. Rorty speculates on the way of thinking which led Danes and Italians to save Jews during the Nazi occupation. An appeal to a common humanity would have been less useful than thinking of particular Jews "as a fellow Milanese, or a fellow Jutlander, or a fellow member of the same union or profession, or a fellow bocce player, or a fellow parent of small children" (1989, pp. 190–1). Curiously, Rorty does not advocate that the Danes and Italians should have thought of particular Jews as 'fellow-Danes' or 'fellow-Italians'. The sort of national identification that Rorty recommends fellow Americans to use is conspicuous by its absence in the hypothetical advice he gives to the Danes and Italians. Perhaps the nationalism of 'others' – Danish or Italian – is less comfortable: it awakens echoes in a way that 'ours' does not; and, of course, it excludes 'us'. Moreover, the problems of the Jews, who were to be considered as fellow Milanese or fellow Jutlanders, arose because they were being defined as outsiders by nationalist ideologies.

In recommending his fellow liberals to address young (American) blacks as 'fellow Americans', Rorty draws upon the nationalist rhetoric of

American mythology – the image of the land of hope. This rhetoric, which is so familiar in both liberal and conservative US politics, recreates the image of America as the special nation, the special community of 'us'. By recommending this rhetoric, Rorty is conserving nationalist mythology for 'our' use, for accomplishing 'our' union. In consequence, nationalism underwrites 'our' liberalism, as it does the Democratic politics of Clinton. Indeed, Rorty, in his essay 'Wild orchids and Trotsky', openly declares that "we Deweyans are sentimentally patriotic about America" (1993a, p. 47). Thus, if Rorty recommends that 'we' start from where 'we' are, then 'we' start from 'our' homeland. And this homeland is to be cherished with patriotic pride as the best of societies.

## The Western Alliance

Rorty recommends that a particular way of doing philosophy and of doing politics should be 'our' way – the way of the Western democracies. 'We' should give up grand theorizing, and adopt a non-ideological pragmatism which matches 'our' place and times. After all, "our society has, tacitly, given up on the idea that theology or philosophy will supply general rules" for solving the problems of politics (1991, pp. 206–7). But which is 'our' society? Have all the Western societies given up on philosophy, or is one society in the vanguard, showing the way to the rest, just as 'we pragmatists' are leading the way in philosophy?

When Rorty praises John Dewey, he situates his own pragmatism both intellectually and nationally. In *Philosophy and the Mirror of Nature* (1979) Rorty claimed that Dewey is one of the three most important philosophers of the twentieth century, the other two being Wittgenstein and Heidegger. Recently, Dewey seems to have pulled in front of his two European rivals (1991, p. 16). He is now described more simply as "my hero" (1993b, p. 3). The point is not that Rorty chooses an American as his philosophical hero, but that he praises Dewey for representing specifically American characteristics. In 'Wild orchids and Trotsky', Rorty directly associates himself with Dewey's vision of America: "I see America pretty much as Whitman and Dewey did, as opening a prospect of illimitable democratic vistas" (p. 32). Here again, the more technical themes are repeating ideas expressed in the *New York Times* article.

One of Rorty's main recommendations is to de-throne philosophy from the exalted place it has claimed for itself. He argues that 'we' should let philosophy take second place to democracy, for nothing is more important than the preservation of liberal institutions (see for instance, 1987b, pp. 567f.). In his essay 'The priority of democracy to philosophy', Rorty reminds readers of the intellectual and cultural history behind his essay's title. Dewey "admired the American habit of giving democracy priority over philosophy"; Rorty also points out that Emerson thought Dewey's pragmatism to be "characteristically American" (1990, p. 294). According to Rorty, Dewey was accused of "blowing up the optimism and flexibility" of the American way of life into a whole philosophical system. Rorty comments: "So he did, but his reply was that *any* philosophical system is going to be an attempt to express the ideals of *some* community's way of life." In this way, Dewey was able to expatiate on "the special advantages" of his community "over other communities" (Rorty, 1987a, pp. 49–50, emphases in original).

Here, Rorty's championing of Dewey involves a roundabout rhetoric, appropriate for texts such as philosophical works, which, unlike the *New York Times*, are addressed to multinational audiences. His approval of Dewey (and his quoting, with apparent approval, what others said about Dewey's Americanism) enables Rorty to repeat praise for the American way of doing things, whilst not directly uttering the praise himself. According to others (Emerson, unnamed critics, Dewey himself), Dewey's pragmatism is typically American; and, according to Rorty, 'we' Deweyans praise such pragmatism. If Rorty had himself drawn out the implied connections, he would be claiming that his own philosophy of pragmatism is characteristically American and that he, Rorty, by praising (American) pragmatism, is praising the special advantages of his community (nation) over other communities (nations). That thought is too nationalist to be uttered directly, at least in philosophical texts addressed across national boundaries to an audience of 'we philosophers' or 'we postmoderns'. It would undermine the hegemonic aspiration to speak for 'us' liberals in the other Western democracies. Nevertheless, the thought remains scattered within the philosophical text, waiting to be assembled.

## Speaking for the Whole World

The voice of hegemony must seek a wider audience of 'us'. Rorty constantly argues that 'we' should extend 'ourselves'. In fact, he claims that this drive to incorporate 'others' distinguishes his tolerant ethnocentrism from pig-headed varieties. 'Ours' is an ethnocentrism of inclusion rather than exclusion. He urges that 'we' "keep trying to expand our sense of 'us' as far as we can": 'we' should try to note the similarities between 'us' and marginalized people "whom we still instinctively think of as 'they' rather than 'us' " (1991, p. 196). The good intentions and the humanitarian tolerance are undeniable, especially in relation to internal US politics, where, as has been seen, expanding the sense of 'we' involves emphasizing a sense of nationality. Nevertheless, Rorty specifically applies his message to the world at large (see, for example, Rorty, 1991, pp. 212f.). The movement of the categorization is significant. 'We' change 'them' from 'them' into 'us'. 'They' are the ones to be incorporated and recategorized, while 'we' remain 'ourselves' with the same self-identity. In fact, 'we' may not need to change 'ourselves' for "Western social and political thought may have had the last *conceptual* revolution it needs" (1991, p. 63).

'We' have ambitions to spread 'ourselves' – 'our' message, 'our' way of politics – across the globe. 'Our' time has come, for 'we pragmatists' should see "the history of humanity . . . as the gradual spread of certain virtues typical of the democratic West" (1991, p. 216). 'We' hope to incorporate all others into 'our' way of doing things: "Deweyan pragmatists urge us to think of ourselves as part of a pageant of historical progress which will gradually encompass all of the human race" (1991, p. 219). If Rorty (1993b, p. 3) has written of "the great social hope which permeates the democratic societies – the hope for a co-operative global utopia", then this utopia is going to need 'us' to advance its cause: and this requires 'us' to remain 'us', taking pride in 'our' particular nation and its heritage.

In such writings, it is possible to identify a tone suited to the new *Pax Americana*. The philosophy distances itself from the rhetoric of the Cold War. It discards certainty, even denying that it is philosophy in the old sense. It claims to have a supposedly non-ideological message for supposedly non-ideological times. The American way – the way of non-ideological pragmatism – is recommended for all. On a number of occasions, Rorty has criticized French philosophy for being too theoretical, too wedded to the universalism of the Enlightenment. But, as he says, the issue is wider than philosophy for he is responding to a "massive phenomenon", which is "the post-war failure of American nerve" and "the loss of America's hopes to lead the nations" (1991, p. 77).

Although Rorty does not explicitly reclaim the role for his nation, his rhetoric implies a reclamation. 'We' hope to spread 'ourselves', and 'our' way, across the globe, for 'we' are the force of historical progress. If 'we' succeed, 'we' will lead the nations. In this way, Rorty writes of his hope that "America will continue to set an example of increasing tolerance and equality" (1993a, p. 45). He does not specify to whom this example is being set, nor who 'they', the followers of 'our' example, should be. But the rest of the world can be assumed.

## The Text as Flag

There, in philosophical outline, is the nationalism of the *Pax Americana*. The familiar clichés of the politician, or the newspaper editorial, calling for greater patriotism, can, if required, be given an intellectual justification from the 'sage' of the times. This philosophical nationalism, unlike some other forms, does not speak with narrow ferocity. Instead, it draws its moral force to lead the nations from its own proclaimed reasonableness. The global ambitions are to be presented as the voice of tolerance ('our' tolerance), even doubt ('our' doubt, 'our' modesty). All the while, 'we' are to keep a sense of 'ourselves'. And a sense of 'others': the mad and the bad, who cling to dangerous absolutes, opposing 'our' pragmatic, non-ideological politics. It should be noted how easily new enemies – the religious fundamentalists, particularly Islamic fundamentalists, and also the misguided extremists within 'our' own homeland – can replace old Soviet demons in this ideological matrix.

It has become customary for cultural analysts to treat objects, such as flags, as if they were texts. The process can be reversed, so that the text appears as a flag. Rorty's texts, with their drum-beat of 'we's, seek to enrol 'us', his readers, in their literary march. Rorty's flag (or his collection of flags for every 'us') may be vastly preferable to other flags – such as those of the religious fundamentalists or the ethnic cleansers. However, if the text is a flag, then its patterns must be read. Between the printed lines are white stripes; at a metaphorical squint, Rorty's words are striped with warning red. White stars on a blue background twinkle among his marginalia. And together they beckon 'us' with charm, tempting 'us' to leave 'our' dreams behind.

# 8

# Concluding Remarks

This book has been urging again and again: 'Look and see the constant flaggings of nationhood.' Often unnoticed, these flaggings are not hidden. They are unlike the messages from the unconscious mind, which, according to Freudian theory, are repressed from consciousness, and leave only oblique outward traces. Freud, as is well known, proposed that a complex training was necessary to enable people to read the signs of the unconscious. The flaggings of nationhood are quite different. Their unobtrusiveness arises, in part, from their very familiarity. Shameful desires have not driven them from conscious awareness. No course of formal instruction is required to notice the flaggings. Instead, there need be only a conscious willingness to look towards the background or to attend to the little words.

Previous chapters have drawn attention to various sorts of flaggings. Richard Rorty's philosophy, which at first glance might appear to be the voice of sophisticated, cosmopolitan irony, was described as a textual flag: if one looks closely, one can see the pages of his philosophy waving gently in support of the United States. Then, there is the world of professional wrestling, two generations after Roland Barthes' famous essay. Today, the theatre of wrestling might appear as a grotesque parade of hyper-masculinity or just good fun, depending on personal taste. But there is more. National flags are part of the display. In particular, the American Stars and Stripes can be waved to the sound of global cheers or merely displayed as a necessary part of wrestling's environment.

Flagging is not confined to bouts of philosophy or to the syllogisms of wrestling. It spreads beyond such restricted, specialist domains. The media of mass communication bring the flag across the contemporary hearth. Daily newspapers and logomanic politicians constantly flag the world of nations. They routinely use a deixis of little words. 'Here', 'us' and 'the' are so easy to overlook. They are not words to grab the attention, but they perform an important task in the business of flagging. Banally, they address 'us' as a national first person plural; and they situate 'us' in the homeland within a world of nations. Nationhood is the context which must be assumed to understand so many banal utterances. Even 'the weather', so familiar and so concrete a concept, is routinely nationalized in this way. Cumulatively, such flaggings provide daily, unmindful reminders of nationhood in the contemporary, established nation-state. It is no wonder, then, that national identity is seldom forgotten.

Once one starts looking for flaggings, they seem to be ubiquitous. As the television newscaster mentions a foreign country, an emblematic flag flashes on to the screen. The Hollywood traffic cop stopping the car which carries hero and heroine on their adventures has an emblem of state stitched to his upper arm. The newspaper addresses 'us', its readers, as if 'we' are all nationals of the same state: it tells 'us' of 'home' news. Earlier chapters have offered examples of flaggings which were gathered almost haphazardly, as if a handful of fruit had been quickly grabbed from the edge of a ripe orchard. There is much systematic, empirical work to be done. Taxonomies of flaggings could be constructed to list the different genres and their customary rhetorical strategies; and the extent of flaggings in different domains, and in different nations, could be calculated. Above all, the lives of citizens in established nations need to be profiled, in order to document the nature and number of flaggings which the average person might encounter in the course of a typical day. In short, the serious business of classification and calculation has barely begun.

What is the point of doing all this tabulation, one might ask. Why bother to notice signs which are not struggling for attention and which often provide the means for directing awareness to much more interesting things? Shouldn't we listen to what the newscaster is saying, rather than concentrate on the routine graphics? Why spend time on the cop's arm, when we can watch the stunning good looks of hero and heroine? And why spoil the wrestling match by concentrating upon the flags, when there is so much else to notice, and so much else to object to?

The short answer is that by noticing the flaggings of nationhood, we are noticing something about ourselves. We are noticing the depths and mechanisms of our identity, embedded in routines of social life. These rhetorical episodes continually remind us that we are 'us' and, in so doing, permit us to forget that we are being reminded. And, if we look closely, we not only see reminders of 'ourselves'; we see reminders of 'them' and foreignness. What is so familiar that it hardly warrants a second glance can, then, begin to look strange. Not only are 'we' (and 'them') flagged, but so is the homeland; and the world as a world of homelands is also conveyed. A banal mysticism, which is so banal that all the mysticism seems to have evaporated long ago, binds 'us' to the homeland – that special place which is more than just a place, more than a mere geophysical area. In all this, the homeland is made to look homely, beyond question and, should the occasion arise, worth the price of sacrifice. And men, in particular, are given their special, pleasure-saturated reminders of the possibility of sacrifice.

There is a further reason for looking carefully. We are not just noticing our own identity, or even the identity of others. All those identities do not float in some sort of free psychological space. Identities are forms of social life. National identities are rooted within a powerful social structure, which reproduces hegemonic relations of inequity. Moreover, the nation-state is rooted in a world of such states. To quote Anthony Giddens, the nation-state remains a 'power-container'. The power, in its ultimate form, is direct physical power, amassed in unprecedented quantities. Nations collectively possess weaponry sufficient to destroy the globe. Even in times of economic stress, states continue to devote vast resources to armaments. Currently, for example, in Britain public spending on what is conventionally called 'defence' is double that on education (*Guardian*, 30 November 1994). There is little remarkable about these proportions: across the globe they are reproduced in nation after nation. 'Defence', in this context, means national defence and the weaponry for defence is nationally controlled and nationally possessed.

This needs to be borne in mind when observing the banal symbols of nationhood. It also should be remembered when considering the claim that the nation-state is withering away, as the world moves from a system of sovereign states into some sort of global, postmodern village; or when the world is imagined to be moving from masculine patriarchal states towards an unbounded feminine future. There are, to be sure, signs of change and old boundaries are being opened up. Information is transmitted electronically across state borders without let or hindrance. A new politics of identity seems, at first sight, to challenge old nationalist hegemonies; new faces, and new diversities, are to be found in the pictures of national identity. Even American Presidents are talking about a new world order. But the last gives a clue that nationhood has by no means disappeared. The new world order is itself flagged as a national order, in which one nation will be *primus inter pares* and its culture experienced as a universal culture.

Nationalism, as has been argued, never spoke with a straightforwardly simple voice. It always used the syntax of hegemony, claiming an identity of identities. Today, claims about a 'world community' or a 'new global order' are being made on behalf of the most powerful nation. As they are made, so an identity of interests is asserted: 'our' interests are the interests of the whole world. Military forces, bearing national colours, are deployed to support these interests. This is said as a caution against the confident assertion that global processes are out-dating national ones in the postmodern world. Information technology, which is supposedly helping to undermine nationhood, is today being developed for military purposes, making weaponry ever more sophisticated. Those who proclaim the death of nationhood do not specify what will be done with all the armaments of states. Theoretical predictions cannot wish it away. The rockets, missiles and tanks are not suddenly going to be piled outside to rust in the rain.

To be sure, there will be changes in the structures of nations. States today are not as they were at the end of the nineteenth century. And, just as surely, the age of nationhood will pass eventually. History has created nations and, in time, it will unmake them. New forms of community will emerge, for the past is never repeated exactly. Perhaps the universal forms, which Rorty's philosophy enjoins us to forget, will have their time in the future. Maybe, nations are already past their heyday and their decline has already been set in motion. But this does not mean that nationhood can yet be written off, and its flaggings dismissed as pastiche or nostalgia.

The future today looks increasingly unclear. The last part of the twentieth century has seen profound international changes, which have caught most professional predictors unawares. The collapse of communism, the ending of *apartheid*, the recognition of Israel by Arab countries are events which, ten years before their occurrence, seemed unthinkable. If shifts of power produce vacuums, then these seem to be filled by those who are willing to yield weaponry in the cause of nationhood. And the United States of America, showing few signs of immediately following the Holy Roman Empire or Aztec polities into the graveyard of history, flags its global ambitions. These are reflected within a global culture, which even possesses its speciality products of philosophy.

Certainly, the ideal of nationhood today continues to exert its hold over the political imagination; it continues to be reproduced as the cause worth more than individual life; and it frames the practice of political democracy. Even if the structures of nationhood start to fragment, as theorists of the postmodern predict, it is optimistic to believe that the vast armaments will lie unused, while the entities they supposedly defend are supplanted. Perhaps, at that moment, nationalism will be at its most dangerous. Then, the credits accumulated by routine deposits of flaggings will be called upon.

Amid the uncertainty, one thing can be asserted with confidence. Today, innumerable signs of nationhood are being flagged. Tomorrow, there will be further flaggings, too, around the world. Countless national flags will be unceremoniously raised and lowered on their poles. This much, at least, we know. But it is unclear where the sequence is leading in the long term and what further calls for sacrifice will be made. If the future remains uncertain, we know the past history of nationalism. And that should be sufficient to encourage a habit of watchful suspicion.

# References

Abrams, D. and Hogg, M.A. (eds) (1991). *Social Identity Theory*. New York: Springer Verlag.

Achard, P. (1993). Discourse and social praxis in the construction of nation and state, *Discourse and Society*, 4, 75–98.

Adorno, T.W., Frenkel-Brunswik, E., Levinson, D.J. and Sanford, R.N. (1950). *The Authoritarian Personality*. New York: Harper and Row.

Agnew, J. (1989). Nationalism: autonomous force or practical politics? Place and nationalism in Scotland. In C.H. Williams and E. Kofman (eds), *Community Conflict, Partition and Nationalism*. London: Routledge.

Ahmed, A.S. (1992). *Postmodernism and Islam*. London: Routledge.

Akioye, A. (1994). The rhetorical construction of radical Africanism at the United Nations, *Discourse and Society*, 5, 7–32.

Altemeyer, B. (1981). *Right-Wing Authoritarianism*. Winnipeg: University of Manitoba Press.

Altemeyer, B. (1988). *Enemies of Freedom*. San Francisco: Jossey Bass.

Anderson, B. (1983). *Imagined Communities*. London: Verso.

Anderson, P. (1992). Science, politics, enchantment. In J.A. Hall and I.C. Jarvie (eds), *Transition to Modernity*. Cambridge: Cambridge University Press.

Anonymous (1916). *British Historical and Political Orations*. London: J.M. Dent.

Arendt, H. (1963). *Eichmann in Jerusalem: A Report on the Banality of Evil*. New York: Viking Press.

Aristotle. (1909). *Rhetoric*. Cambridge: Cambridge University Press.

Ashmore, M., Edwards, D. and Potter, J. (1994). The bottom line: the rhetoric of reality demonstrations, *Configurations*, 2, 1–14.

Atkinson, J.M. (1984). *Our Masters' Voices*. London: Methuen.

Augoustinos, M. (1993). 'Celebration of a Nation': representations of Australian national identity *Papers on Social Representations*, 2, 33–9.

Aulich, J. (1992). Wildlife in the South Atlantic: graphic satire, patriotism and the Fourth Estate. In J. Aulich (ed.), *Framing the Falklands War*. Buckingham: Open University Press.

Bachelard, G. (1969). *The Poetics of Space*. Boston: Beacon Press.

Bagehot, W. (1873). *Physics and Politics*. London: Henry S. King.

Bailyn, B. (1988). *The Peopling of North America: An Introduction*. New York: Vintage Books.

Bairstow, T. (1985). *Fourth-Rate Estate*. London: Comedia.

Bakhtin, M.M. (1981). *The Dialogic Imagination*. Austin: University of Texas.

Bakhtin, M.M. (1986). *Speech Genres and Other Late Essays*. Austin: University of Texas.

Baldwin, S. (1937). *On England*. Harmondsworth: Penguin.

Balibar, E. (1991). 'Is there a neo-racism'? In E. Balibar and I. Wallerstein, *Race, Nation, Class*. London: Verso.

Banton, M. (1994). Modelling ethnic and national relations, *Ethnic and Racial Studies*, 17, 1–20.

Bar-Tal, D. (1989). Delegitimization: the extreme case of stereotyping and prejudice. In D. Bar-Tal, C. Graumann, A.W. Kruglanski and W. Stroebe (eds), *Stereotyping and Prejudice*. New York: Springer Verlag.

Bar-Tal, D. (1990). *Group Beliefs*. New York: Springer Verlag.

Bar-Tal, D. (1993). Patriotism as fundamental beliefs of group members, *Politics and the Individual*, 3, 45–62.

Barker, M. (1981). *The New Racism*. London: Junction Books

Barnett, A. (1982). *Iron Britannia*. London: Allison and Busby.

Barthes, R. (1975). *The Pleasure of the Text*. New York: Farrar, Straus and Giroux.

Barthes, R. (1977). *Roland Barthes*. Basingstoke: Macmillan.

Barthes, R. (1983a). Inaugural lecture, Collège de France. In S. Sontag (ed.), *Barthes: Selected Writings*. London: Fontana.

Barthes, R. (1983b). Myth today. In S. Sontag (ed.), *Barthes: Selected Writings*. London: Fontana.

Barthes, R. (1983c). The world of wrestling. In S. Sontag (ed.), *Barthes: Selected Writings*. London: Fontana.

Baudrillard, J. (1983). *Simulations*. New York: Semiotext(e).

Baudrillard, J. (1988). *America*. Harmondsworth: Penguin.

Bauman, Z. (1992a). *Intimations of Postmodernity*. London: Routledge.

Bauman, Z. (1992b). Soil, blood and identity, *Sociological Review*, 40, 675–701.

Bauman, Z. (1993). *Postmodern Ethics*. London: Routledge.

Beattie, G. (1988). *All Talk*. London: Weidenfeld & Nicolson.

Beattie, G. (1993). *We Are the People*. London: Mandarin.

Beck, U. (1992). *Risk Society*. London: Sage.

Bellah, R.N., Madsen, R., Sullivan, W.M., Swidler, A. and Tipton, S.M. (1986). *Habits of the Heart*. New York: Harper and Row.

Benjamin, W. (1970). *Illuminations*. London: Fontana.

Bentham, J. (1789/1982). *An Introduction to the Principles of Morals and Legislation* (ed. J.H. Burns and H.L.A. Hart). London: Methuen.

Berkowitz, L. (1993). *Aggression: its Causes, Consequences and Control*. New York: McGraw Hill.

Berlin, I. (1991). *The Crooked Timber of Humanity*. New York: Alfred A. Knopf.

Bernstein, R. (1987). One step forward, two steps backward: Richard Rorty on liberal democracy and philosophy, *Political Theory*, 1987, 15, 538–63.

Bhabha, H. (1990). Introduction: narrating the nation. In H. Bhabha (ed.), *Nation and Narration*. London: Routledge.

Bhabha, H. (1992). Postcolonial authority and postmodern guilt. In L. Grossberg, C. Nelson and P. Treichler (eds), *Cultural Studies*. London: Routledge.

Bhaskar, R. (1992). *Philosophy and the Idea of Freedom*. Oxford: Basil Blackwell.

Bhavnani, K.-K. and Phoenix, A. (1994). Shifting identities shifting racisms: an introduction, *Feminism and Psychology*, 4, 5–18.

Billig, M. (1978). *Fascists: a Social Psychological View of the National Front*. London: Harcourt Brace Jovanovich.

Billig, M. (1985). Prejudice, categorization and particularization: from a perceptual to a rhetorical approach, *European Journal of Social Psychology*, 15, 79–103.

Billig, M. (1987a). *Arguing and Thinking*. Cambridge: Cambridge University Press.

Billig, M. (1987b). Anti-semitic themes and the British far left: some social-psychological observations on indirect aspects of the conspiracy tradition. In C.F. Graumann and S. Moscovici (eds), *Changing Conceptions of Conspiracy*. New York: Springer Verlag.

Billig, M. (1989a). The extreme right: continuities in the anti-semitic conspiracy tradition. In R. Eatwell and N. O'Sullivan (eds), *The Nature of the Right*. London: Pinter.

Billig, M. (1989b). The argumentative nature of holding strong views: a case study, *European Journal of Social Psychology*, 19, 203–22.

Billig, M. (1990a). Collective memory, ideology and the British Royal Family. In D. Middleton and D. Edwards (eds), *Collective Remembering*. London: Sage.

Billig, M. (1990b). Rhetoric of social psychology. In I. Parker and J. Shotter (eds), *Deconstructing Social Psychology*. London: Routledge.

Billig, M. (1991). *Ideology and Opinions*. London: Sage.

Billig, M. (1992). *Talking of the Royal Family*. London: Routledge.

Billig, M. and Edwards, D. (1994). La construction sociale de la mémoire, *La Recherche*, 25, 742–5.

Billig, M. and Golding, P. (1992). The hidden factor: race, the news media and the 1992 election, *Representation*, 31, 36–8.

Billig, M., Condor, S., Edwards, D., Gane, M., Middleton, D. and Radley, A.R. (1988). *Ideological Dilemmas: A Social Psychology of Everyday Thinking*. London: Sage.

Birch, A.H. (1989). *Nationalism and National Integration*. London: Unwin Hyman.

Bloch, M. (1973). *The Royal Touch*. London: Routledge and Kegan Paul.

Bocock, R. (1974). *Ritual in Industrial Society*. London: George Allen & Unwin.

Boose, L.E. (1993). Techno-muscularity and the 'boy eternal': from quagmire to the Gulf. In M. Cooke and A. Woollacott (eds), *Gendering War Talk*. Princeton, NJ: Princeton University Press.

Boswell, J. (1906). *The Life of Samuel Johnson*. London: J.M. Dent.

Bourdieu, P. (1990). *The Logic of Practice*. Cambridge: Polity Press.

Bowen, G.L. (1989). Presidential action and public opinion about U.S. Nicaraguan policy: limits to the 'Rally "Round the Flag" Syndrome', *P.S.*, 200, 793–800.

Bowers, J. and Iwi, K. (1993). The discursive construction of society, *Discourse and Society*, 4, 357–93.

Brass, P.R. (1991). *Ethnicity and Nationalism*. New Delhi: Sage.

Braudel, F. (1988). *The Identity of France:* vol. 1. *History and Environment*. London: Collins.

Breuilly, J. (1985). Reflections on nationalism, *Philosophy of the Social Sciences*, 15, 65–75.

Breuilly, J. (1992). *Nationalism and the State*. Manchester: Manchester University Press.

Brewer, M. (1979). Ingroup bias in the minimal intergroup situation: a cognitive-motivational analysis, *Psychological Bulletin*, 86, 307–24.

Brody, R.A. (1991). *Assessing the President*. Stanford, CA: Stanford University Press.

Brown, D. (1989). Ethnic revival: perspectives on state and society, *Third World Quarterly*, 11, 1–18.

Brown, P. and Levinson, S.C. (1987). *Politeness: Some Universals in Language Use*. Cambridge: Cambridge University Press.

Brown, R. (1988). *Group Processes*. Oxford: Basil Blackwell.

Brown, R.H. (1977). *A Poetic for Sociology*. Cambridge: Cambridge University Press.

Brown, R.H. (1994). Reconstructing social theory after the postmodern critique. In H.W. Simons and M. Billig (eds), *After Postmodernism*. London: Sage.

Brunt, R. (1992). Engaging with the popular: audiences for mass culture and what to say about them. In L. Grossberg, C. Nelson and R. Treichler (eds), *Cultural Studies*. London: Routledge.

Burke, K. (1969). *A Rhetoric of Motives*. Berkeley, CA: University of California Press.

Burrows, J. (1990). Conversational politics: Rorty's pragmatist apology for liberalism. In A. Malachowski (ed.), *Reading Rorty*. Oxford: Basil Blackwell.

Cannadine, D. (1983). The context, performance and meaning of ritual: the British monarchy and 'the invention of tradition'. In E. Hobsbawm and T. Ranger (eds), *The Invention of Tradition*. Cambridge: Cambridge University Press.

Capitan, C. (1988). Status of women' in French revolutionary/liberal ideology. In G. Seidel (ed.), *The Nature of the Right*. Amsterdam: John Benjamins.

Castles, S. and Kosack, G. (1985). *Immigrant Class Structure in Western Europe*. Oxford: Oxford University Press.

Chaney, D. (1993). *Fictions of Collective Life*. London: Routledge.

Chomsky, N. (1994). An island lies bleeding, *Guardian* (2), 5 July, pp. 6–9.

Clark, P. (1983). *The English Alehouse: a Social History, 1200–1830*. London: Longman.

Clifford, J. (1992). Travelling cultures. In L. Grossberg, C. Nelson and P. Treichler (eds), *Cultural Studies*. London: Routledge.

Coakley, J. (ed.) (1992). *The Social Origins of Nationalist Movements*. London: Sage.

Cohen, R. (1992). Migration and the new international division of labour. In M. Cross (ed.), *Ethnic Minorities and Industrial Change in Europe and North America*. Cambridge: Cambridge University Press.

Cohn, N. (1967). *Warrant for Genocide*. London: Chatto Heinemann.

Coles, R. (1986). *The Political Life of Children*. Boston, MA: Atlantic Monthly Press.

Colley, L. (1992). *Britons*. New Haven, CT: Yale University Press.

Comay, R. (1986). Interrupting the conversation: notes on Rorty, *Telos*, 67, 119–30.

Comrie, B. (1990). *The Major Languages of Western Europe*. London: Routledge.

Condor, S. (1989). 'Biting into the future': social change and the social identity of women. In S. Skevington and D. Baker (eds), *The Social Identity of Women*. London: Sage.

Condor, S. (in press). Unimagined community? some social psychological issues concerning English national identity. In G. Breakwell and E. Lyons (eds), *Changing European Identities*. Oxford: Pergamon.

Connor, W. (1978). A nation is a nation, is a state, is an ethnic group, is a. . . , *Ethnic and Racial Studies*, 1, 377–400.

Connor, W. (1993). Beyond reason: the nature of the ethno-national bond, *Ethnic and Racial Studies*, 16, 373–89.

Conover, P.J. and Sapiro, V. (1993). Gender, feminist consciousness and war, *American Journal of Political Science*, 37, 1079–99.

Csikszentmihalyi, M. and Rochberg-Halton, E. (1981). *The Meaning of Things*. Cambridge: Cambridge University Press.

Cumberbatch, G. and Howitt, D. (1989). *A Measure of Uncertainty*. London: John Libbey.

Cunningham, H. (1986). The language of patriotism, 1750–1914. In J. Donald and S. Hall (eds), *Politics and Ideology*, Milton Keynes: Open University Press.

Der Derian, J. (1989). The boundaries of knowledge and power in international relations. In J. Der Derian and M.J. Shapiro (eds), *International/Intertextual Relations*. Lexington, MA: Lexington Books.

Der Derian, J. (1993). S/N: international theory, Balkanization and the new world order. In M. Ringrose and A.J. Lerner (eds), *Reimagining the Nation*. Buckingham: Open University Press.

Deutsch, K. (1966). *Nationalism and Social Communication*. Cambridge, MA: MIT Press.

Devine, P.G. (1989). Stereotypes and prejudice: their automatic and controlled components, *Journal of Personality and Social Psychology*, 56, 5–18.

Dillon, G.M. (1989). *The Falklands, Politics and War*. New York: St Martin's Press.

Dittmar, H. (1992). *The Social Psychology of Material Possessions*. Hemel Hempstead: Harvester/Wheatsheaf.

Doob, L. (1964). *Patriotism and Nationalism*. New Haven, CT: Yale University Press.

Dumont, L. (1992). Left versus right in French political ideology: a comparative approach. In J.A. Hall and I.C. Jarvie (eds), *Transition to Modernity*. Cambridge: Cambridge University Press.

Eagleton, T. (1991). *Ideology: an Introduction*. London: Verso.

Eco, U. (1987). *Travels in Hyperreality*. London: Picador.

Edelman, M. (1977). *Political Language: Words that Succeed and Policies that Fail*. New York: Academic Press.

Edwards, D. (1991). Categories are for talking, *Theory and Psychology*, 1, 515–42.

Edwards, D. and Potter, J. (1992). *Discursive Psychology*. London: Sage.

Edwards, D. and Potter, J. (1993). Language and causation: a discursive action model of description and attribution, *Psychological Review*, 100, 23–41.

Edwards, J. (1985). *Language, Society and Identity*. Oxford: Basil Blackwell.

Edwards, J. (1991). Gaelic in Nova Scotia. In C.H. Williams (ed.), *Linguistic Minorities, Society and Territory*. Clevedon: Multilingual Matters.

Eiser, J.R. (1986). *Social Psychology*. Cambridge: Cambridge University Press.

Elias, N. (1978). *The History of Manners*. Oxford: Basil Blackwell.

Elias, N. and Dunning, E. (1986). *Quest for Excitement*. Oxford: Basil Blackwell.

Elklit, J. and Tonsgaard, O. (1992). The absence of nationalist movements: the case of the Nordic area. In J. Coakley (ed.), *The Social Origins of Nationalist Movements*. London: Sage.

Eller, J.D. and Coughlan, R.M. (1993). The poverty of primordialism: the demystification of ethnic attachments, *Ethnic and Racial Studies*, 16, 181–202.

Elshtain, J.B. (1987). *Women and War*. Brighton: Harverster Press.

Elshtain, J.B. (1993). Sovereignty, identity, sacrifice. In M. Ringrose and A.J. Lerner (eds), *Reimagining the Nation*. Buckingham: Open University Press.

Entessar, N. (1989). The Kurdish mosaic of discord, *Third World Quarterly*, 11, 83–100.

Eriksen, T.H. (1993). *Ethnicity and Nationalism*. London: Pluto Press.

Essed, P. (1994). Contradictory positions, ambivalent perceptions: a case study of a black woman entrepreneur, *Feminism and Psychology*, 4, 99–118.

Fairclough, N. (1992). *Discourse and Social Change*. Cambridge: Polity Press.

Farr, R. (1993). Theory and method in the study of social representations. In G.M. Breakwell and D.V. Canter (eds), *Empirical Approaches to Social Representations*. Oxford: Clarendon Press.

Featherstone, M. (1990). Perspectives on consumer culture, *Sociology*, 24, 5–22.

Featherstone, M. (1991). *Consumer Culture and Postmodernism*. London: Sage.

Finn, G. (1990). In the grip? A psychological and historical exploration of the social significance of freemasonry in Scotland. In T. Gallagher and G. Walker (eds), *Sermons and Battle Hymns: Protestant popular culture in Modern Scotland*. Edinburgh: Edinburgh University Press.

Finn, G. (1993). Constraints on conspiracy ideologies. Paper given at Social Section of British Psychological Society Conference, Oxford, September 1993.

Fiori, G. (1990). *Antonio Gramsci: Life of a Revolutionary*. London: Verso.

Firth, R. (1973). *Symbols: Public and Private*. London: George Allen & Unwin.

Fishman, J.A. (1972). *Language and Nationalism*. Rowley, MA: Newbury House.

Fitzgerald, T.K. (1992). Media, ethnicity and identity. In P. Scannell, P. Schlesinger and C. Sparks (eds), *Culture and Power*. London: Sage.

Fleischman, S. (1991). Discourse as space/discourse as time: reflections on the metalanguage of spoken and written discourse, *Journal of Pragmatics*, 16, 291–306.

Forbes, H.D. (1986). *Nationalism, Ethnocentrism and Personality*. Chicago: Chicago University Press.

Foucault, M. (1972). *The Archaeology of Knowledge*. London: Tavistock.

Foucault, M. (1986). Panopticism. In P. Rabinow (ed.), *The Foucault Reader*. Harmondsworth: Penguin.

Fowler, R. (1991). *Language in the News*. London: Routledge.

Franco, J. (1988). Beyond ethnocentrism: gender, power and the Third World intelligentsia. In C. Nelson and L. Grossberg (eds), *Marxism and the Interpretation of Culture*. London: Macmillan.

Fraser, N. (1989). *Unruly Practices*. Cambridge: Polity Press.

Freeman, M. (1992). *Nationalism: For and Against*. Colchester: Department of Government, University of Essex.

Friedman, J. (1988). Cultural logics of the global system: a sketch, *Theory, Culture and Society*, 5, 447–60.

Fromm, E. (1942). *Fear of Freedom*. London: Routledge & Kegan Paul.

Fukuyama, F. (1992). *The End of History and the Last Man*. Harmondsworth: Penguin.

Gallie, W.B. (1962). Essentially contested concepts. In M. Black (ed.), *The Importance of Language*. Englewood Cliffs, NJ: Prentice Hall.

Gellner, E. (1983). *Nations and Nationalism*. Oxford: Basil Blackwell.

Gellner, E. (1987). *Culture, Identity and Politics*. Cambridge: Cambridge University Press.

Gellner, E. (1993). Nationalism. In W. Outhwaite and T. Bottomore (eds), *Blackwell Dictionary of Twentieth-Century Thought*. Oxford: Basil Blackwell.

Gergen, K.J. (1982). *Towards Transformation in Social Knowledge*. New York: Springer Verlag.

Gergen, K.J. (1985). The social constructionist movement in modern psychology, *American Psychologist*, 40, 266–75.

Gergen, K.J. (1989). Social psychology and the wrong revolution, *European Journal of Social Psychology*, 19, 463–84.

Gergen, K.J. (1991). *The Saturated Self*. New York: Basic Books.

Ghiglione, R. (1993). Paroles de meetings. In A. Trognon and J. Larrue (eds), *Pragmatique du Discours Politique*. Paris: Armand Colin.

Giddens, A. (1985). *The Nation-State and Violence*. Cambridge: Polity Press.

Giddens, A. (1987). *Social Theory and Modern Sociology*. Cambridge: Polity Press.

Giddens, A. (1990). *The Consequences of Modernity*. Cambridge: Polity Press.

Gilbert, G.M (1951). Stereotype persistence and change among college students, *Journal of Abnormal and Social Psychology*, 46, 245–54.

Giles, H., Mulac, A., Bradac, J.J. and Johnson, P. (1987). Speech accommodation. In M. McGlaughlin (ed.), *Speech Communication Yearbook*, vol. 10. Newbury Park, CA: Sage.

Gillett, G. and Harré, R. (1994). *The Discursive Mind*. London: Sage.

Gilroy, P. (1992a). The end of antiracism. In J. Donald and A. Rattansi (eds), *'Race', Culture and Difference*. London: Sage.

Gilroy, P. (1992b). Cultural studies and ethnic absolutism. In L. Grossberg, C. Nelson and R. Treichler (eds), *Cultural Studies*. London: Routledge.

Giroux, H.A. (1993). Living dangerously – identity politics and the new cultural racism, *Cultural Studies*, 7, 1–28.

Goffman, E. (1981). *Forms of Talk*. Oxford: Basil Blackwell.

Golby, J.M. and Purdue, A.W. (1984). *The Civilisation of the Crowd: Popular Culture in England, 1750–1900*. London: Batsford.

Gould, A. (1993). Pollution rituals in Sweden: the pursuit of a drug-free society. Paper presented to Conference of Social Policy Association, Liverpool, July 1993.

Gramsci, A. (1971). *Prison Notebooks*. London: Lawrence & Wishart.

Graumann, C.F. and Moscovici, S. (eds) (1987). *Changing Conceptions of Conspiracy*. New York: Springer Verlag.

Greenfeld, L. (1992). *Nationalism: Five Roads to Modernity*. Cambridge, MA: Harvard University Press.

Griffin, C. (1989). 'I'm not a women's libber but . . . ': Feminism, consciousness and identity. In S.Skevington and D. Baker (eds), *The Social Identity of Women*. London: Sage.

Grimes, B.F. (1988). *Ethnologue: Languages of the World*. Dallas: Sumner Institute of Linguistics.

Gruber, H. (1993). Evaluation devices in newspaper reports, *Journal of Pragmatics*, 19, 469–86.

Gudykunst, W.B. and Ting-Toomey, S. (1990). Ethnic identity, language and communication breakdowns. In H. Giles and W.P. Robinson (eds), *Handbook of Language and Social Psychology*. Chichester: John Wiley.

Gunew, S. (1990). Denaturalizing cultural nationalisms: multicultural readings of Australia. In H.K. Bhabha (ed.), *Nation and Narration*. London: Routledge.

Hackett, R.A. and Zhao, Y. (1994). Challenging a master narrative: peace protest and opinion/editorial discourse in the US press during the Gulf War, *Discourse and Society*, 5, 509–41.

Hagendoorn, L. (1993a). Ethnic categorization and outgroup exclusion: cultural values and social stereotypes in the construction of ethnic hierarchies, *Ethnic and Racial Studies*, 16, 26–49.

Hagendoorn, L. (1993b). National and cultural fragmentation after the Cold War. Paper presented at UNESCO Conference on 'Cultural Identity and Development in Europe', June 1993, Middelburgh, Netherlands.

Hagendoorn, L. and Hraba, J. (1987). Social distance toward Holland's minorities: discrimination amongst ethnic outgroups, *Ethnic and Racial Studies*, 10, 317–33.

Hagendoorn, L. and Kleinpenning, G. (1991). The contribution of domain-specific stereotypes to ethnic social distance, *British Journal of Social Psychology*, 30, 63–78.

Hainsworth, P. (1992). The extreme right in post-war France: the emergence and success of the Front national. In P. Hainsworth, (ed.), *The Extreme Right in Europe and the USA*. London: Pinter.

Hall, C. (1992). Missionary stories: gender and ethnicity in England in the 1830s and 1840s. In L. Grossberg, C. Nelson and P. Treichler (eds), *Cultural Studies*. London: Routledge.

Hall, S. (1975). Introduction. In A.C.H. Smith, *Paper Voices*. London: Chatto & Windus.

Hall, S. (1988a). The toad in the garden: Thatcherism among the theorists. In C. Nelson and L. Grossberg (eds), *Marxism and the Interpretation of Culture*. London: Macmillan.

Hall, S. (1988b). Authoritarian populism. In B. Jessop, K. Bonnett, S. Bromley and T. Ling (eds), *Thatcherism*. Cambridge: Polity Press.

Hall, S. (1991a). Old and new identities, old and new ethnicities. In A.D. King (ed.), *Culture, Globalization and the World-System*. Basingstoke: Macmillan.

Hall, S. (1991b). The local and the global: globalization and ethnicity. In A.D. King (ed.), *Culture, Globalization and the World-System*. Basingstoke: Macmillan.

Hall, S. and Held, D. (1989). Citizens and citizenship. In S. Hall and M. Jacques (eds), *New Times*. London: Lawrence & Wishart.

Hallin, D.C. (1994). *We Keep America on Top of the World*. London: Routledge.

Haralambos, M. and Holborn, M. (1991). *Sociology: Themes and Perspectives*, 3rd edn. London: Collins.

Harding, J., Kutner, B., Proshansky, H. and Chein, I. (1954). Prejudice and ethnic relations. In G. Lindzey (ed.), *Handbook of Social Psychology*. Cambridge, MA: Addison Wesley.

Harkabi, Y. (1980). *The Palestinian Covenant and its Meaning*. London: Vallentine Mitchell.

Harré, R. (1991). The discursive production of selves, *Theory and Psychology*, 1, 51–64.

Harris, N. (1990). *National Liberation*. London: I.B. Taurus.

Harris, R. (1985). *Gotcha! The Media, the Government and the Falklands Crisis*. London: Faber.

Hartley, J. (1992). *Teleology: Studies in Television*. Routledge: London.

Harvey, D. (1989). *The Condition of Postmodernity*. Oxford: Basil Blackwell.

Haugen, E. (1966a). Dialect, language, nation, *American Anthropologist*, 68, 922–35.

Haugen, E. (1966b). *Language Conflict and Language Planning*. Cambridge, MA: Harvard University Press.

Hawkins, J.A. (1990). German. In B. Comrie (ed.), *The Major Languages of Western Europe*. London: Routledge.

Hazani, M. (1993). Netzah Yisrael, symbolic immortality and the Israeli–Palestinian conflict. In K. Larsen (ed.), *Conflict and Social Psychology*. London: Sage.

Held, D. (1989). The decline of the nation state. In S. Hall and M. Jacques (eds), *New Times*. London: Lawrence & Wishart.

Held, D. (1992). The development of the modern state. In S. Hall and B. Gieben, *Formations of Modernity*. Cambridge: Polity Press.

Heller, A. (1991). The ironies beyond philosophy: on Richard Rorty's *Contingency, Irony and Solidarity*, *Thesis Eleven*, 28, 105–12.

Heller, Z. (1993). Hurt Feelin's, *Independent on Sunday, Review*, 11 April, pp. 2–5.

Helms, C.M. (1981). *The Cohesion of Saudi Arabia*. London: Croom Helm.

Heritage, J. (1984). *Garfinkel and Ethnomethodology*. Cambridge: Polity Press.

Heritage, J. and Greatbach, D. (1986). Generating applause: a study of rhetoric and response in party political conferences, *American Sociological Review*, 92, 110–57.

Hertz, F. (1944). *Nationality in History and Politics*. London: Routledge & Kegan Paul.

Hewison, R. (1986). *The Heritage Industry*. London: Methuen.

Hey, V. (1986). *Patriarchy and Pub Culture*. London: Tavistock.

Hill, D. (1966). *Fashionable Contrasts: Caricatures by James Gillray*. London: Phaidon Press.

Hinsley, F.H. (1986). *Sovereignty*. Cambridge: Cambridge University Press.

Hitler, A. (1972). *Mein Kampf*. London: Hutchinson.

Hitler, A. (1988). *Hitler's Table-Talk* (ed. H. Trevor-Roper). Oxford: Oxford University Press.

Hobsbawm, E.J. (1992). *Nations and Nationalism since 1780*. Cambridge: Cambridge University Press.

Hobsbawm, E.J. and Ranger, T. (eds) (1983). *The Invention of Tradition*. Cambridge: Cambridge University Press.

Hogg, M.A. and Abrams, D. (1988). *Social Identifications*. London: Routledge.

Holland, P. (1983). The page three girls speak to women, too, *Screen*, 24, 84–102.

Holquist, M. (1990). *Dialogism: Bakhtin and his World*. London: Routledge.

Hroch, M. (1985). *Social Preconditions of National Revival in Europe*. Cambridge: Cambridge University Press.

Husbands, C.T. (1992). Belgium: Flemish legions on the march. In P. Hainsworth (ed.), *The Extreme Right in Europe and the USA*. London: Pinter.

Hutnik, N. (1991). *Ethnic Minority Identity: a Social Psychological Perspective*. Oxford: Oxford University Press.

Ignatieff, M. (1993). *Blood and Belonging: Journeys into the New Nationalism*. London: Chatto & Windus.

Ihonvbere, J.O. (1994). The 'irrelevant' state, ethnicity and the quest for nationhood in Africa, *Ethnic and Racial Studies*, 17, 42–60.

Inglehart, R. (1991). Trust between nations: primordial ties, societal learning and economic development. In K. Reif and R. Inglehart (eds), *Eurobarometer*. Basingstoke: Macmillan.

James, C.L.R. (1964). *Beyond a Boundary*. London: The Sportsmans Book Club.

James, C.L.R. (1989). *Cricket*. London: Allison and Busby.

Jameson, F. (1991). *Postmodernism, or the Cultural Logic of Late Capitalism*. London: Sage.

Jamieson, K.H. (1988). *Eloquence in an Electronic Age*. Oxford: Oxford University Press.

Janowitz, M. (1983). *The Reconstruction of Patriotism*. Chicago: University of Chicago Press.

Jennings, H. and Madge, C. (1987). *May 12 1937: Mass Observation Day Survey*, London: Faber.

Jessop, B., Bonnett, K., Bromley, S. and Ling, T. (1988). *Thatcherism*. Cambridge: Polity Press.

Johnson, D. (1993). The making of the French nation. In M. Teich and R. Porter (eds), *The National Question in Europe in Historical Context*. Cambridge: Cambridge University Press.

Johnson, D.M. (1994). Who is we?: constructing communities in US–Mexico border discourse, *Discourse and Society*, 5, 207–32.

Johnson, G.R. (1987). In the name of the fatherland: an analysis of kin term usage in patriotic speech and literature, *International Political Science Review*, 8, 165–74.

Jones, A. (1994). Gender and ethnic conflict in ex-Yugoslavia, *Ethnic and Racial Studies*, 17, 115–34.

Jowell, R., Brook, L., Prior, G. and Taylor, B. (1992). *British Social Attitudes: the 9th Report*. Aldershot: Dartmouth.

Jowell, R., Witherspoon, S. and Brook, L. (1987). *British Social Attitudes: the 1978 Report*. Aldershot: Gower.

Karlins, M., Coffman, T.L. and Walters, G. (1969). On the fading of social stereotypes: studies in three generations of college students, *Journal of Personality and Social Psychology*, 13, 1–16.

Katz, D. and Braly, K. (1935). Racial prejudice and racial stereotypes, *Journal of Abnormal and Social Psychology*, 30, 175–93.

Katz, J. (1980). *From Prejudice to Destruction: Anti-semitism, 1700–1933*. Cambridge, MA: Harvard University Press.

Kedourie, E. (1966). *Nationalism*. London: Hutchinson.

Kennedy, P. (1988). *The Rise and Fall of the Great Powers*. London: Unwin Hyman.

Kiernan, V. (1993). The British Isles: Celt and Saxon. In M. Teich and R. Porter (eds), *The National Question in Europe in Historical Context*. Cambridge: Cambridge University Press.

Kitromilides, P.M. (1979). The dialectic of intolerance: ideological dimensions of ethnic conflict, *Journal of the Hellenic Diaspora*, 6, 5–30.

Kornblum, W. (1988). *Sociology in a Changing World*. New York: Holt, Rinehart & Winston.

Kosterman, R. and Feshbach, S. (1989). Toward a measure of patriotic and nationalistic attitudes, *Political Psychology*, 10, 257–74.

Kristeva, J. (1991). *Strangers to Ourselves*. Hemel Hempstead: Harvester/Wheatsheaf.

Kristeva, J. (1993). *Nations without Nationalism*. New York: Columbia University Press.

Krosnick, J.A. and Brannon, L.A. (1993). The impact of the Gulf War on the ingredients of Presidential evaluations: multidimensional effects of political involvement, *American Political Science Review*, 87, 963–75.

Ladurie, E. Le R. (1978). *Montaillou: Cathars and Catholics in a French Village, 1294–1324*. London: Scolar Press.

Langer, E.J. (1989). *Mindfulness*. Reading, MA: Addison Wesley.

Lash, S. (1990). *The Sociology of Postmodernism*. London: Routledge.

Lather, P. (1992). Postmodernism and the human sciences. In S. Kvale (ed.), *Psychology and Postmodernism*. London: Sage.

Lather, P. (1994). Staying dumb? feminist research and pedagogy with/in the postmodern. In H.W. Simons and M. Billig (eds), *After Postmodernism*. London: Sage.

Lauerbach, G.E. (1989). 'We don't want war . . . but:' speech act schemata and inter-schemata inference transfer, *Journal of Pragmatics*, 13, 25–51.

Layton-Henry, Z. (1984). *The Politics of Race in Britain*. London: George Allen & Unwin.

Levine, H.B. (1993). Making sense of Jewish ethnicity: identification patterns of New Zealanders of mixed parentage, *Ethnic and Racial Studies*, 6, 323–44.

LeVine, R.A. and Campbell, D.T. (1970). *Ethnocentrism: Theories of Conflict, Ethnic Attitudes and Group Behavior*. New York: John Wiley.

Lincoln, B. (1989). *Discourse and the Construction of Society*. New York: Oxford University Press.

Linell, P. (1990). The power of dialogue dynamics. In I. Markova and K. Foppa (eds), *The Dynamics of Dialogue*, New York: Harvester/Wheatsheaf.

Linz, J.J. (1985). From primordialism to nationalism. In E.A. Tiryakin and R. Rogowski (eds), *New Nationalisms of the Developed West*. Boston, MA: Allen & Unwin.

Lipset, S.M. and Raab, E. (1970). *The Politics of Unreason*. London: Heinemann.

Lister, R. (1994). Dilemmas in engendering citizenship. Paper presented at Crossing Borders Conference, Stockholm, May 1994.

Lyotard, J.-F. (1984). *The Postmodern Condition*. Manchester: Manchester University Press.

Macionis, J.J. (1989). *Sociology*. Englewood Cliffs, NJ: Prentice Hall.

Magnusson, W. (1990). The reification of political community. In R.B.J. Walker and S.H. Mendlovitz (eds), *Contending Sovereignties*. Boulder, CO: Lynne Reinner.

Maitland, K. and Wilson, J. (1987). Pronominal selection and ideological conflict, *Journal of Pragmatics*, 11, 495–512.

Mann, M. (1986). *The Sources of Social Power*, vol. 1. Cambridge: Cambridge University Press.

Mann, M. (1988). European development: approaching a historical explanation. In J. Baechler et al. (eds), *Europe and the Rise of Capitalism*. Oxford: Basil Blackwell.

Mann, M. (1992). The emergence of modern European nationalism. In J.A. Hall and I.C. Jarvie (eds), *Transition to Modernity*. Cambridge: Cambridge University Press.

Marvin, C. (1991). Theorizing the flagbody: symbolic dimensions of the flag, *Critical Studies in Mass Communication*, 8, 119–38.

Marx, K. and Engels, F. (1968). *The Communist Manifesto*. In *Selected Works of Marx and Engels*. London: Lawrence & Wishart.

Marx, K. and Engels, F. (1970). *The German Ideology*. London: Lawrence & Wishart.

Mass Observation (1987). *The Pub and the People* (first published 1943). London: Cresset Library.

Maynard, S.K. (1994). Images of involvement and integrity: rhetorical style of a Japanese politician, *Discourse and Society*, 5, 233–61.

McCauley, C., Stitt, C.L. and Segal, M. (1980). Stereotyping: from prejudice to prediction, *Psychological Bulletin*, 87, 195–208.

McCloskey, D. (1985). *The Rhetoric of Economics*. Brighton: Harvester/Wheatsheaf.

McCrone, D. (1992). *Understanding Scotland: the Sociology of a Stateless Nation*. London: Routledge.

McDonald, M. (1993). The construction of difference: an anthropological approach to stereotypes. In S. Macdonald (ed.), *Inside European Identities*. Providence, RI: Berg.

McKinlay, A., Potter, J. and Wetherell, M. (1993). Discourse analysis and social representations. In G.M. Breakwell and D.V. Canter (eds), *Empirical Approaches to Social Representations*. Oxford: Clarendon Press.

McLellan, D. (1986). *Ideology*. Milton Keynes: Open University.

Melucci, A. (1989). *Nomads of the Present*. London: Hutchinson Radius.

Mercer, K. (1992). '1968': periodizing postmodern politics and identity. In L. Grossberg, C. Nelson and P. Treichler (eds), *Cultural Studies*. London: Routledge.

Meyrowitz, J. (1986). *No Sense of Place*. Oxford: Oxford University Press.

Michael, M. (1991). Some postmodern reflections on social psychology, *Theory and Psychology*, 1, 203–21.

Michael, M. (1992). Postmodern subjects: towards a transgressive social psychology. In S. Kvale (ed.), *Psychology and Postmodernism*. London: Sage.

Michael, M. (1994). Discourse and uncertainty: postmodern variations, *Theory and Psychology*, 4, 383–404.

Miliband, R. (1987). Class analysis. In J.H. Turner and A. Giddens (eds), *Social Theory Today*. Cambridge: Polity Press.

Miller, D. (1986). *Material Culture and Mass Consumption*. Oxford: Basil Blackwell.

Monimambo, S. (1971). In MPLA liberated areas. In J. Gerassi (ed.), *Towards Revolution*. London: Weidenfeld & Nicolson.

Monopolies and Mergers Commission (1993). *The Supply of National Newspapers*. London: HMSO.

Morley, D. (1992). *Television, Audiences and Cultural Studies*. London: Routledge.

Moscovici, S. (1983). The phenomenon of social representations. In R. Farr and S. Moscovici (eds), *Social Representations*. Cambridge: Cambridge University Press.

Moscovici, S. (1987). Answers and questions, *Journal for the Theory of Social Behaviour*, 17, 513–29.

Mühlhäusler, P. and Harré, R. (1990). *Pronouns and People*. Oxford: Basil Blackwell.

Murdock, G. (1993). Communications and the constitution of modernity. *Media, Culture and Society*, 15, 521–39.

Murphy, J.J. (1974). *Rhetoric in the Middle Ages*. Berkeley, CA: University of California Press.

Nairn, T. (1977). *The Break-Up of Britain*. London: New Left Books.

Nairn, T. (1988). *The Enchanted Glass*. London: Radius.

Nelson, J.S., Megill, A. and McCloskey, D.N. (eds) (1987). *The Rhetoric of the Human Sciences*. Madison: University of Wisconsin.

Nofsinger, R.E. (1991). *Everyday Conversation*. Newbury Park, CA: Sage.

Norris, C. (1993). *The Truth About Postmodernism*. Oxford: Oxford University Press.

O'Donnell, H. (1994). Mapping the mythical: a geopolitics of national sporting stereotypes, *Discourse and Society*, 5, 345–80.

Orfali, B. (1990). *L'Adhésion au Front National*. Paris: Editions Kimé.

Orwell, G. (1962). *Inside the Whale and Other Essays*. Harmondsworth: Penguin.

Ó Tuathail, G. and Agnew, J. (1992). Geopolitics and discourse: practical geopolitical reasoning in American foreign policy, *Political Geography*, 11, 190–204.

Pedic, F. (1989). Effect on social self-esteem of nationalist appeals in corporate image advertisements, *Australian Journal of Psychology*, 41, 37–47.

Pedic, F. (1990). Persuasiveness of nationalistic advertisements, *Journal of Applied Social Psychology*, 20, 724–38.

Perelman, C. (1979). *The New Rhetoric and the Humanities*. Dordrecht: D. Reidel.

Perelman, C. and Olbrechts-Tyteca, L. (1971). *The New Rhetoric*. University of Notre Dame Press: Indiana.

Perrin, W.G. (1922). *British Flags: their Early History and their Development at Sea*. Cambridge: Cambridge University Press.

Petrosino, D. (1992). National and regional movements in Italy: the case of Sardinia. In J. Coakley (ed.), *The Social Origins of Nationalist Movements*. London: Sage.

Pettigrew, T.F. (1979). The ultimate attribution error: extending Allport's cognitive analysis of prejudice, *Personality and Social Psychology Bulletin*, 5, 461–75.

Pilger, J. (1994). *Distant Voices*. London: Vintage.

Plotnicov, L. and Silverman, M. (1978). Jewish ethnic signalling: social bonding in contemporary American society, *Ethnology*, 17, 407–23.

Poliakov, L. (1974). *The Aryan Myth*. London: Chatto Heinemann.

Postman, N. (1987). *Amusing Ourselves to Death*. London: Methuen.

Potter, J. and Wetherell, M. (1987). *Discourse and Social Psychology*. London: Sage.

Potter, J., Edwards, D. and Wetherell, M. (1993). A model of discourse in action, *American Behavioral Scientist*, 36, 383–401.

Quattrone, G.A. (1986). On the perception of a group's variability. In S. Worchel and W.G. Austin (eds), *Psychology of Intergroup Relations*. Chicago: Nelson Hall.

Rae, J. and Drury, J. (1993). Reification and evidence in rhetoric on economic recession: some methods used in the UK press, final quarter 1990, *Discourse and Society*, 4, 357–94.

Rathzel, H. (1994). Harmonious 'Heimat' and disturbing 'Auslander', *Feminism and Psychology*, 4, 81–98.

Reader, W.J. (1988). *At Duty's Call: a Study in Obsolete Patriotism*. Manchester: Manchester University Press.

Reich, W. (1990). Understanding terrorist behavior: the limits and opportunities of psychological inquiry. In W. Reich (ed.), *Origins of Terrorism*. Cambridge: Cambridge University Press.

Reicher, S. (1993). Stating the nation: an argumentative approach to the definition and salience of national identities. Paper delivered at Conference of European Association of Experimental Social Psychology, Lisbon, September, 1993.

Renan, E. (1990). What is a nation? In H.K. Bhabha (ed.), *Nation and Narration*. London: Routledge.

Retzinger, S.M. (1991). *Violent Emotions*. Newbury Park, CA: Sage.

Ricoeur, P. (1986). *Lectures on Ideology and Utopia*. New York: Columbia University Press.

Riddell, P. (1993). *Honest Opportunism*. London: Hamish Hamilton.

Roberts, J.M. (1974). *The Mythology of the Secret Societies*. St Albans: Paladin.

Roberts, J.M. (1985). *The Triumph of the West*. London: British Broadcasting Corporation.

Robertson, R. (1990). After nostalgia? Wilful nostalgia and the phases of globalization. In B.S. Turner (ed.), *Theories of Modernity and Postmodernity*. London: Sage.

Robertson, R. (1991). Social theory, cultural relativity and the problem of globality. In A.D. King (ed.), *Culture, Globalization and the World-System*. Basingstoke: Macmillan.

Robertson, R. (1992). *Globalization: Social Theory and Global Culture*. London: Sage.

Rogowski, R. (1985). Causes and varieties of nationalism: a rationalist account. In E.A. Tiryakian and R. Rogowski (eds), *New Nationalisms of the Developed West*. Boston, MA: Allen & Unwin.

Roosens, E.E. (1989). *Creating Ethnicity*. London: Sage.

Rorty, R. (1979). *Philosophy and the Mirror of Nature*. Princeton, NJ: Princeton University Press.

Rorty, R. (1987a). Science as solidarity. In J.S. Nelson, A. Megill and D.N. McCloskey (eds), *The Rhetoric of the Human Sciences*. Madison: University of Wisconsin.

Rorty, R. (1987b). Thugs and theorists: a reply to Bernstein, *Political Theory*, 15, 564–80.

Rorty, R. (1989). *Contingency, Irony and Solidarity*. Cambridge: Cambridge University Press.

Rorty, R. (1990).The priority of democracy to philosophy. In A. Malachowski (ed.), *Reading Rorty*. Oxford: Basil Blackwell.

Rorty, R. (1991). *Objectivity, Relativism, and Truth*. Cambridge: Cambridge University Press.

Rorty, R. (1993a). Wild orchids and Trotsky. In M. Edmundson (ed.), *Wild Orchids and Trotsky*. New York: Penguin Books.

Rorty, R. (1993b). In a flattened world, *London Review of Books*, 8 April, p. 3.

Rorty, R. (1994). The unpatriotic academy, *New York Times*, 13 February, p. E15.

Rosch, E. (1978). Principles of categorization. In E. Rosch and B. Lloyd (eds), *Cognition and Categorization*. Hillsdale, NJ: Erlbaum.

Rosenberg, S.D. (1993). The threshold of thrill: life stories in the skies over South-East Asia. In M. Cooke and A. Woollacott (eds), *Gendering War Talk*. Princeton, NJ: Princeton University Press.

Rotberg, R.I. (1966). African nationalism: concept or confusion, *Journal of Modern African Studies*, 4, 33–46.

Rothbart, M. and Hallmark, W. (1988). Ingroup-outgroup differences in the perceived efficacy of coercion and conciliation in resolving social conflict, *Journal of Personality and Social Psychology*, 55, 248–57.

Ruhlen, A. (1987). *A Guide to the World's Languages*, vol. I: *Classification*. Stanford, CA: Stanford University Press.

Ruzza, C.E. (1993). Collective identity formation and community integration in the Lega Lombarda. Paper delivered at Changing European Identities Conference, Farnham, Surrey, April 1993.

Said, E.W. (1983). *The World, the Text and the Critic*. London: Verso.

Sampson, E.E. (1993). *Celebrating the Other*. Hemel Hempstead: Harvester/Wheatsheaf.

Sanders, D., Ward, H., Marsh, D. and Fletcher, T. (1987). Government popularity and the Falklands War, *British Journal of Political Science*, 17, 281–313.

Scheff, T.J. (1990). *Microsociology: Discourse, Emotion and Social Structure*. Chicago: Chicago University.

Scheff, T.J. (1995). *Bloody Revenge: Nationalism, War and Emotion*. Boulder, CO: Westview Press.

Schiller, H. (1993). Not yet the postimperialist era. In C. Roach (ed.), *Communication and Culture in War and Peace*. Newbury Park, CA: Sage.

Schlesinger, P. (1991). *Media, State and Nation*. London: Sage.

Schmidt, W. (1993). The nation in German history. In M. Teich and R. Porter (eds), *The National Question in Europe in Historical Context*. Cambridge: Cambridge University Press.

Schwartz, B. (1986). Conservatism, nationalism and imperialism. In J. Donald and S. Hall (eds), *Politics and Ideology*. Milton Keynes: Open University Press.

Schwartz, B. (1987). *George Washington: the Making of an American Symbol*. New York: Free Press.

Schwartzmantel, J. (1992). Nation versus class: nationalism and socialism in theory and practice. In J. Coakley (ed.), *The Social Origins of Nationalist Movements*. London: Sage.

Seton-Watson, H. (1977). *Nations and States*. Boulder, CO: Westview Press.

Shapiro, M.J. (1990). Representing world politics: the sport/war intertext. In J. Der Derian and M.J. Shapiro (eds), *International/Intertextual Relations*. Lexington, MA: Lexington Books.

Sheffer, G. (1988). *Modern Diasporas in International Politics*. Aldershot: Croom Helm.

Sherrard, C. (1993). Gender and aesthetic response: sports reporting. Paper presented at conference of British Psychological Society, London, December 1993.

Sherry, J.F. (1991). Postmodern alternative: the interpretive turn in consumer research. In T. Robertson and H. Kassarjian (eds), *Handbook of Consumer Research*. Englewood Cliffs, NJ: Prentice Hall.

Shils, E. (1985). Sociology. In A. Kuper and J. Kuper (eds), *The Social Science Encyclopedia*. London: Routledge.

Shotter, J. (1993a). *The Cultural Politics of Everyday Life*. Milton Keynes: Open University Press.

Shotter, J. (1993b). *Conversational Realities: Studies in Social Constructionism*. London: Sage.

Shotter, J. (1995). In conversation: joint action, shared intentionality and ethics, *Theory and Psychology*, 5, 49–74.

Shotter, J. and Gergen, K. (eds) (1989). *Texts of Identity*. London: Sage.

Sifry, M.L. and Cerf, C. (eds) (1991). *The Gulf War Reader: History, Documents, Opinions*. New York: Times Books.

Sigelman, L. and Conover, P.J. (1981). Dynamics of presidential support during international conflict situations, *Political Behavior*, 3, 303–18

Silverstein, B. and Flamenbaum, C. (1989). Biases in the perception and cognition of the actions of enemies, *Journal of Social Issues*, 45, 51–72.

Slater, D. (1994). Exploring other zones of the post-modern: problems of ethnocentrism and differences across the North–South divide. In A. Rattansi and S. Westwood (eds), *Modernity, Identity and Racism*. Cambridge: Polity Press.

Smith, A.D. (1981). *The Ethnic Revival*. Cambridge: Cambridge University Press.

Smith, A.D. (1986). *The Ethnic Origins of Nations*. Oxford: Basil Blackwell.

Smith, A.D. (1990). Towards a global culture?, *Theory, Culture and Society*, 7, 171–91.

Smith, A.D. (1994). The problem of national identity: ancient, mediaeval and modern, *Ethnic and Racial Studies*, 17, 374–99.

Smith, M. (1982). Modernization, globalization and the nation-state. In A.G. McGrew (ed.), *Global Politics*. Cambridge: Polity Press.

Snyder, L.L. (1976). *Varieties of Nationalism: a Comparative Study*. Hinsdale, IL: Dryden Press.

Sollors, W. (1986). *Beyond Ethnicity*. Oxford: Oxford University Press.

Sparks, C. (1992). The popular press and political democracy. In P. Scannell, P. Schlesinger and C. Sparks (eds), *Culture and Power*. London: Sage.

Sparks, C. and Campbell, M. (1987). The inscribed reader of the British quality press, *European Journal of Communication*, 2, 455–72.

Spivak, G.C. (1988). Can the subaltern speak? In C. Nelson and L. Grossberg (eds), *Marxism and the Interpretation of Culture*. London: Macmillan.

Stangor, C. and Ford, T.E. (1992). Accuracy and expectancy-confirming processing orientations and the development of stereotypes and prejudice, *European Review of Social Psychology*, 3, 57–90.

Stringer, P. (1990). Prefacing social psychology: a textbook example. In I. Parker and J. Shotter (eds), *Deconstructing Social Psychology*. London: Routledge.

Sumner, W.G. (1906). *Folkways*. Boston, MA: Ginn.

Surel, J. (1989). John Bull. In R. Samuel (ed.). *Patriotism*, vol. III: *National Fictions*. London: Routledge.

Taguieff, P.-A. (1988). *La Force du Préjugé*. La Découverte: Paris.

Tajfel, H. (1969). The formation of national attitudes: a social psychological perspective. In M. Sherif (ed.), *Interdisciplinary Relationships in the Social Sciences*. Chicago: Aldine.

Tajfel, H. (1970). Aspects of ethnic and national loyalty, *Social Science Information*, 9, 119–44.

Tajfel, H. (1974). Social identity and intergroup behaviour, *Social Science Information*, 13, 65–93.

Tajfel, H. (1981). *Human Groups and Social Categories*. Cambridge: Cambridge University Press.

Tajfel, H. (ed.) (1982). *Social Identity and Intergroup Relations*. Cambridge: Cambridge University Press.

Taylor, D.M. and Moghaddam, F.M. (1994). *Theories of Intergroup Relations*. Westport, CT: Praeger.

Taylor, J. (1992). Touched with glory: heroes and humans in the news. In J. Aulich (ed.), *Framing the Falklands War*. Buckingham: Open University Press.

Taylor, P.M. (1992). *War and the Media: Propaganda and Persuasion in the Gulf War*. Manchester: Manchester University Press.

Taylor, S.J. (1991). *Shock! Horror! The Tabloids in Action*. London: Corgi Books.

Tehranian, M. (1993). Ethnic discourse and the new world dysorder: a communitarian perspective. In C. Roach (ed.), *Communication and Culture in War and Peace*. Newbury Park, CA: Sage.

Tham, H. (1993). Drug control as a national project. Paper presented at Fourth International Conference of Drug Related Harm, Rotterdam, March 1993.

Thompson, J.B. (1984). *Studies in the Theory of Ideology*. Cambridge: Polity Press.

Touraine, A. (1985). Sociological intervention and the internal dynamics of the Occitanist Movement. In E.A. Tiryakian and R. Rogowski (eds), *New Nationalisms of the Developed West*. Boston, MA: Allen & Unwin.

Trevor-Roper, H. (1983). The invention of tradition: the Highland tradition of Scotland. In E. Hobsbawm and T. Ranger (eds), *The Invention of Tradition*. Cambridge: Cambridge University Press.

Tseelon, E. (1991). The method is the message: on the meaning of methods as ideologies, *Theory and Psychology*, 1, 299–316.

Tulviste, P. and Wertsch, J.V. (in press). Official and unofficial histories: the case of Estonia, *Journal of Narrative and Life History*.

Turner, B.S. (1987). A note on nostalgia, *Theory, Culture and Society*, 4, 147–56.

Turner, B.S. (1990). The two faces of sociology: global or national, *Theory, Culture and Society*, 7, 343–58.

Turner, J.C. (1984). Social identification and psychological group formation. In H. Tajfel (ed.), *The Social Dimension*. Cambridge: Cambridge University Press.

Turner, J.C., Hogg, M.A., Oakes, P.J., Reicher, S.D. and Wetherell, M. (1987). *Rediscovering the Social Group*. Oxford: Basil Blackwell.

Turner, J.H. and Giddens, A. (eds) (1987). *Social Theory Today*. Cambridge: Polity Press.

Van Dijk, T.A. (1988a). *News Analysis*. Hillsdale, NJ: Lawrence Erlbaum.

Van Dijk, T.A. (1988b). *News as Discourse*. Hillsdale, NJ: Lawrence Erlbaum.

Van Dijk, T.A. (1991). *Racism and the Press*. London: Routledge.

Van Dijk, T.A. (1992). Discourse and the denial of racism, *Discourse and Society*, 3, 87–118.

Van Dijk, T.A. (1993). *Elite Discourse and Racism*. Newbury Park, CA: Sage.

Vincent, N. (1987). Italian. In B. Comrie (ed.), *The World's Major Languages*. London: Routledge.

Voloshinov, V.N. (1973). *Marxism and the Philosophy of Language*. New York: Seminar Press.

Vos, L. (1993). Shifting nationalism: Belgians, Flemings and Walloons. In M. Teich and R. Porter (eds), *The National Question in Europe in Historical Context*. Cambridge: Cambridge University Press.

Voutat, B. (1992). Interpreting national conflict in Switzerland: the Jura question. In J. Coakley (ed.), *The Social Origins of Nationalist Movements*. London: Sage.

Walker, R.B.J. (1990). Sovereignty, identity, community: reflections on the horizons of contemporary political practice. In R.B.J. Walker and S.H. Mendlovitz (eds), *Contending Sovereignties*. Boulder, CO: Lynne Reinner.

Wallerstein, I. (1987). World-systems analysis. In J.H. Turner and A. Giddens (eds), *Social Theory Today*. Cambridge: Polity Press.

Wallerstein, I. (1991). The construction of peoplehood: racism, nationalism, ethnicity. In E. Balibar and I. Wallerstein, *Race, Nation, Class*. London: Verso.

Waterman, S. (1989). Partition and modern nationalism. In C.H. Williams and E. Kofman (eds), *Community Conflict, Partition and Nationalism*. London: Routledge.

Wertsch, J.V. (in press). Struggling with the past: some dynamics of historical representation. In M. Carretero and J. Voss (eds), *Cognitive and Instructional Processes in History and the Social Sciences*. Hillsdale, NJ: Lawrence Erlbaum.

Wertsch, J.V. and O'Connor, K. (in press). Multivoicedness in historical representation: American college students' accounts of the origins of the US, *Journal of Narrative and Life History*.

Wetherell, M. and Potter, J. (1992). *Mapping the Language of Racism*. Hemel Hempstead: Harvester/Wheatsheaf.

White, P. (1991). Geographic aspects of minority language situations in Italy. In C.H. Williams (ed.), *Linguistic Minorities, Society and Territory*. Clevedon: Multilingual Matters.

Wilkins, D.P. (1992). Interjections as deictics, *Journal of Pragmatics*, 18, 119–58.

Williams, F. (1987). Racism and the discipline of social policy: a critique of welfare theory, *Critical Social Policy*, 20, 4–29.

Williams, G. (1991). *The Welsh in Patagonia*. Cardiff: University of Wales Press.

Williams, J.A. (1984). Gender and intergroup behaviour: towards an integration, *British Journal of Social Psychology*, 23, 311–16.

Wilson, J. (1990). *Politically Speaking*. Oxford: Basil Blackwell.

Windisch, U. (1985). *Le Raisonnement et le Parler Quotidiens*. Lausanne: L'Age d'Homme.

Windisch, U. (1990). *Le Prêt-à-Penser*. Lausanne: L'Age d'Homme.

Woodiwiss, A. (1993). *Postmodernity USA*. London: Sage.

Woollacott, A. (1993). Sisters and brothers in arms: family, class and gendering in World War I Britain. In M. Cooke and A. Woollacott (eds), *Gendering War Talk*. Princeton, NJ: Princeton University Press.

Yatani, C. and Bramel, D. (1989). Trends and patterns in Americans' attitude toward the Soviet Union, *Journal of Social Issues*, 45, 13–32.

Young, H. (1993). *One of Us: a Biography of Margaret Thatcher*. London: Pan Books.

Yuval-Davies, N. (1993). Gender and nation, *Ethnic and Racial Studies*, 16, 621–32.

Yuval-Davies, N. (1994). Women, ethnicity and empowerment, *Feminism and Psychology*, 4, 179–97.

Zavalloni, M. (1993a). Ascribed identities and the social identity space: an ego/ecological analysis. Paper delivered at Changing European Identities Conference, Farnham, Surrey, April 1993.

Zavalloni, M. (1993b). Identity and hyperidentities: the representational foundation of self and culture, *Papers on Social Representations*, 2, 218–35.

Zelizer, B. (1989). Saying as collective practice: quoting and differential address in the news, *Text*, 9, 369–88.

Zelizer, B. (1990). Where is the author in American TV news? On the construction and presentation of proximity, authorship and journalistic authority, *Semiotica*, 80, 37–48.

Ziegler, P. (1977). *Crown and People*. London: Collins.

Zubaida, S. (1993). *Islam, the People and the State*. London: I.B. Tauris.

# Name Index

Abrams, D., 65, 66, 67
Achard, P., 107, 116
Adorno, T.W., 79, 137, 166
Agnew, J., 74, 100
Ahmed, A.S., 149
Akioye, A., 85
Altemeyer, B., 137
Anderson, B., 10, 22, 23, 24, 68, 70, 74, 75, 95, 125
Anderson, P., 53
Arafat, Yassar, 41, 64
Arendt, H., 7
Aristotle, 97
Ashmore, M., 107
Atkinson, J.M., 106
Augoustinos, M., 69
Aulich, J., 3, 89, 124

Bachelard, G., 108–9
Bagehot, W., 26, 29
Bailyn, B., 142
Bairstow, T., 110
Bakhtin, M.M., 17, 87, 96
Baldwin, S., 2
Balibar, E., 63, 71
Banton, M., 63–4
Bar-Tal, D., 56–7, 67, 81
Barker, M., 71, 82
Barnett, A., 3, 89, 100
Barruel, Auguste de, 84
Barthes, R., 37, 40, 61, 102, 125, 151–3, 174
Baudrillard, J., 131, 143, 149
Bauman, Z., 53, 130, 135, 136, 140, 141, 157
Beattie, G., 41, 123
Beck, U., 52
Bellah, R.N., 54–5
Benjamin, W., 2
Bentham, J., 84
Berkowitz, L., 123
Berlin, I., 1
Berlusconi, Silvio, 47, 123
Bernstein, R., 157, 165
Bhabha, H., 7, 155

Bhaskar, R., 157, 165
Bhavnani, K.-K., 60, 146
Billig, M., 18, 37, 45, 52, 57, 61, 64, 71, 72, 82, 84, 87, 91, 110, 138, 161
Birch, A.H., 22
Blair, Tony, 104–5, 107, 109
Bloch, M., 29
Bocock, R., 45
Bolivar, Simon, 26
Boose, L.E., 126
Bormann, Martin, 80
Boswell, J., 18
Bourdieu, P., 42
Bowen, G.L., 2
Bowers, J., 53
Braly, K., 80, 81
Bramel, D., 47, 81
Brannon, L.A., 2
Brass, P.R., 62
Braudel, F., 21, 25, 30, 34
Breuilly, J., 67, 133
Brewer, M., 65
Brody, R.A., 2
Brown, D., 27, 140
Brown, P., 106
Brown, R., 65
Brown, R.H., 51
Brunt, R., 143
Burke, K., 98
Burrows, J. 157
Bush, George, 1–4, 5, 7, 9, 21, 75, 88–9, 90, 91, 98, 103, 107, 109, 158, 169

Cable, V., 135
Campbell, D.T., 79
Campbell, M., 111, 119
Cannadine, D., 26, 81
Capitan, C., 25
Castles, S., 130
Cerf, C., 1, 3, 4, 91
Chaney, D., 45
Chilembwe, John, 85
Chirac, Jacques, 104
Chomsky, N., 4
Churchill, Winston, 3

# Subject Index

anthems, national 86
authoritarianism, 137–8

banal nationalism, concept of, 6, 10, 12; distinguished from 'hot' nationalism 43ff; *see also* flagging
Belgium, 13, 15
boundary consciousness, 20–1, 137
British/English identity, 19, 26, 71–2, 78, 99–100, 102, 110, 123

citizenship, 124, 142
colonialism, 85
commemoration, national 45, 46, 50–1, 113–4
Congress of Vienna, 83
conspiracy theory, 84–5
consumer culture, 132–3, 151
Croatia, 42
currency and national symbols, 41–2

deixis, 11, 94, 105–111, 114–119, 144–5, 174
democracy, 47, 93–4, 95, 167
dialect, 31–6; *see also* language and nation

East Timor, 4, 28
enemies, construction of, 91–2
enhabiting nationhood, 42, 43, 69
ethnicity, 46, 47, 48, 63, 69, 135, 145–9
ethnocentrism, 79, 80, 163–5

Falklands/Malvinas War, 2, 3, 81, 89, 100, 124
fascism, 46, 47, 57, 137
flagging nationhood, 8, 11, 38, 93–127, 150–2, 174, 175
flags, 2, 39–43, 86
foreigners, construction of, 79, 80
French identity, 17–18, 25, 26, 27, 28
French Revolution, 25, 88

gender and nation, 119, 123–127
German language, 32–3
globalization, 11, 129–132, 149ff
Gulf War, 1–4, 5, 91, 126

habitus, 42
hegemony, 27, 32, 33, 34, 87ff, 156, 170ff; *see also* syntax of hegemony
homeland, 74–8, 96, 99, 105–111, 117–9

identity, multiple and decentred, 69, 136ff, 166
identity, national, 7, 9, 10, 60–92, 93, 79, 133, 147, 169
identity, politics of, 92, 145–150
identity, psychology of, 8, 17, 60, 65ff, 162–3
imagined communities, 24ff, 68, 70, 77, 95; imagining 'us', 70–3; imagining homelands, 74–8; imagining 'them', 78–83
immigration, 82, 110, 130
internationalism of nationalism, 61, 79–80, 86–7, 90–2, 142ff
Islam, 68, 149
Italy and separatism, 33–4, 35

Kurds, 3, 34

language and nation, 13–36; creation of national languages, 27–31; distinguishing between languages, 33–5; language and national boundaries, 31–6; language and identity, 14–5; language and ideology, 17–8; suppression of minority languages, 27–8; *see also* dialect, syntax of hegemony
left-wing and nationalist politics, 22–3, 104–5
Lombard League, 35

Macedonia, 73
Malaysia, 63–4
Marxism and nationalism, 22–3
mediaeval Europe, 4, 20–1, 30, 31
modernity and nationalism, 19ff, 128–132
multiculturalism, 148, 159
mysticism of 'homeland', 77–8